Ethics and the Global Financial Crisis

In this topical book, Boudewijn de Bruin examines the ethical 'blind spots' that lay at the heart of the global financial crisis. He argues that the most important moral problem in finance is not the 'greed is good' culture, but rather the epistemic shortcomings of bankers, clients, rating agencies and regulators. Drawing on insights from economics, psychology and philosophy, De Bruin develops a novel theory of epistemic virtue and applies it to racist and sexist lending practices, subprime mortgages, CEO hubris, the Madoff scandal, professionalism in accountancy and regulatory outsourcing of epistemic responsibility. With its multidisciplinary reach, *Ethics and the Global Financial Crisis* will appeal to scholars working in philosophy, business ethics, economics, psychology and the sociology of finance. The many concrete examples and case studies mean that this book will also prove useful to policymakers and regulators.

BOUDEWIJN DE BRUIN is Professor of Financial Ethics at the University of Groningen, The Netherlands. He is a consultant with the financial services industry, has taught in various executive MBA programmes across the world and is a regular contributor to the media. He runs a large project on Trusting Banks, with Alex Oliver (University of Cambridge) and financed by the Dutch Research Council (NWO), which draws together philosophers, social scientists, policymakers and finance professionals.

Business, Value Creation, and Society

Series editors

R. Edward Freeman, *University of Virginia*
Jeremy Moon, *Copenhagen Business School*
Mette Morsing, *Copenhagen Business School*

The purpose of this innovative series is to examine, from an international standpoint, the interaction of business and capitalism with society. In the twenty-first century it is more important than ever that business and capitalism come to be seen as social institutions that have a great impact on the welfare of human society around the world. Issues such as globalization, environmentalism, information technology, the triumph of liberalism, corporate governance and business ethics all have the potential to have major effects on our current models of the corporation and the methods by which value is created, distributed and sustained among all stakeholders – customers, suppliers, employees, communities, and financiers.

Published titles:

Fort *Business, Integrity, and Peace*
Gomez and Korine *Entrepreneurs and Democracy*
Crane, Matten and Moon *Corporations and Citizenship*
Painter-Morland *Business Ethics as Practice*
Yaziji and Doh *NGOs and Corporations*
Rivera *Business and Public Policy*
Sachs and Rühli *Stakeholders Matter*
Mansell *Capitalism, Corporations and the Social Contract*
Hemingway *Corporate Social Entrepreneurship*
Hartman *Virtue in Business*

Forthcoming titles:

de Bakker and den Hond *Organizing for Corporate Social Responsibility*
Griffin *Managing Corporate Impacts*
Knudsen and Moon *Visible Hands*
Nyberg and Wright *Corporate Politics and Climate Change*

Ethics and the Global Financial Crisis

Why Incompetence is Worse than Greed

BOUDEWIJN DE BRUIN
University of Groningen

CAMBRIDGE
UNIVERSITY PRESS

CAMBRIDGE
UNIVERSITY PRESS

University Printing House, Cambridge CB2 8BS, United Kingdom

Cambridge University Press is part of the University of Cambridge.

It furthers the University's mission by disseminating knowledge in the pursuit of education, learning and research at the highest international levels of excellence.

www.cambridge.org
Information on this title: www.cambridge.org/9781107028913

© Boudewijn de Bruin 2015

First published 2015

A catalogue record for this publication is available from the British

Library of Congress Cataloguing in Publication data
Bruin, Boudewijn de, 1974–
Ethics and the global financial crisis : why incompetence is worse than greed /
Boudewijn de Bruin.
  pages   cm. – (Business, value creation, and society)
ISBN 978-1-107-02891-3 (hardback)
1. Financial crises – Moral and ethical aspects.   2. Finance – Moral and ethical aspects.   3. Business ethics.   4. Global Financial Crisis, 2008–2009 – Moral and ethical aspects.   I. Title.
HB3722.B78   2015
174′.4–dc23

2014026396

ISBN 978-1-107-02891-3 Hardback

for Katja

jezelf een vraag stellen
daarmee begint verzet

Remco Campert, 'Verzet begint niet met grote woorden'

Contents

Foreword

Professor De Bruin has written an important book. For all of the thousands of pages written on the recent global financial crisis, there is very little solid ethical analysis of the underlying causes and concepts. He makes a critical distinction between the motivation of financial actors and their competence, then argues that most of the analysis of the crisis has been about motivation. In particular, many have called into question the very idea of capitalism as seeking to maximize profits for shareholders. While De Bruin admits that motivation is an important idea, he traces much of the difficulty to incompetence on the part of multiple stakeholders, who have no real motivation to learn about how the basic ideas in finance actually work.

This book breaks important theoretical and practical ground. On the theory front, De Bruin argues that the traditional separation of ethics and epistemology needs to come to an end. His ideas of 'epistemic virtue and vice' are an important addition to our way of thinking about business and ethics. He draws on some cutting-edge philosophers who are working out the view that 'knowledge is virtuously formed true belief'. He goes on to show that this theory can give us a novel interpretation of phenomena like the global financial crisis and the recent work in behavioural economics.

De Bruin speaks to multiple audiences in this book. First of all scholars in the fields of business and society and business ethics will easily begin to see how the rich conceptual apparatus of epistemic virtues has application to a broad range of issues. Scholars in management theory and finance will also be interested in the analysis of how theory can work better. In addition they will gain insight into the basic relationships in finance understood in terms of epistemic virtues and values. But De Bruin also speaks to policymakers. If the main cause of the Great Recession was incompetence, the implications for policy are profound.

This book represents an important step in the project of rewriting the story of business so that we come to see business and value creation as firmly enmeshed in society. By taking on one of the most powerful ways of thinking about business, finance theory and institutions, De Bruin advances the cause that is behind this series, *Business, Value Creation, and Society*. The very purpose of the series is to stimulate new thinking about value creation and trade, and their role in the world of the twenty-first century. We need new scholarship that builds on what we know, yet offers the alternative of a world of hope, freedom and human flourishing. Boudewijn de Bruin has given us such a book.

R. Edward Freeman
University Professor
University of Virginia
Charlottesville, Virginia, USA

Acknowledgements

I should like to thank Rob Alessie, Alrik Baltus, Ron Beadle, John Boatright, Tony Booth, Matthew Braham, Ian Carter, Rutger Claassen, Julian Clarke, Wilfred Dolfsma, Wim Dubbink, Luciano Floridi, Joan Fontrodona, Martin van Hees, Frank Hindriks, Richard Holton, Jacques Jacobs, Sue Jaffer, Ronald Jeurissen, Marc Kramer, Matthew Kramer, Luc Van Liedekerke, Christoph Lütge, Marco Meyer, Seamus Miller, Nick Morris, Laetitia Mulder, Alex Oliver, Martin O'Neill, Onora O'Neill, Christoph Prainsack, Jan-Willem van der Rijt, Jan-Willem Romeijn, Tom Simpson, Alejo Sison, Max Torres, Kees van Veen, David Vines, and my research assistants Arthur Constandse and Sjoerd Norden. I have also learnt a lot from the many stimulating and thoughtful comments I have received from audiences in Amsterdam, Antwerp, Barcelona, Cambridge, Delft, Doorn, Dublin, Groningen, Hamburg, Louvain, Madrid, Nyenrode, Oxford, Paris, Pavia, Rotterdam, Tilburg and Wassenaar.

I should also like to thank Paula Parish and Claire Wood for their kind help at various stages of the writing process.

The last bits of the book were written while spending time in the Faculty of Philosophy of the University of Cambridge, and I am very grateful to the dean, Tim Crane, for his generous hospitality, and to Alex Oliver for inspiring joint work on our project on trust and finance. I thank Clare Hall for providing a pleasant and collegial atmosphere for research.

I gratefully acknowledge generous financial support from the Dutch Research Council (NWO) for project 360–320–10 Trusting Banks, in which the universities of Groningen and Cambridge cooperate. This book is among the first of its outputs.

I acknowledge permission obtained from Damon for reusing 'Epistemische deugden en de wereldwijde financiële crisis', *Filosofie en Praktijk*, 34, 4 (Winter 2013), 5–13, ISSN 0167–2444; from Springer for reusing 'Epistemic virtues in business', *Journal of Business Ethics*, 113,

4 (2013), 583–95, ISSN 0167-4544; from Springer for reusing 'Epistemically virtuous risk management: financial due diligence and uncovering the Madoff fraud', in Christoph Luetge and Johanna Jauernig (eds.), *Business ethics and risk management*, Ethical Economy, 43 (2014), pp. 27–42, ISBN 978-94-007-7440-7; and from the Philosophy Documentation Center for reusing 'Epistemic integrity in accounting: accountants as justifiers in joint epistemic agents', *Business and Professional Ethics Journal*, 32, 1/2 (Spring 2013), 109–30, ISSN 0227-2027.

Introduction

In the *Politics*, Aristotle tells the tale of Thales the Milesian. Thales is one of the first philosophers. Bertrand Russell even goes so far as to write that 'Philosophy begins with Thales.'[1] But he could equally have written 'Finance begins with Thales'; for Thales was an early option trader. The fragment from the *Politics* where Aristotle recounts Thales's story is one of the oldest sources to mention option contracts. Predicting a rich olive harvest, Thales spent a small amount of money to buy the exclusive right to use the olive presses; and when his predictions turned out correct, he sold the right to use the presses to the owners of the olive yards, with a nice margin.

Aristotle thinks it was Thales's intention to show the world that philosophers can effortlessly become as rich as other people, but that because their ambitions lie elsewhere, they generally do not end up very rich, which sounds all very good. But wasn't Thales the first speculator? With a carefully orchestrated media campaign entitled 'Banks: Profiting from Hunger', Oxfam International calls on banks to stop speculative trading in food commodities. Food speculation is quite similar to what Thales did, even if Thales's financial innovation might today be more aptly called a *lease contract*, involving as it does the use of particular assets, whereas food speculation is about the assets themselves, the olives not the presses. Oxfam condemns such activities in unequivocal terms. *Food Speculation: A Matter of Life and Death*, a film lasting only fifty-eight seconds, explains why:

Speculation with food commodities causes the price of corn, wheat and rice to skyrocket. Millions of people in poor countries are being driven into hunger and poverty. Stop gambling with food – curb speculation![2]

---

[1] Russell, *History*, 3.
[2] www.oxfam.org/en/grow/video/2012/food-speculation-matter-life-and-death.

1

What we now call the *global financial crisis*, in 2008 we still called the *credit crunch* or *subprime meltdown*. It is true that the year 2008 marks the collapse of Lehman Brothers as well as the rescue of Bear Stearns, Northern Rock, Merrill Lynch, AIG, Wachovia, Fortis, Lloyds, Royal Bank of Scotland and others. The enormous recessional increase in unemployment, however, was still far ahead of us, and trust in banks in the United States was still at a stunning 69 per cent, according to the renowned Edelman Trust Barometer. Predicting a prolonged recession would have landed you in a pessimist minority camp. It cannot be denied therefore that the Dutch Bankers' Association realized the significance of the 2008 events remarkably quickly. Lehman Brothers had barely collapsed when a committee led by a respected former banker started an investigation and published its results only a few months later in a report entitled 'Restoring trust'.[3] With its exceptionally concrete suggestions, the report did not fail to have impact. The Banking Code, published in September 2009, which has been effective as a code of conduct under civil law since January 2010, is a form of self-regulation springing directly from that report. The worldwide novelty of a Hippocratic oath, which bankers and other financials have to pledge, was suggested by the committee.[4] Moreover, the report gave a serious boost to the development of regulation requiring the financial services industry to refocus on the interests of its clients.

Yet it is only a very natural question to ask: has this report succeeded in realizing the goal encapsulated in its title? Has consumer trust in finance been restored? Before answering this question, it is important to see that, excepting the eccentric idea of an oath for bankers, the committee's attempts are by no means unique in the world. Restoring trust in banking and finance has been the avowed goal of many government and industry committees around the globe. The US Financial Crisis Inquiry Commission Report, published in January 2011, is perhaps the most famous example, but the Turner Review (2009) and the reports of the Vickers Commission (2011) in Britain and the De la Rosière report of the European Commission (2009), among many others, have largely parallel aims.

---

[3] Advisory Committee on the Future of Banks in the Netherlands, 'Restoring trust'.

[4] Anderson and Escher, *The MBA oath*, is another well-known initiative.

Trust and trustworthiness

Consumer trust in banks in 2008 was, as stated, 69 per cent in the United States. In Europe it was lower, at 56 per cent in the Netherlands and 47 per cent in the United Kingdom, for example. But five years later it had declined across the board, as witnessed by figures of 49 per cent in the United States, 31 per cent in the Netherlands and a quite scarifying 22 per cent in the United Kingdom.[5] There is no way to escape the conclusion: trust has declined. Restoring trust has totally failed so far. But this statement may be unduly hasty. The figures have to be interpreted with care, and when trust has left on horseback, it will only return on foot. Perhaps banks need more time. Besides that, we must distinguish between general trust in the banking industry and the trust people place in the bank they bank with. If distrust were as widespread as the statistics claim, many people would keep their money under the mattress. This is something they seem to avoid doing.

More can be gained by looking closely into the concept of trust. Trust, to begin with, is a relation. Mary trusts John. Mary trusts the bank. Person X trusts person or organization Y. The truster and the trustee are not the only elements of the relation. Mary trusts John with something – with the car, for instance. And Mary does not trust John with something else – the dog, for instance. A third relatum is, in addition to all this, the sort of actions Mary trusts or does not trust John to perform. Nor is that all. As Onora O'Neill observes, we are particularly interested in placing trust 'intelligently', and that requires the truster to have good reasons to trust the trustee.[6] Mary trusts John with the car but not the dog because she knows John is a careful driver but not a canophilist.

The observation that rightly placed trust requires good reasons immediately directs our attention to a concept that is probably even more important: *trustworthiness*.[7] Mary trusts John with the car on account of her having reasons to believe that John is trustworthy with the car, but she does not trust him with the dog because she has evidence that with respect to pet sitting he is untrustworthy. For banks and bankers to restore trust, then, requires first of all that they regain their

[5] Edelman Trust Barometer 2013.
[6] O'Neill, 'Trust, trustworthiness, and accountability'. Also see Manson and O'Neill, *Rethinking informed consent in bioethics*.
[7] For a brief summary of O'Neill's position, see www.bbc.co.uk/news/magazine-20627410.

trustworthiness. This is not mere wordplay. Take the idea of a Hippocratic oath for bankers, or the MBA oath developed by Harvard Business School graduates several years ago.[8] To claim that an oath will help restore confidence among consumers throughout society is to claim something that has great initial plausibility. But to claim that an oath will raise the trustworthiness of bankers or general managers betokens a naive sort of optimism concerning the behavioural effects of oath taking.

If I had to summarize all this in two words, they would be: trustworthiness first. A frequently used way to analyse trustworthiness is that it depends on two things, namely, the trustee's motivation and the trustee's competence. Take medicine. What makes a GP trustworthy? First, the doctor has to be motivated to help. Physicians primarily interested in their yachts or the amount of money they earn per hour will *ceteris paribus* be less trustworthy than doctors motivated by care, concern for their patients' wellbeing, altruism and other related values. Yet motivation is insufficient on its own. Trustworthy physicians are also competent. They are capable of making an accurate diagnosis. They know the side effects of the drugs they prescribe. They recognize the boundaries of their own capacities and refer their patients to specialists whenever necessary. They see to it that their knowledge is up to date. A trustworthy medical practitioner, in sum, is both motivated to help and competent to help.

The analysis of trustworthiness in terms of motivation and competence is attractive thanks to its elegant simplicity; it is also a vantage point from which I can describe the contribution of this book to ethics and finance. So far ethicists have almost only focused on things that have to do with motivation. Corporate social responsibility, corporate citizenship, stakeholder theory, ethics management, the triple bottom line of people, planet and profit: all are concerned with ways to describe, explain, understand, curtail or improve the motivations and intentions of managers and employees or of entire business organizations. That these ethics models are themed around motivation is probably not a controversial observation. What these models do, perhaps with the exception of ethics management, is to provide ways to call upon businesses to pay attention not only to economic but also other considerations. The triple bottom line adds social and environmental perspectives to mere economic ones.[9] Stakeholder theory opens our eyes to other

---

[8] Anderson and Escher, *The MBA oath.*   [9] Elkington, *Cannibals with forks.*

parties beyond traditional management theory; it shows managers that business affects competitors, governments and civil society, besides the usual four suspects of shareholders, employees, customers and suppliers.[10] To the economic concerns of an enterprise, corporate social responsibility adds the normative expectations that society has concerning its legal, ethical and philanthropic responsibilities.[11] The most recent branch of the tree, corporate citizenship, asks firms to view themselves as partly contributing to the realization of liberal citizenship rights.[12] It is certainly true that these models facilitate competent ethical decision making among managers in that they offer ready-made formulas to determine those concerns of people, organizations or even ecosystems that they must incorporate in their decisions; and initiatives that follow from philanthropic corporate social responsibility or from corporate citizenship may foster competence among many of a business's stakeholders (a much discussed example in this respect is the British retailer Marks and Spencer's 'Marks and Start' programme, developed to help unemployed and homeless people gain experience and work skills).[13] Competence is not presented as a specific theme here, though.

Moral decision making and moral intensity

It is only in the multifarious techniques of ethics management that competence finds a place, however minor that may still be. Ethics management can take many forms, including corporate mission statements, codes of conduct, ethics training programmes, ethical performance management systems, ethics audits, ethics and compliance officers, ethics committees, ethics hotlines, whistle-blower policies and others. More than in the corporate social responsibility model, these management techniques do address manager and employee competence. The theoretical underpinnings of these techniques include a theory of ethical decision making developed by James Rest and a theory of moral intensity developed by Thomas Jones.[14] Rest distinguished four stages of ethical decision making. People first have to recognize the decision problem as one that has a moral dimension to it; they have to see, that is, that their

---

[10] Freeman, *Strategic management.*   [11] Carroll, *Business and society.*
[12] Matten and Crane, 'Corporate citizenship'.
[13] Crane and Matten, *Business ethics*, 77.
[14] Rest, *Moral development.* Jones, 'Ethical decision making'.

actions may influence other people positively or negatively. Secondly, they have to form an ethical judgement concerning what ought to be done, which requires them to analyse the situation from a moral viewpoint. Thirdly, they have to establish the moral intention to act in conformity with what they judged, in the previous stage, to be the right kind of behaviour. Finally, they have to engage in that behaviour. Unethical behaviour may result from failures at any of the four stages. People may fail to recognize, judge, intend or behave. Whether they succeed or fail depends on motivation and competence, because knowledge or ignorance may as well influence decision making as weakness of will and feelings of control and responsibility. Competence is evidently related to the first two stages. Who is unable to recognize ethics where ethics exist, or who fails to make competent ethical judgements, will likely fail to act ethically.

Particularly in the context of the financial services industry, a second theme is relevant: the moral intensity of the ethical issue. An issue's moral intensity depends on the magnitude of the consequences of the actions and the probability with which they arise, as well as on whether the consequences are concentrated on a group of people or dispersed among them. Moral intensity also depends on whether there is any social consensus about the fact that particular actions are good or evil and whether the consequences and/or people affected by the actions are socially, culturally, psychologically, physically and temporally close to the agent. Roughly speaking, when evil consequences are likely or severe, affect people in close proximity or a large number of people, and when the agent rightly or wrongly perceives this to be the case, then the issue's moral intensity is high.

As Jones convincingly argues, the moral intensity of an issue determines how people proceed at each of the four stages of ethical decision making. Issues with high moral intensity are more frequently recognized as moral issues, they will lead to more sophisticated forms of moral judgement, and they will more often trigger people to form moral intentions and engage in ethical behaviour. This is relevant to ethics management in banking and the rest of the finance industry because unlike the oil industry, the pharmaceutical industry and the nuclear industry, among others, the financial sector's main ethical issues often involve such high levels of detailed technical understanding and detached engagement that their moral intensity is likely to be perceived as rather low. The prototypical image of traders working in front of several computer screens illustrates the point: they are unaware of the consequences of their number-crunching sales techniques. Empirical studies of moral intensity in banking are, to my knowledge, absent, so we should tread carefully here; in my view, the hypothesis just ventured has much to recommend it. The consequences of investment decisions are often remote and they are dispersed over many people. Probability estimates are typically hard to make. Moreover, the technical character of the issues involved means that consensus is often absent.

Trustworthiness will hardly grow where people do not notice ethical issues, and to notice them, they need competence. The sort of competence that is central to this book, however, is not this sort of *ethical* competence. Recall the doctor. The trustworthiness of doctors depends on the extent to which they are able to recognize and judge ethics and deal with hard cases involving informed consent or conflicts of interest. Thinking of the competence of physicians, however, one typically thinks of their suturing skills and knowledge of intestinal disorders, or something like that. It is the analogue of these sorts of skills and knowledge in finance that I am interested in here, for two reasons. One is the surprising dearth of such competence in the financial sector; another is a recent development in philosophy arising out of a rapprochement between ethics and the theory of knowledge: the theory of *epistemic* virtues.

Motivation or competence?

A lack of motivation rather than a lack of competence is still seen as the primary moral determinant of the global financial crisis. Titles such as Alex Brummer's *The crunch: how greed and incompetence sparked the credit crisis*, David Faber's *And then the roof caved in: how Wall Street's greed and stupidity brought capitalism to its knees* and William Fleckenstein's *Greenspan's bubbles: the age of ignorance at the Federal Reserve* may suggest a view focusing both on incompetence (stupidity, ignorance) and on lack of motivation (greed, etc.). But the emphasis in these and similar books overwhelmingly lies on motivation, not competence. And lack of competence there is. First, among customers. Many people across the world have limited knowledge of financial concepts. About a fifth of adult citizens in Britain are unable to understand compound interest, and consequently fail fully to grasp such simple products as a savings account. Generally, levels of *financial literacy*, as it is called, are low, and the lower they are, the less likely it is that people will engage in decent financial planning. American house owners with little knowledge of finance are more likely to face problems repaying their mortgages, not because they may have been saddled with a potentially inappropriate mortgage, but because of issues independent of the terms of the loan.[15] Nor do many people seem to be very interested in acquiring a knowledge of finance. Though it may take weeks for a family to decide on a new kitchen, many people do hardly any research into optimum mortgage terms, often with predictably subprime outcomes.[16] In the vocabulary of epistemic virtue theory, customers often show little curiosity, inquisitiveness or love of knowledge.

But epistemic vice can be found among others than customers alone; among tax professionals, for instance.[17] Tax professionals provide advice concerning the tax returns of business organizations, estimating the probability that if a court of justice had to decide, it would rule favourably. The search technique is disarmingly simple. The professionals try to find judicial precedents. But which precedents? It is only natural to expect them randomly to select a set of relevant court rulings, to distinguish positive and negative decisions, and to divide the number of positive decisions by the total size of the sample. In reality, however, these professionals do not take a random sample. They suffer from the *confirmation bias*, a topic studied in psychology and behavioural economics. The sample they select contains a greater than average number of positive rulings, as a result of which the probability estimate is going to be too optimistic, with predictably unpleasant outcomes for the company filing its tax returns. This is the vice of epistemic injustice – that is, of showing prejudice towards evidence favouring one side of the issue.

Lack of competence is sometimes hard to detect. Consider bonuses, trampled into the mud by many popular writers as a wretched element of a culture of greed supposedly setting the financial sector apart from the rest of the world. The existence of bonuses is typically seen as a prime indicator of an utter lack of motivation among bankers to care for their clients. But a more intelligent accusation relates them not to motivation but to competence. A neat mathematical argument shows

[15] Gerardi et al., 'Mortgage default'.
[16] Courchane et al., 'Subprime borrowers'.
[17] Cloyd and Spilker, 'Tax professionals'.

that when employees receive performance-based compensation, it makes it very difficult if not impossible for their managers to determine whether their professional successes, if they have them, are attributable to skills or to brute luck. Bonuses establish smoke screens between employees and managers, thwarting epistemic virtue and making decent human resource management impossible.

Let me be blunt. Incompetence is likely to be among the key determinants of the global financial crisis. Take mortgage-backed securities, the infamous results of repackaging mortgages, often subprime, with the aim of diminishing risk. Medical practitioners prescribing drugs are expected to understand the risks of the drugs and to have a clear idea of why it is a good idea for their patients to take them; and before taking the drugs, patients read instructions they believe to contain all relevant information, written in ways they can understand. An important form of risk for buyers of mortgage-backed securities is that the borrowers of the underlying mortgages fail to repay them. Some will not repay, but the hope is that this will not happen to all of them, only to a few. The so-called *default correlation* must not be too high.

Credit rating agencies are the main researchers of such risks. They give ratings to bonds and structured debt securities, mortgage-backed securities among them, ranging from top tier triple A to the D of default. When it comes to rating corporate and government bonds, their success rate since the 1920s has been rather impressive; and this is true despite a number of highly publicized scandals (WorldCom, Enron, Tyco, etc.), despite the fact that many economists believe that similar levels of accuracy can be gleaned from much cheaper sources (without the purportedly private information from the issuers that rating agencies claim gives them their competitive edge), and despite the fact that many commentators find that the agencies are embroiled in conflicts of interest arising from the fact that they are paid by the issuers of the securities they rate. Mortgage-backed securities are, however, devastatingly more complex than these plain vanilla bonds. A corporate bond is just a loan to a firm. A mortgage-backed security is a complex amalgam of thousands of house loans structured in fancy yet complex tranches, which makes them more difficult to rate. The rating agencies proved unequal to their task. It was necessary for Moody's, one of the big three rating agencies, to witness the first outbursts of the subprime meltdown to realize that in order to rate mortgage-backed securities it ought to obtain information about what in reality are only the simplest indicators of a mortgage's credit risk, such as its loan-to-value ratio, the credit score of the borrower and the borrower's debt-to-income level.[18] Up to then, Moody's had not found it opportune to examine more than only the *average* mortgage, which contains barely any relevant information at all. It is not surprising, consequently, that Moody's and other raters were later unmasked as twenty-first-century 'alchemists' turning securities with underlying assets of very low, near-junk ratings into gilt-edge triple As.[19] But the consequences of their unconcern for epistemic virtue should not be trivialized. What was rated as gold would have been in much smaller demand had it been rated as junk. As economists phrase it, investor appetite for structured debt securities was significantly increased by the favourable ratings the products obtained from the major rating agencies.[20] No one claims, of course, that the global financial crisis should be attributed to the rating agencies only. That they played a fundamental role is, however, hardly deniable.

Finally, Bernard Madoff. Way ahead of his time when he introduced computer technology in the financial world, he helped set up NASDAQ, the world's first electronic stock market; gained a reputation as one of the biggest market makers on Wall Street, maintaining close connections with supervisory authorities and, until recently, possessing an impeccable status; but behind bars now, guilty of running the largest Ponzi scheme ever. Madoff claimed to be using a penny-plain split strike conversion method merely involving a basket of around thirty-five shares from the S&P 100 index, plus some buying and selling of options or treasury bills. Such a strategy should not be expected to deliver dazzling results; and the returns were indeed not very spectacular if one looked at them month by month. Madoff claimed, however, a yield of about 10 per cent per annum, with only 3 per cent volatility. For split strikes, such figures (it does not matter much now what they exactly mean) are out of the ordinary. With the benefit of hindsight, we can now explain how Madoff arrived at his claim. He was not investing; he was unscrupulously using the money brought in by new depositors to pay the earlier borrowers their promised 10 per cent. That is why he was in

---

[18] J. Mason and J. Rosner, 'Where did the risk go? How misapplied bond ratings cause mortgage backed securities and collateralized debt obligation market disruptions' (2007), papers.ssrn.com/sol3/papers.cfm?abstract_id=1027475.

[19] Benmelech and Dlugosz, 'The alchemy of CDO ratings'.

[20] Pagano and Volpin, 'Credit ratings failures'.

need of cash all the time. And cash he got, from *feeder funds*, so called because they swamped him with the money he wanted, among them funds investing the retirement savings of many people around the globe.

Didn't these funds fathom the fraud? Didn't they do their financial due diligence? The story of the feeder funds is a story of ignorance and serious epistemic ethics shortcomings. The story of how the Madoff scam was detected is, by contrast, a story of epistemic excellence. It is Harry Markopolos's story. Markopolos was working for a finance firm at the time, and was assigned the task of emulating Madoff's putatively successful split strike conversion strategy in order for the firm to encourage its output. A real *quant* or financial mathematician, Markopolos considered this to be a nice mathematical challenge. Solving the puzzle did not lead him to higher returns or lower volatility than Madoff boasted of. Markopolos's quest ended with a very different conclusion: Madoff was lying.

How did Markopolos do it? For a start, he knew his capital asset pricing models and had the skills to use them. But that is a bit of knowledge that almost any feeder fund will have had, we may assume. Markopolos had something else in addition. He had epistemic virtue. He had the epistemic courage and inquisitiveness to ask questions where others kept silent. He was sufficiently epistemically temperate and patient not to rush to unsupported conclusions. He had the epistemic humility and self-awareness to question his own skills, and he was open-minded and impartial enough to ask others to join his research efforts. A combination of traditional mathematical and more qualitative financial due diligence skills reinforced by epistemic virtue is, in my view, what explains why Markopolos succeeded where others failed.

Epistemic virtues

This is all very well as far as it goes to show how incompetence contributed to the collapse of the financial sector. But why should it matter to an ethicist? Aren't competence and all things epistemic the domain of epistemology, the philosophical theory of knowledge, and shouldn't ethicists confine themselves to motivation and all things practical? The present book is built on the premise that maintaining the traditional distinction between ethics and epistemology no longer holds water. Rather what we see is that the two fields are growing closely together. Ethicists increasingly turn to questions about knowledge and belief. Allen

Buchanan, for instance, has argued that philosophers contributing to debates on public policy ought to be more sensitive to the pernicious influence on moral behaviour of false beliefs about factual, as opposed to ethical, matters.[21] Examples abound. False beliefs supported Apartheid and keep supporting racism, ageism, sexism and many other forms of unfair discrimination. False beliefs supported the Zimbabwe-style planned economy and keep supporting many other abhorrent forms of economic policymaking. Finally, false beliefs led to an unjustifiable increase in the appetite for mortgage-backed securities, as we have seen.

Miranda Fricker's writings on epistemic justice go beyond the traditional confines of the philosophical subdisciplines as well.[22] She calls attention to a particular kind of injustice arising when certain people are not taken sufficiently seriously as knowers, as people who gain knowledge. An example of this phenomenon is when people of colour are refused a hearing as witnesses in courts of law, or when a risk manager working for a bank is ridiculed as a 'pessimistic party-pooper' because he warns against excessively optimistic expectations about house price developments.[23] This is not only an injustice to the risk manager; it is also detrimental to the goal of gaining relevant knowledge about, say, the risks certain financial products impose on society.

In turn, the philosophical theory of knowledge has increasingly turned to social, political and moral aspects of knowledge. Echoing the well-known African proverb that it takes a village to raise a child, epistemology no longer studies knowledge acquisition in isolation at the level of the individual epistemic agent only, but incorporates the social context of the agent, or even conceives of social groups as learning entities. Epistemologists have gained insight into expert knowledge and developed theories of civic deliberation and policymaking.[24] They have started working on epistemic democracy and judgement aggregation.[25] These insights have also been used to help us decide on what to believe.[26]

The place where ethics and epistemology come closest together is perhaps the theory of epistemic virtues. Writers such as Jason Baehr, James

---

[21] Buchanan, 'Social moral epistemology'.   [22] Fricker, *Epistemic injustice*.
[23] Contribution by 'gp' to 'Dealbook', *New York Times*, 29 January 2008, dealbook.nytimes.com/2008/01/29/when-risk-management-isnt-just-a-department.
[24] Griffin, 'Motivating reflective citizens'.   [25] List, 'Judgment aggregation'.
[26] Coady, *What to believe now*.

Montmarquet, Robert Roberts and Jay Wood, and Linda Zagzebski have explored new terrain by applying themes from Aristotelian virtue ethics to epistemological questions about the analysis and value of knowledge, offering the radically novel view that knowledge is virtuously formed true belief.[27] Virtue epistemological themes run through the works of St Thomas Aquinas, René Descartes, John Locke, John Stuart Mill and John Dewey, among others, and a concern for epistemic issues can also be discerned in the writings of Alisdair MacIntyre and Bernard Williams; yet as a genuine subfield of philosophy and ethics, the theory of epistemic virtues is only some three decades old.

It is regrettable that this theory has so far attracted little attention from applied ethicists. I believe that the theory of epistemic virtues is best positioned to respond to Buchanan's call for more epistemic engagement from ethicists.[28] The theory of epistemic virtues not only offers a plausible vocabulary with which to hold normative discussions about belief formation practices; it also promises a view according to which epistemic and non-epistemic virtues go together and form a unity for the sake of reaching *eudaimonia*, the *good life*. All this chimes in with developments in applied ethics, where virtue ethics has become as important a normative model as consequentialism and deontology. Virtue ethics has gained increasingly serious and detailed treatment in textbooks in the field and has developed into something much more substantial than what was once considered a mere '*laissez-faire* ethics', only complementary to Kantian and utilitarian approaches.[29] True, the situationist critique of virtue ethics has sparked an impassioned debate about whether the notion of moral character survives psychological scrutiny; and moral character is the key to virtue.[30] And also true, important virtue theoreticians such as Aristotle, Aquinas, Elizabeth Anscombe and Alisdair MacIntyre have not always spoken warmly

---

[27] Baehr, *Inquiring mind*. Montmarquet, *Epistemic virtue*. Roberts and Wood, *Intellectual virtues*. Zagzebski, *Virtues of the mind*.

[28] Marcum, 'The epistemically virtuous clinician', Pritchard, 'Virtue epistemology' and Schwab, 'Epistemic humility and medical practice' are applications in medical ethics. A special issue of the *Journal of Philosophy of Education*, 47, 2 (2013) has been devoted to virtue epistemology and education. Rawwas et al., 'Epistemology and business ethics' is an empirical study of epistemic virtues in business.

[29] Nash, *Good intentions aside*. Also see Whetstone, 'How virtue fits'.

[30] Alzola, 'Character and environment'. Doris, 'Persons'. Harman, 'No character'. Solomon, 'Victims of circumstances?'.

about business and/or capitalism.[31] Nevertheless, a fascinating and imaginative body of literature has started applying virtue ethics to such diverse themes as corporate governance, corporate entities and teams, customers, management, the marketing of corporate social responsibility, meaningful work, networking, supply chains, the theory of the firm, as well as on a more theoretical level to the capabilities approach of Amartya Sen and Martha Nussbaum, the common good, economic theory, love, the market, and the separation thesis, which is the thesis that business and morality are worlds apart.[32] Not to mention the attractions of virtue ethics to ethics programmes, consultancy and executive education.

Some may surmise that the fact that the theory of epistemic virtues has found little application shows that virtue theory has still not entirely succeeded in catching up with its two main competitors. A more plausible explanation, I believe, is that until very recently the theory of epistemic virtues (also known as *virtue epistemology*) was studied at a very high level of abstraction, motivated largely by epistemological rather than ethical concerns. A casual glance at the literature reveals that virtue ethical approaches to epistemic ethics are not behind consequentialism and deontology, however; indeed, they may be ahead of them. Virtue theory is more than ready to take up the epistemic gauntlet, and this is only strengthened by a wave of related and relevant empirical and theoretical research in psychology, economics, sociology and other fields.

Take research on knowledge management first. Knowledge management is directed at coordinating processes around the use of knowledge and information in organizations.[33] Often inspired by work in the philosophical theory of knowledge, knowledge management theorists develop concrete insights into how business enterprises can capture knowledge that is tacitly available in employees (estimated to be about

---

[31] Dobson, 'Alisdair MacIntyre's business ethics'. Wicks, 'MacIntyre'.
[32] Sison, *Corporate governance*. Gowri, 'On corporate virtue'. Moore, 'Corporate character'. Palanski et al., 'Team virtues'. Bull and Adam, 'Customer relationship management'. Moore, 'Management'. Van de Ven, 'Marketing of CSR'. Beadle and Knight, 'Meaningful work'. Melé, 'Management'. Drake and Schlachter, 'Supply chain collaboration'. Fontrodona and Sison, 'The nature of the firm'. Bertland, 'Capabilities'. Arjoon, 'Dynamic theory'. Sison, 'Common good theory'. Baker, 'Virtue and behavior'. Argandoña, 'Love in firms'. Harris, 'Is love a virtue?'. Graafland, 'Markets'. Hartman, 'The separation thesis'.
[33] Dalkir, *Knowledge management*.

80 per cent of knowledge in an organization) rather than codified for general use, and how employees can create knowledge. They develop strategies to stimulate knowledge sharing and knowledge dissemination among employees, and they study processes contributing to successful knowledge acquisition and application. Knowledge management theorists and practitioners do not seem to use virtue theoretical vocabulary, but with their focus on the *learning organization*, their aims and techniques are often quite close to those of the virtue epistemologist.[34]

A second line of research is behavioural economics, a result of confronting traditional economics and finance methods and models with psychological concepts, theories and experiments. Historically the subject probably started when Daniel Kahneman and Amos Tversky tried to find psychologically plausible alternatives to decision theory based on the postulate of expected utility maximization.[35] They and other researchers demonstrated the relevance of framing effects, mental accounting, the use of heuristics instead of mental computation, and numerous cognitive obstacles related to overconfidence, confirmation bias, belief perseverance, anchoring, the gambler's fallacy, the home bias, herding and what have you, of which the relevance to finance is well explained in Robert Shiller's best-selling *Irrational Exuberance*. So what behavioural economics shows is that when people and organizations strive for epistemic perfection they will face many challenges.

Warning and outline

Before I proceed with a brief survey of the chapters to come, a warning is perhaps in order. This book develops a new view of ethics in finance by bringing together various streams of research, including virtue epistemology and behavioural economics. In common with most books on applied ethics, this book is written for a fairly broad audience including philosophers and ethicists just as much as economists, sociologists, psychologists and practitioners from the world of finance. My ambition is at the same time to contribute to a burgeoning literature on epistemic virtues by showing the real-life relevance of such virtues and to suggest paths of future research on the intersection of behavioural finance,

---

[34] Senge, *The fifth discipline*. Also see Conner and Clawson, *Learning culture*.
[35] Kahneman, *Thinking fast and slow* is a popular introduction. Also see Shefrin, *Beyond greed and fear*.

organizational design and epistemic virtue theory. Another aim is to offer input to policymaking. Scattered throughout the book I have included observations supporting the view that promoting epistemic virtue is feasible, and I make concrete suggestions as to how to do so. When I explain philosophy, philosophers may want to move ahead, and the same applies to financial economists and finance practitioners when I explain finance. I have tried to keep the level of technicality to a minimum, which some readers may find has led to unacceptable simplification at several points, but I have not been able to avoid using such concepts as *eudaimonia*, justification, moral hazard, diversification and confirmation bias. Note, moreover, that in spite of the logical order of the book, much of the material can fairly easily be read in isolation.

Chapter 1 introduces the main ideological and normative assumptions that underlie the book. I first examine whether one can assign a purpose to banks and other financial organizations in the sense in which hospitals and housing corporations are commonly held to have purposes; or should we rather conceive of banks as the sole nexus of contracts between shareholders, directors, employees and clients? Is it, in other words, the purpose of a bank to please its shareholders or its clients, or even society at large? The strategy used in the book is to adopt assumptions that are as minimal as possible in order that my argument shall be convincing. Reading too much of a function into banks risks losing readers who may advocate views à la Milton Friedman and others whose primary interests are in contracts and shareholder value. But if I find too little of a function or purpose in banks, macro-prudential regulation is much harder to defend; for if banks lack purpose, why not let them go bust when they are unable to support themselves? I adopt an austere view of function. The final part of the first chapter is used to introduce what I call the *argument for liberty*, which has been used by politicians ranging from Ronald Reagan and Margaret Thatcher to Tony Blair and Bill Clinton in favour of a regime of mostly deregulatory policies in the 1980s and afterwards. The argument holds that increasing the freedom of choice that citizens have with respect to, for instance, retirement planning or health insurance enlarges the scope for taking personal responsibility for satisfying their needs and wants. I show, however, that an essential precondition of this argument is effectively overlooked by theoreticians as well as politicians, namely, that in order for an increase in freedom of choice to lead to increased responsibility and desire satisfaction, citizens must have accurate beliefs about their freedom of choice. This epistemic condition often remains unsatisfied. Governments, and business enterprises even more frequently, invoke the argument for liberty to defend their economic activities. This is part and parcel of seeing oneself as instrumental to the maximization of welfare by way of one's contributions to a perfectly competitive market. Consistency requires, therefore, that when one invokes the ideology of perfect competition one also has to accept the epistemic premise, and not only accept it, but also actively contribute to its realization. To do that, epistemic virtues are necessary.

Chapter 2 develops a theory of epistemic virtues tailored to the world of business. I start with a brief introduction setting aside various views of epistemic virtues that can be found in the literature, zooming in particularly on a recent proposal by Jason Baehr.[36] I argue that Baehr's proposal, albeit attractive in its own right, is less suited to applications in business and other more commonplace contexts. It is too intellectualist. I argue that rather than conceiving of epistemic virtues as contributing to personal intellectual worth, as Baehr has it, such virtues help people to achieve particular goals; these virtues have *instrumental* epistemic value. This settles the question of what epistemic virtues do. The second topic broached is how virtues do what they do. I set out a traditional Aristotelian or Thomasian view of virtues as motivators and enablers, which I describe in a consequentialist (perhaps more precisely: decision-theoretic) way that owes much to Julia Driver.[37] Epistemic virtues motivate people to perform virtuous actions by affecting their preferences, and they enable people to perform virtuous actions by removing internal obstacles influencing their choice sets. The mere idea of virtues motivating and enabling people may seem out of place in an epistemological domain, and that is why I subsequently engage in a brief discussion of the sorts of actions at stake. *Epistemic actions*, as I call them, are analysed as a triad of inquiry, belief adoption and justification, and all three components can be performed more or less virtuously. All this is finally used to give us a deeper understanding of what epistemic virtues are.

The main epistemic virtues are individually explained in a number of separate chapters. Roughly, the idea is that Chapters 3, 5 and 7 introduce self-regarding virtues, corporate virtues and other-regarding virtues, which are related to customers, banks and rating agencies, respectively. I shall discuss them here first. Chapters 4, 6 and 8, in

---

[36] Baehr, *Inquiring mind.*   [37] Driver, *Uneasy virtue.*

turn, are case studies. Chapter 3 starts with a number of claims that are well established in the empirical literature. Most people do not know much about finance, and this lack of financial literacy leads to numerous suboptimal financial decisions. Sometimes financial illiteracy is the result of a lack of quantitative skills or low IQ. Often, however, it seems to be the consequence of a lack of interest or discipline. Chapter 3 defends the claim that epistemic virtues are needed to generate financial literacy, and it relates epistemic virtues to biases uncovered by researchers in behavioural economics and psychology. This yields an illustration of how epistemic virtues motivate and enable. They influence preferences and internal obstacles in such a way that biases are less likely to come to the fore. I should emphasize that this claim is rather tentative, and that more empirical research is dearly needed. Work on debiasing strategies suggests, however, that this hypothesis is not too far-fetched. I start with curiosity or love of knowledge and discuss, among other things, the predilection among laypeople to listen to friends, acquaintances and self-proclaimed experts venturing their opinions on the Internet rather than consumer organizations such as Which? or *Consumer Reports*. I look at epistemic courage and examine epistemic justice and open-mindedness in relation to the confirmation bias as well as to racist prejudices among consumers of insurance policies. I relate epistemic temperance (the virtue of not adopting beliefs too hastily) to empirical research on investors witnessing a decrease in the returns on their investments after an increase in information. I turn to epistemic humility (the virtue of giving way to experts whenever justified) and discuss the relevance to epistemic ethics of research into managerial hubris as well as the notorious fall of Nobel-laureate-run hedge fund Long-Term Capital Management.

Chapter 5 examines epistemic virtue at the level of the corporation. The study of corporate entities covered by umbrella titles such as *social ontology, collective intentionality* or *corporate responsibility* has made impressive progress in the past decade or two, also when it comes to corporate virtues. Corporate epistemic virtues form largely unexplored terrain, though. Related, but also in stark contrast to extant work by Reza Lahroodi, Chapter 5 develops a theory of epistemic virtues that applies to corporations, corporate entities par excellence.[38] I borrow freely not only from Lahroodi's work, but also from such authors as

---

[38] Lahroodi, 'Collective epistemic virtues'.

Peter French, Margaret Gilbert and Seamus Miller, all of whom have made significant contributions to the theory of corporate entities.[39] My starting point is that even if ascribing a function or purpose to an entire business corporation is almost always out of the question owing to the austere ideological assumptions on which I want to base my argument, individual employees and work groups or teams come with clear roles within organizations. Often these roles are prescribed by law. It is, for instance, the role of the managing director or chief executive officer (CEO) to direct the firm with a keen eye to the interests of the shareholders. They thus have fiduciary duties towards shareholders enshrined in corporate law. Probably more common are extra-legal function descriptions that are internal to the firm. In either case, I argue, functions demand that certain epistemic virtues are particularly prominent. It benefits all to have all epistemic virtues, but a chemist working in the research and development department of a pharmaceutical company, for instance, needs a love of knowledge more intensely than the salesperson selling the drugs. The view I defend in Chapter 5 is that corporate epistemic virtue is, to begin with, a matter of ensuring that the individual employees possess the individual epistemic virtues that are relevant to the function they fulfil within the organization, or *virtue-to-function matching*. But possession is not enough. A second precondition is that the firm offers what I call *organizational support for virtue*. Non-executive directors can only fulfil their task to supervise the firm critically if they have sufficient room to obtain and process information. Typically, however, they do not have these opportunities, and even the most curious directors will fail to do their jobs excellently. Finally, I show that epistemic virtues are incorporated in the firm by means of clever *organizational remedies against vice*, mitigating individual epistemically unvirtuous behaviour that it is difficult or impossible to eradicate by hiring epistemically virtuous employees or providing organizational support.

Chapter 3 examines the clients and argues that they benefit from epistemic virtues, and, more strongly, that whenever policymakers support liberalization by preaching personal responsibility for needs satisfaction, the assumption is that clients do practise virtue. Chapter 5 subsequently shows what it means for a corporation to embody epistemic virtue. So far I have primarily provided a conceptual analysis of individual and corporate epistemic virtue and related it to empirical

---

[39] French, *Corporate ethics*. Gilbert, *On social facts*. Miller, *Moral foundations*.

findings. I have not so much addressed the normative issue as the circumstances in which epistemic virtue may be morally required. Epistemic virtues may be nice character traits that it may be in our own interest to acquire, but what grounds do we have for requiring others to acquire them? And what grounds do we have to criticize others for their epistemic vices? Up to some point, answers to these questions follow immediately from function descriptions. Insufficiently inquisitive research analysts are criticized precisely because they do not live up to the expectations that come with the function of being a research analyst. But what about banks? If a corporation is merely a nexus of voluntary contracts of freely consenting people, who is going to say that this nexus should be a blueprint of epistemic virtue? Why object to a group of people preferring to do business in unintelligent ways? To make out a case for corporate epistemic virtue in banks is certainly easier once we adopt the view that banks fulfil a function that places them almost at the level of governments. Perhaps what they do is protect private property in the form of deposits, distribute freedom over a person's life cycle, guarantee liberal citizenship rights, consonant with corporate citizenship ideals. How far such an argument can go should not detain us here. It is important, however, to show that epistemic virtue is not a straightforward normative requirement across all cases. In Chapter 7, I consider a case where a massive moral and political appeal for epistemic virtue seems warranted at first glance. It concerns the credit rating agencies. These agencies, as we have seen, provide information about the credit risk of corporate and government debt as well as structured debt securities. It seems that if there is one player on the world stage of finance that not just benefits but is morally obliged to practise epistemic virtue, it is the rating agencies. To warn against what I call *outsourcing epistemic responsibility*, Chapter 7 considers the consequences of government regulation that fails to encourage epistemic virtue.

Finally, the case studies. Case studies are often seen as investigations of one single case with the explicit aim of helping us to understand a larger class of similar cases, as well as to develop new theories or further explore or 'test' existing theories.[40] In the context of this book, the cases also fulfil two other functions. First, they provide illustrations in the sense that, more than the theoretical chapters, they show epistemic virtue theory in action. Secondly, they are ethical studies in their own

---

[40] Brigley, 'Case studies'. Gerring, *Case study research*. Ruzzene, 'Case studies'.

right. They examine three important topics relevant to a fair appraisal of the origins of the global financial crisis, namely, subprime clients, financial due diligence and the accountancy profession. Chapter 4 focuses on subprime clients. It starts with an analysis of the complexity of subprime loan terms and the failure of clients to grasp that complexity. I examine the sort of epistemic virtues that were missing and also investigate whether outsourcing the epistemic work to financial advisers should be recommended. The second case study, in Chapter 6, looks into the financial world itself and considers financial due diligence. Financial due diligence is what banks and other financial institutions have to do to ascertain the potential risks of investments they make on behalf of their clients. Part of it is quantitative work using elementary models from financial economics as well as more qualitative methods. As we have seen, however, financial due diligence failed hopelessly as an insurance against the biggest Ponzi scheme in the history of finance. Chapter 6 illustrates the claim defended in the book that without epistemic virtues, quantitative and qualitative research will hardly do what it is supposed to do. The last case study, in Chapter 8, examines the accountancy profession. Like the credit rating agencies, chartered accountants or certified public accountants are there to inform potential investors and/or the tax office of particular aspects of the financial situation of firms. Like the agencies, the accountants are not paid by the beneficiaries of their services (the investors or the tax office) but by the firms they audit. This leads, in the words of one commentator, to a situation no different from when butchers hired their own meat inspectors 'with the power to set their prices and fire [their inspectors] if they do not like the inspection reports issued'.[41] In Chapter 7, I defend the view that in the end no normative case for epistemic virtue can be pleaded if all we assume is that governments happen to use credit rating agencies in prudential regulation. One ingredient of my argument is that the information value of raters is disputed among economists, and epistemically virtuous governments should therefore not coerce banks, pension funds and other institutional investors to use them as a source of information on credit risk. The information value of chartered accountants, however, is much more broadly accepted, and unlike credit rating agencies, they are not only designated by law as official

---

[41] Armstrong, 'Ethical issues in accounting', 155.

sources of information, but also regulated by law. Rather than arguing for a kind of laissez-faire with respect to accountancy or defending a more revolutionary but difficult-to-realize alternative compensation scheme, I show that accountants should be seen as part of a joint epistemic agent, together with corporate management, and that a number of epistemic virtues result from this view.

1 | *Financial ethics: virtues in the market*

On 13 September 1970, *New York Times Magazine* published an op-ed article provocatively entitled 'The social responsibility of business is to increase its profits'. It would turn its author into the most prominent colour guard of shareholder wealth maximization.[1] In this piece, Milton Friedman, six years later awarded the Nobel Prize in economics, inveighed against what he called 'unadulterated socialism'.[2] He believed that 'socialist' tendencies were present among many businesspeople of his time, claiming as they did that business is not only about making profit but also about achieving certain social ends. Friedman provided the 'socialist' businesspeople with an alternative as simple as it was powerful. Business, he said, is about maximizing shareholder wealth, and nothing else.

Simple or simplistic? In the writings of Friedman's opponents and many of his followers surely this view has often been reduced to the idea that in business 'anything goes'. Nor has Friedman done too much to allay potential misgivings on this point, as he and his followers have been quite proud to accept being turned into relentless laissez-fairists. The view is much more subtle, though; it is in any case subtle enough to use as a plausible default position about the responsibilities of corporations. To begin with, Friedman does not mean to say that shareholder interests trump everything. Law is a restrictive factor, which has lexicographic priority over the shareholders; no business strategy should be adopted if it clashes with the law, whatever pain the shareholders suffer as a result of opportunity lost. Tax evasion and illegal pollution are prohibited, for instance, despite the obvious negative effects on profit generation. This is true of ethics as well. Even though ethics is mentioned only twice, Friedman is clear enough to stipulate that ethics too has lexicographic priority over the interests of the shareholders. Now Friedman was acutely aware of the fact that ethics and law may differ

---

[1] Friedman, 'Social responsibility'.   [2] Friedman, 'Social responsibility'.

from context to context, and that is why he prefers to refer to the 'basic rules of society' rather than law and ethics. This undoubtedly smacks of relativism. The fact that turning a blind eye to human rights abuses in order to propagate profitability is unacceptable to Friedman shows, however, that despite intricate questions about international ethics, his position is powerful enough to indict contemporary multinational companies that violate these rights.

It is misguided to view Friedman's article as a plea against ethics in business. But what, then, were his aims? With indeed perhaps a little too much Cold War rhetoric, Friedman directed his arrows at a movement that started in the 1960s to promote the idea of corporate social responsibility. As I mentioned briefly in the Introduction, advocates of corporate social responsibility maintain that firms have responsibilities beyond the mere business-economic. Summarized by Archie Carroll's four-storey pyramid of corporate social responsibilities, the idea is that society 'requires' firms, as he puts it, to discharge not only business-economic but also legal responsibilities; that society, moreover, 'expects' them to meet ethical responsibilities; and that society 'desires' them to undertake philanthropic responsibilities.[3] Given what I said about the lexicographic priority of ethics and law, Friedman in a sense accords a slightly firmer place to ethics and law than corporate social responsibility. It is only economic concerns that form the ground floor of Carroll's corporate social responsibility, and law, ethics and philanthropy are built thereon. It is the 'basic rules of society' (ethics and law) that form the basis of Friedman's model, and shareholder wealth comes thereafter. So the controversy between Friedman and the commenders of corporate social responsibility is chiefly concerned with top-floor responsibilities – that is, with philanthropy.

Friedman's argument

It is not so much that Friedman rejects philanthropy as such. He does not rule out that people have 'feelings of charity' and he does not rule out that people may decide to start a company for an 'eleemosynary purpose' such as a hospital or school.[4] He does not even rule out spending money on charitable projects when this generates value to the shareholders. Organizing day care for children, building houses for

---

[3] Carroll, 'The pyramid'.   [4] Friedman, 'Social responsibility'.

labourers, financing sports facilities in the community may all enhance profit making. But then such activities stay firmly attached to the basis of corporate social responsibility, the economic responsibilities. What he does reject, though, is when shareholders' money is used for philanthropic purposes without their explicit consent (unlike the hospital) or without there being a business-economic rationale behind it (unlike workers' housing).

Corporate responsibility

What was Friedman's argument? A useful reconstruction sees Friedman as making three claims.[5] First, he finds fault with the idea that corporations can be bearers of responsibility in a way that is irreducible to the individual responsibilities of directors, managers, employees and other people taking part in or dealing with the business enterprise. Responsibility, Friedman seems to think, is closely connected to being human, and corporations are not human beings. This is not to say that we end up in a vacuum where nothing or no one is responsible for what a company does, but for Friedman the responsibility for corporate actions must always be reduced to the responsibilities of individual human actors; and plainly, without corporate responsibility there is no corporate social responsibility.

Shareholders

Friedman next considers the responsibilities of a salient group of decision makers: the firm's directors. He defends a second claim, which says that the sole responsibility of a firm's management is to act in the interests of the shareholders. It is here that Friedman flies into the teeth of the philanthropists. When the directors of a firm decide to sponsor a museum or sports club, they steal from the shareholders. Part of the earnings, however small, are not used in ways that benefit the shareholders in terms of dividend or additional investments; part of the earnings are used to benefit artists, art lovers or sportspersons, without the shareholders' consent. That is what Friedman finds objectionable.

It is important to realize that this second claim is essentially an argument from law; it is not an argument based on the concept of equity

---

[5] See, e.g., the lucid discussion by Crane and Matten, *Business ethics*, 46–61.

or on the ethics of shareholders; it depends for its validity on the way corporate law has been shaped during the past two centuries. The capacious legal template of the public limited company or corporation endows directors with fiduciary duties towards the shareholders of the firm. It is a historical accident that rather than the eleemosynary firm (hospital, school, etc.) it was the profit-seeking firm that formed the main inspiration driving developments in corporate law. This accident is understandable, and I believe we need not be deeply worried about history here. In a world with different laws, however, Friedman's second claim falls.

That is not to say that opposition to this template is entirely absent. Jack Welsh, former CEO of General Electric, has called shareholder wealth maximization a 'dumb idea'.[6] Some legal scholars claim that courts of justice have not even always ruled in ways consistent with this idea. Lynn Stout, for instance, has defended the view that corporate law categorizes shareholders not so much as owners but more as contractors very much on a par with bondholders, employees and suppliers.[7] Courts have afforded managers ample space for discretionary judgements about balancing the interests of various other stakeholders. It is indeed quite clear that shareholders own equity in a company in a very different way than they own, say, their house, their land or their art collection. Let us grant that Stout is right. Then it is only when a company is bought by another company or when a company goes bankrupt that shareholder ownership gets a specific meaning, offering special protection to shareholders at the expense of bondholders and other interested or affected parties.

The legal argument that underlies Friedman's view may be less convincing in the end than many people have thought, but Friedman's other contributions to the debate are still strong. To begin with, if the discretionary decisions that courts allow boards to make are about cases where boards let the 'basic rules of society' prevail over the interests of shareholders, Stout may have succeeded in arguing against *ruthless* shareholder value maximization, but not against shareholder wealth maximization with lexicographic respect for law and ethical custom. Courts are in that case fully consistent with Friedman's view, because what they do is allow management room to take on these legal and ethical responsibilities even when that does not maximize shareholder

[6] Mazzucato, 'Towards a fairer capitalism'.   [7] Stout, *The shareholder value myth*.

wealth. Only if courts allow management to engage in supererogatory shareholder-value-slashing philanthropy will there be a serious case against Friedman's second claim.

Job requirements

Even then Friedman has an answer. For two independent reasons, solving social problems is not, for him, the responsibility of corporations in the first place. One reason is the empirical observation that the capacities that make people good managers do not necessarily make them good policymakers. Directing a firm is very different from leading a country. The nefarious idea of *UK plc*, viewing the state as a corporation to be run by a government of CEOs and CFOs, is consigned to the waste-paper basket. The second leg of Friedman's charge against the idea of corporations assuming social responsibilities is conceptually much stronger; it is that making business instead of politics responsible for addressing social issues endangers democratic legitimacy. For all the cynical remarks that the most significant political act of many citizens is not carried out in the polling booths but in the supermarket where they vote on brands, it is indisputably true that managers are not hired by a democratic selection procedure.[8] Managers are not accountable to their rank and file and they can exclude whole segments of the population from their philanthropic endeavours at will. A manager sponsoring sports not arts will not be brought to book; a local government official taking such a decision, however, will fortunately need to provide a clear justification.

Despite serious criticism of Friedman's position, I work on the assumption that he is right. This is primarily for methodological reasons. Assumptions have to be made, and I prefer to make assumptions that are as minimal as possible. More substantive assumptions about corporations, shareholders, law and morality would alienate advocates of unadorned shareholder wealth maximization. Making minimal assumptions does not risk losing readers with more substantive views about these themes; the risk is smaller at any rate. More concretely, I want to be able to say something normative about epistemic virtues in business without having to commit myself to the idea that business has to take on any other obligations than those entailed by Friedman's view. This may look like a hopeless project. Most theorists writing on finance and ethics have

---

[8] Klein, *The shock doctrine.*

therefore adopted a decidedly more ponderous view of the function of finance. For my purpose, minimal assumptions are enough.

A theory of the firm

It is now important briefly to review some of the arguments that have been given in defence of the legal template of the public limited company or corporation. Let us start with the influential definition by Michael Jensen and William Meckling describing a corporation as a mere 'legal fiction' or 'artificial construct' allowing a particular kind of organization to be treated in law as an individual.[9] This is a good starting point because, as Lynn Stout has also observed, Jensen and Meckling were building on Friedman's suggestion here, among others.[10] In a recent monograph, Jensen put it thus:

> The public corporation is the nexus for a complex set of voluntary contracts among customers, workers, managers, and the suppliers of materials, capital, and risk bearing. This means that the parties contract, not between themselves bilaterally, but unilaterally with the legal fiction called the *corporation*, thus greatly simplifying the contracting process. The rights of the interacting parties are determined by law, the corporation's charter, and the implicit and explicit contracts with each individual.[11]

Seeing a firm as nothing more than a complex system of interwoven voluntary contracts need not lead to a hierarchical notion of capitalist firms. John Stuart Mill once argued that when the level of education increases among workers they turn away from the hierarchical master–servant view of the firm to form 'associations of labourers'.[12] They form cooperatives with or without suppliers of capital and develop firms that supersede the traditional capitalist model. But this idea 'barely outlived Mill', as Gerald Gaus writes.[13]

Hierarchy of command

It is, ironically, a utilitarian or consequentialist explanation that shows why Mill's idea has not caught on.[14] As Ronald Coase famously showed, a

---

[9] Jensen and Meckling, 'Theory of the firm', 310.
[10] Another predecessor is Alchian and Demsetz, 'Economic organization'.
[11] Jensen, *A theory of the firm*, 1.   [12] Mill, *Political economy*.
[13] Gaus, 'Capitalism', 90.   [14] Gaus, 'Capitalism'.

hierarchical relation of control is essential to the corporation.[15] Without
a hierarchical command structure in which a manager instructs workers
on what to do, capitalists have to find a party willing and able to carry
out every single task they deem necessary, negotiate contracts with them
and later monitor their work. This leads capitalists to incur search and
transaction costs and to encounter a number of agency problems. It is
these costs and problems that are significantly mitigated by organizing
the firm in a hierarchical manner by hiring people to do the work instead
of contracting it all out. Coase's argument had to remain fairly speculative until it was backed by empirical findings. Seventy years of subsequent research on corporate governance (how is the firm organized?)
and corporate performance (how much profit is made?) have indeed
considerably refined and corroborated Coase's view. The core of his
speculation remains valid. With only a few exceptions, hierarchical
corporate governance structures considerably outdo other forms of
organization.

Corporate law

But does that mean that shareholder wealth maximization is unequivocally a good thing to pursue? It goes without saying that a hierarchical
command structure does not entail a shareholder-interests-first mentality;
the defence of Jensen and Meckling's 'legal fiction' has to go further than
Coase's observations. Comparative legal research shows that corporate
law in almost all jurisdictions offers a template of a legal entity close to the
corporation. John Armour, Henry Hansmann and Reinier Krankman
single out five characteristics that are universally adopted.[16] A corporation is a *legal person* in that it can enter into contracts itself, own
property, delegate authority to other persons and can sue or be sued.
Moreover, it only has so-called *limited liability*. The function of these two
provisions is called *asset partitioning*. Legal personality shields the assets
of the company from the creditors of the individual owners of the
company, which has the advantage that without such provisions creditors, when they have claims on shareholders of the company that are
unable to repay their debts, could take security on the company's assets,
endangering the firm. Limited liability conversely shields the private

---

[15] Coase, 'Nature of the firm'.   [16] Armour et al., 'Corporate law'.

assets of the shareholders of the company from creditors with claims on the company. Shareholders of broken companies will not have to pay their remaining debts. The conditions of *transferability of shares* and *investor ownership* determine that unlike, for example, partnerships, the shares of a company can be freely traded, and ensure that shareholders have a right to its residual earnings and a right to control the firm. The right to control, however, is a right that shareholders do not exercise all by themselves, as the final condition holds that the owners *delegate control* to an elected *board of directors*.

   In the end, the way company law statutes fix the meaning of the legal fiction of the public limited company across the globe is not merely motivated by the Coasian outlook of a firm as a command structure in which owners delegate management to a board of directors keeping tabs on the employees' decision making. It also owes much to a utilitarian outlook on law that sees the purpose of corporate law as developing legal templates enabling people to maximize social or Pareto efficiency. This utilitarian argument depends on whether maximizing shareholder value, as corporate law sees fit, brings us closer to this utilitarian ideal, and scholars dispute the issue. It is more than disingenuous to claim that empirical data support the efficiency argument for the public limited company.[17] Yet corporate law is not inextricably bound to use utilitarian models. Nothing in law requires it to foster efficiency. Frank Easterbrook and David Fischel's classic treatment of the economic structure of corporate law provides an alternative. Rather than defending corporate law in terms of its potential to contribute to efficiency, they view it as a set of ready-made and standard-form contracts that are attractive to participants for whatever reasons they might have. The attraction of the precise characteristics with which the law has endowed corporations (legal personality, limited liability, etc.) is derived from the fact that, the two authors claim, these are terms that participants would have negotiated had they been able to do so at low or zero cost; in other words, corporate law is seen as the outcome of a hypothetical negotiation between self-interested, autonomous people. It is 'enabling rather than directive'.[18] Easterbrook and Fischel allow alternative ways to form business enterprises, and from this they draw the conclusion that the question of what is the purpose of the corporation is moot. Any purpose is acceptable, or

[17] Jones and Felps, 'Shareholder wealth maximization' offer a critical evaluation.
[18] Easterbrook and Fischel, *Corporate law*, 15.

even no purpose at all. But this does not seem completely true as long as most firms stick to the standard-form setup provided by corporate law; in the absence of any additional clauses to contracts or without communication between the various constituents of the firm, a failure to maximize shareholder wealth is a reason for 'legitimate complaint' from equity investors – for breach of contract, that is.[19]

A company's goals

There are, however, many other reasons to question whether corporations can be said to have any goal at all. In a nexus of contracts contractors will have individual reasons for participation that are highly unlikely to converge. This is obvious for managers (seeking the thrill of it), members of Rhinelandish supervisory boards (wishing to remain in contact with the business world when they are close to retirement age) and employees (depending on their wages for their wealth, wellbeing or survival). But it is no less obvious for many different kinds of shareholders, including pension funds (demanding stable long-term profitability), hedge funds (perhaps even betting on the firm's demise as they are shorting the company) and private investors (speculating on short-term increases of the share price). It makes sense to explain individual contractors' decisions to participate in a nexus of contracts in terms of individual purposes; yet we should avoid ascribing grand overarching goals to corporations, be they shareholder maximization or otherwise. People contracting with firms will have purposes, and certain firms may be contractually organized in such a way that the purposes of particular contractors (shareholders are the prime example) receive more weight. But it is a category mistake to derive a corporate purpose from these multifarious individual purposes. The workers at the drilling and production platform in the Magnus oilfield in the North Sea are there for money or adventure. They have not taken their jobs owing to a desire to increase the wealth of holders of British Petroleum equity shares.

Altogether this may be seen as an astonishing move in a virtue theoretic argument. It may be that utilitarianism rather indirectly supports the idea that firms should not be ascribed the purpose of

---

[19] Easterbrook and Fischel, *Corporate law*, 36.

generating Pareto efficiency as long as the empirical data cannot be adequately lined up. It may also be that a deontological argument more directly supports corporate purposelessness owing to its insistence on the autonomy of freely contracting individual human beings. But virtue theory is, by contrast, renowned for its more constructive and substantive stance on purpose in business. One of the first philosophers applying virtue ethics to this issue, Robert Solomon, set up a theory according to which corporations are communities of people sharing a view of two overarching goals: to produce goods and services of decent quality and to realize profit for shareholders.[20] Rather than deriving a common goal by combining the individual ends of individually contracting individual human beings, Solomon suggests that the goals of individual directors, managers and employees are derived from the common goal that constitutes the corporation as a community of practice. This is important first of all because it may be slightly odd to study epistemic virtues without a commitment to virtue ethics. Is it possible, one may wonder, to defend normative claims about epistemic virtues of, say, bankers or their clients without appealing to a foundational normative virtue ethical view of the purpose of finance? With a virtue ethical underpinning of finance, a normative epistemic argument is decidedly easier. It is easier, for instance, to defend the claim that bank employees have to embrace epistemic virtue if we adopt the view that they work together to develop quality financial services. If we see them as individually contracting people with disparate motives this may be more difficult. But here again I prefer to use the methodology of adopting reasonably minimal normative assumptions. I believe that a virtue epistemic account has much to recommend it even if one disagrees with the virtue ethicist about the common good of business. Even under the austere view of the corporation as a nexus of contracts or a generator of Pareto efficient wealth, epistemic virtues are essential. How far one can require people to practise epistemic virtues is certainly a matter of debate. In particular, as I argue in Chapter 7, the normative requirements on epistemic virtue for credit rating agencies are much less extensive than might be derivable from a thoroughly virtue ethical point of departure. That virtue ethicists may want to use the present approach to argue for more far-reaching epistemic obligations is, however, perfectly consistent with making minimal assumptions.

[20] Solomon, *Ethics and excellence.*

The economics of banking

This discussion of the purpose of the firm is also relevant for another reason. One only needs to follow recent discussions of bank regulation to see that the overwhelming majority of commentators and policy-makers hold to the view that the world of finance is truly special. When Delta Airlines, Polaroid, WorldCom and Enron went bankrupt, they just went bankrupt. When a bank gets into trouble, there is a chance that it will be rescued, and in many countries the chance is quite good. Despite the collapse of Lehman Brothers and other less heavily publicized business failures in the financial services industry, many governments have provided state aid to tottering banks. They have nationalized banks. They have forced healthy banks to take over the sick ones. They have injected capital or agreed to stand surety for the bank's ailing liabilities. They have developed depositor protection schemes. Hardly any industry gets so much help from the government as the financial sector. There is no shortage of popular arguments in support of state aid, either. Reference is made to the Long Depression, the Great Depression, Black Monday, Black Wednesday and many other crises and crashes with execrable consequences. It is claimed that letting a bank fail leads to contagion effects in which sick banks drag down healthy ones in their fall. It is said that without state support no one sensible would deposit money in a bank account any longer. It is even argued that finance is the great facilitator of economic growth and happiness and that finance firms ought to be protected by the tax payer in return for the salutary work they do as liegemen of the economy.

These arguments do not hit home, though. Finance undeniably does a lot of good, and without banks or insurance companies our lives would look quite different. That is also true of the pharmaceutical industry, however. In some sense, and unlike the pharmaceutical industry, things that banks do are things we could also do ourselves. What marks banks as different is essentially that they do these things vastly more efficiently than a do-it-yourself approach could ever aspire to. It is helpful briefly to elaborate on this point. At its simplest, a bank is an intermediary between people with a surplus of money and people with a deficit. The standard way to explain why these people, potential depositors and borrowers, want to make use of the services of a bank is that banks exploit economies of scale and scope to do things more efficiently. To begin with, depositors typically want small amounts of money to be deposited for short periods of time, whereas borrowers often need large sums of money for more extended periods of time. Banks can pool these numerous small deposits and lend the money to fewer borrowers without running the risk of being unable to repay depositors who request their money. This is called *maturities transformation* because banks match the maturity dates of the loans to expected peaks in depositor demand. In addition to this, banks also *reduce risk*. Unlike solo depositors lending their money to one particular borrower, banks diversify their portfolios and lend to very different kinds of borrowers using the funds for very different kinds of activities, and unlike the do-it-yourselfer, banks can hire experts to research potential borrowers to estimate their risk characteristics in ways that individual lenders are hardly capable of doing with equal thoroughness. Thirdly, banks decrease *search* and *transaction* costs in that prospective depositors and borrowers do not need to do work to find each other and do not have to spend a lot on writing loan contracts.

This is all very fine, but from the fact that banks can do things more efficiently than individual people with money surpluses and deficits one cannot, I believe, derive a special place for banks among other businesses. Yet the upshot of this brief excursion into the economics of banking is not entirely negative; it also shows that more than in other sectors, an important part of the banks' added value derives from their superior epistemic position. It is not only because they have more money than individual depositors that they can get a better mix of risk and return; it is also because they know more: about finance, about the economy, about their clients and about how to screen them.

So far, then, we have encountered two arguments showing why epistemic concerns are important in finance. The first stems from a theory of the firm. Whether one adopts a substantive view according to which management and employees work together for the common good of quality services and shareholder value, or a minimal view according to which a firm is nothing other than a nexus of contracts, without expertise, skills, knowledge and information the common good will hardly be reached and the contractual obligations will hardly be met. Not all firms are similar in this respect, though, and a second argument can be gained from inspecting the particular sort of services that finance firms provide. Using a traditional economics of banking view, finance is essentially intermediation between people with money surpluses and people with money deficits. Intermediaries have epistemic advantages with respect to maturities transformation and the like, which suggests that epistemic virtues are a serious element of human capital. But is this all there is to epistemic issues in finance? An important and often overlooked culprit in the global financial crisis is the clients. Most scorn has been heaped upon bankers, hedge fund managers, raters and regulators. Clients have been described as innocent, if not slightly dewy-eyed, victims of the financial institutions' avarice, egoism and pitilessness. The idea that clients may have to bear part of the burden of blame seems to be heresy to most commentators. Chapters 3 and 4 examine in more detail the predicament of many customers facing increasing responsibilities to organize their own financial affairs. Here I present some information on the ideological background of this development, and its concomitant epistemic assumptions.

An argument for liberty

Let me turn now to the *argument for liberty*. The drift of this argument is that liberalization (in the guise of privatization, deregulation and the like) leads to increased freedom of choice for consumers because they assume personal responsibility for satisfying their needs and desires. The argument underlay the so-called *neoliberal* overhaul of much of the financial sector in Britain and America in the 1980s and 1990s, and inspired policymaking in other sectors such as education, health care, mass media, telecommunication, transport and water, and in countries ranging from China and India to Mexico and Ghana and post-apartheid South Africa.[21] With a little more precision, the argument can be represented thus. The first premise covers an assumption about the value to consumers of increasing preference satisfaction and personal responsibility:

1. It is a good thing to increase the personal responsibility consumers have for satisfying their own preferences.

The second premise postulates a connection between increasing freedom of choice and increasing personal responsibility for preference satisfaction:

---

[21] A partial sample from the literature on liberalization includes Driskill, 'The argument for free trade', Harvey, *A brief history of neoliberalism*, Katrougalos, 'Constitutional limitations of privatization', Moloney, 'Financial services and markets', Quiggin, *Zombie economics* and Steger and Roy, *Neoliberalism*.

2. Increasing freedom of choice leads to an increase in the personal responsibility consumers have for satisfying their own preferences.

The third premise connects liberalization (privatization, deregulation, etc.) to freedom of choice:

3. Liberalization increases consumer freedom of choice.

I admit this is an abstract rendering of an argument that has been analysed and criticized in more detail in the literature on regulation. It is my purpose here neither to examine the intricacies of its internal logical structure, nor to evaluate the plausibility of the three premises in much detail. Without doubt, its supposed proximity to neoliberal ideology has led many commentators to criticize the argument. Despite the relevance of such discussions, my interest in the argument is mainly driven here by the project of finding a normative starting point of epistemic virtue. I do think of the argument as potentially a quite powerful source of policymaking, but only if a number of epistemic assumptions be satisfied, which it is the unwarranted tendency of many commentators and policymakers to neglect. For consumers to enjoy and exploit freedom of choice, possessing knowledge of their choice options is essential, and these epistemic assumptions lead us immediately to requirements of practising epistemic virtue. Turning to a closer examination of these assumptions, which I shall do shortly, would only be moderately relevant, though, if hardly any politician, policymaker or academic ever defended any of the three premises above. It is therefore important to point out that they do have their advocates. The argument for liberty has indeed been a powerful force in developments that have shaped the financial sector in the United Kingdom, the United States and other western countries since the 1980s. In line with its first premise, purchasers of financial services are viewed as people bearing responsibility for the satisfaction of their own preferences. The Pew Research Center has even gathered the people most intensely affected by these increased responsibilities under the rubric of the *sandwich generation*.[22] Rather than leaving the responsibility for financial decisions to the state or to employers, sandwichers have to decide all this for themselves. This reasoning inspired, among many other things, the privatization of

[22] www.pewsocialtrends.org/2013/01/30/the-sandwich-generation.

pension schemes in the United Kingdom and the liberalization of legal regulations on mortgage lending in the United States.[23]

Politics

Consider some examples. In the United Kingdom, a 1988 law permitted employees to opt out of occupational pension schemes that had hitherto been mandatory. In the United States, the 1980 Depository Institutions Deregulation and Money Control Act turned the sale of subprime mortgages into a legitimate business, accomplishing this by abandoning the setting of upper limits on mortgage rates on the grounds that this brings house ownership within the reach of people who would never qualify for prime mortgages because of their income or poor credit score.[24] In the same country, but in an entirely different domain, the 1996 Personal Responsibility and Work Opportunity Reconciliation Act required, among other things, single mothers to find a job in order to assume personal responsibility for their lives. These are examples illustrating how politicians and policymakers link liberalization, privatization and related forms of deregulation to personal responsibility, thereby adopting the logic of the argument for liberty. But do policy-makers have anything on offer when it comes to justifying its premises? In the course of a detailed study of personal responsibility, Alexander Brown states that politicians 'are not averse to drawing on moral and political philosophy to make arguments about why personal responsi-bility matters'; he even quotes Tony Blair, the former British prime minister, as advocating a society 'where more opportunities, and more choices, are matched by a greater responsibility for people to help themselves'.[25] So let us first consider Premise 1 in the light of Brown's observations. Although politicians do not typically use the terminology, Premise 1 is indebted to the theoretical framework of decision theory, which many academics favouring the argument adopt, either implicitly or explicitly. A theory of rational decision making, it sees consumers as rational agents maximizing their expected utility. For such agents, increasing preference satisfaction is by definition a good thing.

---

[23] See, e.g., Duménil and Lévy, *The crisis of neoliberalism* and Engel and McCoy, 'Tales of three markets'.

[24] Dietz and Haurin, 'Micro-level consequences'.

[25] Brown, *Personal responsibility*, 77.

Arguments

Now why does one have to bear personal responsibility for one's own preference satisfaction? Brown detects two sorts of arguments that have made their way into politics. One line explains the value of personal responsibility for preference satisfaction in terms of an ideal of fairness and that it is unfair to make other people responsible for a person's preference satisfaction. Brown considers Blair to be a proponent of this view. The tenor of this argument derives the value of a person S's responsibility *ex negativo* from the claim that if S were not responsible for satisfying her own needs and desires, someone else, T, would be; and this the argument considers to be unfair. Another line cleaves to the view that S's personal responsibility is valuable to S herself as part of what it means to be a human being. Brown traces this second view back to another former prime minister, Margaret Thatcher, who argued that 'the virtues of hard work and self-reliance' are valuable in themselves as part of the good life.[26]

It is one thing to believe that it is valuable for oneself or other people to assume responsibility for maximizing one's expected utility. It is quite another thing to argue that increasing freedom of choice leads to an increase in such responsibility, a proposition Premise 2 is intended to capture. An original defence along this line is given by Thomas Hurka.[27] In a nutshell, Hurka asks us to imagine a situation in which an option A is added to the set of actions from which one is free to choose. Besides that, option A has a consequence, C, that was impossible to reach by performing actions in the original set of options. Hurka goes on to argue that someone performing A is responsible for having established C, whereas someone not performing A is responsible for excluding consequence C.[28] As a result, the addition of action A to a set of options has increased the decision maker's personal responsibility with respect to establishing or excluding consequence C.

This is the outline of a fairly plausible way to defend Premise 2. What about Premise 3, that is, the claim that liberalization (in the form of privatization, deregulation, etc.) increases freedom of choice? Advocates of deregulation often defend Premise 3 by means of a reduction to

---

[26] Brown, *Personal responsibility*, 78.   [27] Hurka, 'Why value autonomy?'
[28] This goes a bit fast, ignoring as it does the role of causal factors. For expository purposes I abstract from these details. A treatment of responsibility in the context of business is Gibson, *Ethics and business*, 95–124.

absurdity showing that the alleged opposite of liberalization – regulation – *decreases* freedom. Ned Dobos provides a detailed and critical discussion of this argument to which the present discussion is indebted.[29] Protectionist regulation of the American car industry in the Reagan era established import restrictions on Japanese cars, which curtailed consumer freedom of choice. This is because as a result of the regulations, the price of Japanese cars increased by $900 on average, whereas the price of American cars increased by only $300 on average. Given one's budget constraints, an increase in the price of a particular product decreases one's freedom in the sense that it decreases the number of consumption bundles one can afford. In this case, for instance, the option of buying a Japanese car rather than an American car and spending the remaining $600 on a weekend in New York City (and simultaneously keeping the rest of the expenditures the same as in the deregulated scenario) is no longer available. Tariffs and related forms of regulation decrease freedom, and consequently, winding these things back, which is what liberalization does, increases freedom.

Epistemic preconditions for liberty

This has been a quick survey of how liberalization (privatization, deregulation, etc.) has been defended and why this has influenced policymaking. My purpose, however, is not to evaluate the plausibility of the argument for liberty, but to show how its advocates often fail to take care of an assumption that has to do with processing information, forming beliefs and acquiring knowledge. In essence my strategy is to show that Premise 2 makes implicit assumptions about what consumers know about their choice options. Without knowledge of the consumption bundles one can choose, increasing one's freedom of choice does not have the desired effect of increasing personal responsibility for the satisfaction of one's preferences. Premise 2 states that increasing freedom of choice leads to an increase in the personal responsibility for satisfying their own desires that consumers face. To see that this presupposes an epistemic condition, imagine that a new kind of retirement product is introduced to the market. This assuredly increases consumer

---

[29] Dobos, 'Neoliberalism', 65–6. The case was first developed in Williams, 'Free markets', from which Dobos quotes.

freedom. Imagine, however, that consumers are unaware of the increased freedom. Then obviously there is no increase in the personal responsibility consumers have for the satisfaction of their preferences, because the choice situation, from their point of view, is the same as before. A decision-theoretic framework allows us to make this argument more explicit. A decision problem as decision theory conceives of it has someone choose an action only when it maximizes expected utility. The standard elements of a decision situation are: (i) the *actions* that someone can choose and their various possible *consequences*; (ii) the person's *preferences*, represented by a utility function, over all possible outcomes of all available actions; and (iii) the person's *beliefs* about the likelihood of certain consequences obtaining. From the perspective of decision theory, it is completely transparent that how far people succeed in satisfying their preferences depends on the accuracy of their beliefs. Suppose an action is available, but one does not see or believe that it is; or suppose that a particular highly desired consequence is reachable with high probability, but one underestimates the probability of reaching it. Then one is likely to end up not satisfying one's preferences in the best way possible. It is undeniable that the better a person's beliefs, the higher the expected utility.

Responsibility

It is fairly trivial that epistemic assumptions are essential for preference satisfaction. It is slightly less straightforward if the primary value we discern in consumer freedom is not so much preference satisfaction but responsibility. Yet here too an increase in freedom of choice only contributes to increasing the alleged good effects of responsibility (fairness, hard work, self-reliance and whatever other values Blair, Thatcher and their like have invoked in defence of liberalization) if people are aware of their increased freedom. Suppose, for example, that fairness is what drives the argument and that fairness requires that performing certain activities is my responsibility rather than the responsibility of others. In order to perform the actions that it is my responsibility to perform, I have to be aware of the fact that I am free to perform these actions. Otherwise it is unfair to criticize me for not performing them. Here, however, an interesting twist arises if we adopt Hurka's responsibility defence. Hurka stressed that responsibility should not only include responsibility for the consequences of the action I decide to carry out, but also for the consequences of the actions I decide *not* to carry out. Increasing freedom of choice by one action, A, increases such responsibility even if I never perform A. To be responsible for omitting A, however, I should know that I have gained the freedom to do A. If responsibility is what buttresses the argument for liberty, even gaining knowledge about actions one does not perform should be welcomed.

In decision-theoretic parlance, the epistemic presupposition concerns knowledge about the following three items: available actions, possible consequences and the probabilities of these consequences arising. That may sound overly abstract. What does it mean, for consumers of financial services, to know the products and services that finance firms are offering? It means that they possess knowledge about the characteristics of these products, that is, about what consequences may result from their decision to buy them and how likely these consequences are. For instance, pondering their retirement plans, people have to know the kinds of pensions they can choose, what the differences are between them with respect to the money they receive, the risks they run and how likely it is that, for instance, a retirement product will pay out a guaranteed sum of money, or whether there is a chance that the payout will be less. Though saying that the argument for liberty is committed to a number of epistemic assumptions may not be particularly deep, these assumptions are not always perfectly satisfied, to put it mildly. Owing to tenacious asymmetries of power and knowledge, the commodification of financial services that accompanied the privatization of the financial sector does not, for instance, seem to have benefited consumers a great deal.[30] In the 1980s many British citizens switched from State earnings related pension schemes (Serps) to alternative non-government schemes. In many cases they did that merely on the unreasonable and unjustified suspicion that state pensions had an uncertain future. They made their decisions without having a satisfactory understanding of what they chose, what alternative schemes were open to them and how these schemes differed. A significant number of citizens made the wrong decision.[31] Similar results hold for the American mortgage market, where failures to grasp the complexities of mortgage pricing or credit scoring partly explain why many borrowers chose the wrong products.[32]

---

[30] Burton, *Financial services*.   [31] Aldridge, 'Cultural capital'.
[32] Hynes and Posner, 'Law and economics of consumer finance'.

I must emphasize that, unlike policymakers, most economists working on regulation acknowledge the importance of these epistemic concerns. The received view is that bank regulation should aim at decreasing information and transaction costs of consumers. Unlike extreme laissez-faire political economy, the received view admits that governments can play fruitful roles in overcoming market failures. But unlike the other extreme of complete state intervention, the received view sees the primary role of regulation as one of intervening with informational policies rather than endowing supervisory officials with significant powers to interfere with a bank's daily decision making. The received view favours informational policies directed at removing asymmetries of information and other market failures of epistemic origin. Removing asymmetries of information goes some way to satisfying the epistemic assumptions of the argument for liberty; it should be stressed, however, that in contrast to much of the regulation literature, I am not so much concerned here with the mere availability of information as with processing information and gaining knowledge. To return to two earlier examples, there was plenty of information available on pension plans and credit scoring, but a significant number of people did not access or process – or did not know how to access or process, or did not know that they could access or process – the information adequately. It was a lack of knowledge not a lack of information that resulted in their choosing the wrong pensions or mortgages.

Criticism

Before turning to a closer examination of epistemic virtue in the next chapter it is important to make two observations. The first is that there are many grounds to criticize the argument for liberty. Taking issue with Premise 1, psychological studies suggest that a superabundance of alternatives for consumers impedes their ability to choose.[33] The sheer number of options leads them to take decisions that satisfy them less than what they would have chosen had they had less freedom. Other scholars attack Premise 3. They argue that many forms of deregulation do not increase consumer choice unless they are accompanied by severe re-regulation. Without consumer protection laws, anti-trust legislation and other ways to mitigate deregulation, greater freedom for business

---

[33] A popular account of these problems is Schwartz, *Paradox of choice*.

does not lead to greater freedom for consumers. But re-regulation, these scholars lament, is often absent.[34] These and similar observations are very important for the cogency of my claim that the argument for liberty only works if the epistemic assumptions hold true. The research may be interpreted as pointing out that I have been too optimistic in suggesting that once people have sufficient knowledge of their decision situation they will choose optimally. Under such a reading, too much knowledge rather discapacitates people for choice. I do not think, however, that this is the most natural way to interpret these research findings. Rather I think that the findings support my claim that people need genuine knowledge to benefit from increased freedom. When we are over-whelmed by choice it is because we cannot see the wood for the trees and lack full knowledge of our decision situation. The mere number of alternatives is not what disables us; what disables us is what sets apart the connoisseur from the ignorant. Most of us know how to buy cereals, cars or clothes. It is when we do not know how to distinguish alter-natives that we may start feeling overpowered and unable to choose.

Another worry to be addressed before turning to epistemic virtue is that one might ask how likely it is that the financial services industry accepts the argument. The methodological strategy I use is to adopt a set of assumptions that is as minimal as possible to be consistent with the self-image of the industry. When the industry lobbies against restric-tions of freedom of enterprise, it typically does so on the grounds that such restrictions diminish its ability to contribute to generating Pareto efficiency; lifting such restrictions increases consumer wealth and well-being because it allows the industry to help people allocate resources optimally over time. Much of the regulation of the financial sector is imbued with this view. But this view commits the industry to the argu-ment for liberty, and consequently the industry has to accept willy-nilly that it must not frustrate but support making the epistemic assumptions true. These commitments may surprise the industry, but the only escape is to adopt a radically different concept of itself. It is not clear, however, that adopting such a different self-concept is to its advantage, because if banks, insurance companies, pension funds and other financial firms are no longer seen as contributing to Pareto efficiency by means of freedom for citizens, governments may soon withdraw the many privileges the industry enjoys and start treating it as they treat other business sectors.

---

[34] Griffith-Jones et al., *Time for a visible hand.*

Summary

This chapter has introduced a number of core normative assumptions employed in the book. The first question I addressed was whether banks and other finance firms have a purpose just in the same way as hospitals or schools. I made clear that for methodological reasons I attempt to make minimal ideological assumptions, and that is what led me to examine Milton Friedman's theory of the function of the firm. Following Friedman, firms were conceived of as entities that must maximize shareholder value, provided ethics and law be respected – and this, we saw, is a serious extra condition that has lexicographic priority over maximizing profit. These ideas were reinforced by homing in on the theory of the firm as developed by economists, and by examining the way in which corporate law deals with firms. I showed that there is a clear correlation between corporate governance (how is the firm organized?) and corporate performance (is the firm profitable?) in that firms with hierarchical command structures generally outdo others. And I showed how corporate law describes the public limited company or corporation as a 'legal fiction' satisfying the conditions of legal personhood, limited liability, transferability of shares, investor ownership and delegated management.

The last part of the chapter introduced the argument for liberty, used by such politicians as Reagan, Clinton, Thatcher and Blair in defence of many deregulatory policies that saw the light during their governments. According to this argument, increasing freedom of choice enlarges the scope people have for assuming personal responsibility for satisfying their preferences. What often goes unnoticed is, however, that for more freedom to lead to more responsibility and satisfaction, accurate beliefs about freedom of choice are essential. A failure of this epistemic requirement to hold true gives a partial explanation of why numerous deregulatory policies have not brought the benefits their inventors had hoped for. To defend their policies and activities, governments and businesses still often embrace the argument for liberty: they see the free and perfectly competitive market as an essential motor to maximizing welfare. The upshot of my argument about liberty is that such a defence cannot be consistently offered without accepting the epistemic assumptions – and without contributing to their realization. To realize them, epistemic virtues are necessary, and that is what I shall turn to now.

2 | *Epistemic ethics: virtues of the mind*

In mainstream analytic philosophy, virtue theory started with Elizabeth Anscombe's classic paper 'Modern Moral Philosophy'. Preceded by, among others, Vladimir Jankélévitch and Josef Pieper, a German philosopher writing about courage in the first years of the Nazi regime, and followed by such authors as Alisdair MacIntyre and Robert Solomon, virtue theory rapidly developed, inside and outside analytic philosophy, into the main third normative ethical ideal.[1] The theory of *epistemic* virtues is of much more recent date. In the fourth quarter of the twentieth century two strands of virtue epistemology arose almost at the same time. A faculty-based or reliabilist version of virtue epistemology was pioneered by Ernest Sosa, who suggested that such cognitive faculties as vision, hearing and memory are to be thought of as conducive to the truth, that is, as ensuring or at least enlarging the reliability of our beliefs and judgements.[2] A character-based or responsibilist version, by contrast, was put forward by Lorraine Code, who promoted the view that a number of epistemic or intellectual character traits or virtues contribute to our reaching epistemic goods such as knowledge, understanding and wisdom.[3]

Sosa's faculty-based virtue epistemology stays close to a founding father of virtue theory, Aristotle. According to Aristotle, moral virtues (or virtues of character) and intellectual virtues (or virtues of thought) are different. For Aristotle, virtues of thought are dispositions that assist us to ensure that our soul 'truths', as he called it: the soul must decide correctly which propositions or statements to affirm and deny.[4] These intellectual virtues are the famous five of craft, science, prudence, wisdom and understanding (or sense). Faculty-based virtue epistemology

---

[1] Jankélévitch, *Traité des vertus*. Pieper, *Tapferkeit*. MacIntyre, *After virtue*. Solomon, 'Corporate roles'.
[2] Sosa, 'The raft and the pyramid'.   [3] Code, 'Responsibilist epistemology'.
[4] Aristotle, *Ethica Nicomachea*, VI 3 1139b.

is not concerned with the virtues of character but rather with the virtues of thought, or variants thereof. Character-based virtue epistemology, on the other hand, studies dispositions to steer the middle course between two extremes and explains the importance of these dispositions for finding *eudaimonia*. Character-based virtue epistemology finds its inspiration in the conviction that epistemic virtues are a particular kind of virtue of character, applying as they do to such epistemic activities as inquiry and the maintenance and transmission of knowledge. Epistemic virtues are, for the character-based virtue epistemologist, very much on a par with Aristotelian moral virtues, though philosophers disagree about whether they are identical. It requires courage of a corporation's management, the argument goes, to invest in research and development activities that have uncertain outcomes. It requires justice or fairness or open-mindedness of a non-executive director or member of a supervisory board to give an equal hearing to the views of management, employees and others. It also requires temperance or sobriety of a stock market analyst to interpret the scattered data and rumours and gossip about a company embarking on a flotation.

Without doubt the exploration of a faculty-based strand à la Sosa has led to a number of interesting discoveries in epistemology. Yet its relevance to ethics is limited owing to its being primarily concerned with *inborn* qualities; from a normative ethical point of view, capacities that can be *acquired* are what matter most. What are the most important epistemic virtues? Several authors have come up with taxonomies of epistemic virtue. I am profoundly indebted to Jason Baehr, James Montmarquet, Robert Roberts and Jay Wood, and Linda Zagzebski, despite the fact that at places I suggest different terminology and theory.[5] The prime epistemic motivator virtue is *love of knowledge*, which can be traced at least as far back as Augustine's *studiositas*. Love of knowledge is complemented by epistemic *courage*. Epistemically courageous people dare to subject their beliefs to thorough scrutiny and continue their inquiry irrespective of potential resistance or disdain from others until they have reached a conclusion. They keep trying to answer the questions they ask and are not deterred by the fact that this

---

[5] Baehr, *Inquiring mind*. Montmarquet, *Epistemic virtue*. Roberts and Wood, *Intellectual virtue*. Zagzebski, *Virtues of the mind*.

may graphically reveal their ignorance or expose them to some degree of ridicule or danger. Epistemically *temperate* or sober-minded people are disposed to avoid zealous adoption of beliefs without any good evidence, but they also shun an inert uninterestedness (not the same as disinterestedness, which is a virtue) that leads them to be unwilling to adopt any beliefs at all. Temperate consumers are sceptical enough to take with a grain of salt what salespeople tell them, for instance, but they are not so sceptical as never to believe anyone or anything. Epistemic *justice* and its variants such as open-mindedness are a readiness to confront one's ideas with those of others, and they include an active awareness of one's epistemic shortcomings and fallibility. Epistemically just people want to hear both sides of a story and do not draw any firm conclusions as long as they have only partial evidence concerning an issue. They do not reject particular bits of information on such irrelevant grounds as that they have been provided by, for instance, members of an ethnic minority. Epistemic *humility* is the disposition to avoid being overly confident and arrogant concerning one's knowledge and not to presume authority over a certain knowledge domain just because of one's hierarchical relationship to another person. Directors claiming to know more about a financial model than employees simply because they are directors betray epistemic arrogance, for example, also called *hubris*, an epistemic vice. These virtues are *self-directed* in that they affect the way people practising them process information and acquire knowledge. *Other-directed* epistemic virtues govern the way their possessors influence the belief formation practices of other people. Epistemic *generosity*, in particular, is a disposition to share one's knowledge freely with others, but not in a way that unjustifiably harms one's own interests.

Instrumental epistemic value

I shall attend more directly to the individual epistemic virtues in greater detail in the chapters that follow. Here I outline a theory of what epistemic virtues are conceptually. The Aristotelian view of virtues conceives of them as stable dispositions to steer between two extremes, with respect to particular actions or emotions, which can be acquired, and which promote *eudaimonia*, the good life. This is the standard conception of virtue. For genuinely Aristotelian epistemic virtues an argument should be offered showing they fit this format. Jason Baehr is the author of one of the most recent approaches.[6] His is based on a notion of *personal intellectual worth* to which cultivating epistemic virtues contributes and which, Baehr seems to claim, is part of building *eudaimonia*. Epistemically virtuous people have a positive orientation towards epistemic goods such as knowledge, understanding and wisdom, and a negative orientation towards epistemic bads such as false beliefs, ignorance, lack of understanding and irrationality. It is this attitude that drives their virtuous epistemic behaviour.[7]

This account is not without problems, though, at any rate when the aim is to apply the theory of epistemic virtues to business. At a crucial juncture in his book, Baehr asks us to imagine a person whose motivation for acting in an epistemically virtuous manner is 'rooted entirely in a desire for money, fame, or some other questionable end', and he describes the person as possessing 'intellectual character traits that are reliable in the world in question, but would not, in so far as he is motivated strictly by money, fame, or the like, be an intellectually good or better person in the relevant sense'.[8]

Intellectualism and psychology

To begin with, I find Baehr's insinuation against a desire for money problematic. Rather than being a 'questionable end', the acquisition of money is a very basic and, if you wish, honourable end, especially if it is motivated instrumentally. To realize our goals, we need to finance them, and to finance them, we need money in almost all cases.[9] Without money, numerous ends that Baehr hesitates to set aside as 'questionable' will never be reached. Be that as it may, a second and more important objection can be levelled. I do not consider it to be particularly plausible that our attempts to gain information and form true beliefs are motivated primarily by our desire to reach the cognitive states of knowledge, understanding or wisdom for their own sake. Most of our epistemic urges seem to me to stem more instrumentally from our desires to obtain

---

[6] Baehr, *Inquiring mind*.
[7] Baehr, *Inquiring mind* uses the term *intellectual virtue*. Such terminology has unpleasant intellectualist connotations, suggesting, e.g., that these virtues are especially important to rather high-end sorts of belief formation. Hence I use *epistemic virtue*.
[8] Baehr, *Inquiring mind*, 124–5.
[9] This view is defended with vigour by Shiller, *Good society*.

or realize certain non-epistemic goods. There are scarcely any non-epistemic goods that can be realized without knowledge, and that covers most of the cases in which we are engaged in the epistemic activity of inquiry. To realize our goals, we need knowledge, and to obtain knowledge, we need epistemic virtue. It is no indication of a lack of epistemic virtue if one acts virtuously primarily with these instrumental goals in mind. Scientists and saints may be primarily interested in knowledge for its own sake. Businesspeople, consumers and many others have a decidedly instrumental perspective on epistemic goods.

To be fair, a similar disdain for run-of-the-mill, instrumentally useful knowledge can be found in the writings of other virtue epistemologists. Discussing love of knowledge, Roberts and Wood, for instance, recommend the reading of such magazines as *Atlantic Monthly* or *New York Review of Books*.[10] Nor is intellectualism the only difficulty we have to overcome in applying epistemic virtue theory more broadly. Another is that it remains somewhat unclear what precise mechanism secures the desired psychological orientation towards epistemic goods and bads. Epistemic virtues are claimed to determine a person's psychological orientation towards epistemic goods and bads, and it is interesting to know how they accomplish this. Even though Baehr hints at various theoretical possibilities at various stages in his argument, he does not make an explicit connection to empirical work in psychology. Again, Baehr's aim was not to develop a psychologically viable theory of epistemic virtues for business, so he can hardly be blamed for not having addressed this issue. Before applying an otherwise appealing theory to business, however, the *problem of intellectualism* and the *problem of psychological mechanism* must be solved first.

To solve the problem of intellectualism, I start with a view of epistemic virtues as contributing not so much intrinsically valuable personal intellectual goods, but rather instrumentally valuable epistemic goods as means to *eudaimonia*. In contrast to the personal intellectual worth view of epistemic virtue, I focus on *instrumental epistemic value*. To solve the problem of psychological mechanism, three further ingredients are needed: a notion of virtue as *motivating* and *enabling* people to act virtuously; a view of the sort of *actions* to which epistemic virtues apply; and a view derived from *behavioural economics* about what happens when epistemic virtues motivate and enable people to perform

---

[10] Roberts and Wood, *Intellectual virtues*, 159.

epistemic actions. I cover the first two ingredients in this chapter. I turn to behavioural economics in the next chapter, which examines individual epistemic virtues in more detail.

According to Baehr's view of personal intellectual worth, people are intellectually good or better as far as they possess a positive orientation towards what it is intellectually good to have, become or do, and possess a negative orientation towards intellectual bads. Baehr makes clear that he adheres to the view that personal intellectual worth is largely dependent on a person's being intrinsically motivated to reach epistemic goods. One loves knowledge, wisdom and understanding for their own sake, and despises ignorance, false belief and irrationality because they are bad in and of themselves.

Intrinsic or instrumental value?

It is not necessary, however, to attach intrinsic value to epistemic goods and intrinsic disvalue to epistemic bads. Such a position, as I have said, undermines the applicability of epistemic virtue theory. Reaching epistemic goods and avoiding epistemic bads is as important for businesspeople, for instance, as it is for those seeking to enlarge their personal intellectual worth, but unlike the latter, businesspeople have instrumental reasons to seek knowledge. True beliefs rather than false beliefs will further the development of new products and services. Beliefs based on evidence rather than mere speculation or guesswork will provide a firm foundation on which to implement business strategies. Understanding the characteristics of a particular market and its participants allows businesspeople to respond most effectively to market pressures and consumer demand. Wisdom, finally, allows managers to take a long-term perspective and to address the spiritual or religious concerns of their employees more adequately.

The personal intellectual worth view takes the intellectually good person as its point of departure; the approach I advance here starts from a person seeking not only an intellectually or epistemically good life, but a good life as a whole. Such a person also has a positive orientation to knowledge, understanding and other epistemic goods and a negative orientation to epistemic bads, but only as far as is necessary for the realization of non-epistemic goods that the good life requires. Looking at epistemic goods as means to *eudaimonia* entails that epistemic goods without such instrumental value are not the things that an epistemically virtuous person aspires to by necessity. No need exists to gain these epistemic goods whenever the knowledge, wisdom or understanding does not play a part in something else with value. This may sound like a severe restriction, but this view has considerable advantages here over the personal intellectual worth view.

For a start, it does not presuppose that epistemically virtuous people *avoid* epistemic goods if they are not instrumentally useful. The view is neutral with respect to these issues and one may still seek to follow epistemic pursuits for their own sake, unless they obstruct living well. Moreover, most knowledge is instrumentally useful in one way or another, so the restriction does not reach as far as one might think. It is not true, however, that any sort of epistemic behaviour sanctioned by way of its contribution to personal intellectual worth is acceptable from the perspective of instrumental epistemic value. This is explained by a second difference from Baehr's view. Focusing on instrumental epistemic value allows a more ready explanation of the fact that the knowledge, wisdom or understanding that virtuous people aim at depends on what they want to do with it; and similarly, instrumental epistemic value makes it easier to understand why the levels of certainty, justification and warrant that epistemic virtue requires depend on what people want to do with the beliefs. Unlike personal intellectual worth, instrumental epistemic value can provide a precise explanation of why people may virtuously settle for a lower degree of justification when they set up surveys for marketing purposes than when they conduct survey research as academic marketing researchers, or when they investigate the potential side effects of a new medication or the risks of nuclear energy. Deploying high justificatory standards even as a marketer is virtuous for Baehr, but may be an unvirtuous waste of intellectual and other resources once we look at it from an instrumental point of view. In contrast to Baehr's viewing the standards of justification as dependent on the epistemic goods sought, I propose to make the standards of justification dependent on the non-epistemic goods for which knowledge, truth and justification are means to an end.

Motivation and enablement

I have shown that viewing epistemic virtues as contributing to instrumental epistemic value is more serviceable than the personal intellectual worth view when considering applications of epistemic virtues to business and other domains, but I have not addressed the second problem, which concerns the psychological mechanism explaining how epistemic virtues influence epistemic behaviour. As I have said, three ingredients are necessary to tackle this problem. We need a theory of motivation and enablement, a theory of epistemic actions, and a behavioural economics approach linking the first two ingredients. To begin with, owing to a view that goes back to Aquinas, a virtue is a virtue because it enables us to do something, because it motivates us to do something, or because it does both.[11] A virtue motivates people to perform particular actions through influence on their desires, preferences, wishes and goals; and a virtue enables people to do certain things through the removal of internal obstacles they have against performing virtuous actions.[12] Most virtues do both. They enable and they motivate.[13]

Courage

Courage illustrates how virtues enable. Imagine that at some point in time person S has not yet acquired courage. S is a coward at that moment. He sees a child drowning in a raging river. He has his mobile phone ready, so he can ring the emergency number 999 (let us call this action A), and were it not for his cowardice, he could have jumped in the water and attempted to rescue the child (action B), or he could have called one of the tourists nearby and asked them to help (action C). But being the coward that he is, he neither jumps nor calls but only rings 999. The coastguard arrives only barely in time. Shocked by the sight of the guards' resuscitation attempts and the child's suffering, S decides to work on his lack of courage, and succeeds. At a later point in time he has acquired the virtue, and as though he were to be put to the test, he again sees a child drowning. He waits no longer, searches for a place where he can safely jump into the water, swims out and rescues the child.

Courage has enabled S to rescue the child and to perform other actions requiring courage by removing what one could call *internal obstacles* to the performance of such actions. The treatment of epistemic virtues in the next chapter shows that internal obstacles often arise from so-called *behavioural biases* leading us to behave suboptimally with

---

[11] Aquinas, *Summa theologiae*, I–II q.57.
[12] Pouivet, 'Moral and epistemic virtues'.   [13] Driver, *Uneasy virtue*.

respect to investigative activities and other forms of belief formation. For the purpose of illustration, however, I focus on a non-epistemic instance of courage. In the beginning, S was blocked by his cowardice from performing actions B and C; his choice situation was a singleton set containing action A only. Acquiring courage subsequently led to the removal of these internal obstacles, as a result of which his choice set at the later point in time contained the actions B and C besides A.

Generosity

Courage illustrates how virtues enable. Generosity shows how they motivate. S starts as a Scrooge spending nothing on anyone – 'Bah, humbug!' Haunted by the three ghosts of Christmas, he decides that it is time for a change and acquires liberality. It works. On Christmas we see him treating his relatives, neighbours and his clerk's family with generosity and concern. Liberality has not so much removed obstacles to performing generous actions. It is wrong, for example, to describe S as initially incapable of giving. Rather, he initially had no preference whatsoever for giving; he was miserly in wanting to keep his money. What the three ghosts did was make him change his preferences to become motivated to be generous.

Two things have to be said about this very succinct virtue theory. I must say something about the theory of the mean (virtues lie in the middle of two extremes) and also about the idea that most virtues motivate and enable. First, the examples discussed so far only consider one vice, that is, one extreme of the virtue. I looked at a move from cowardice to courage, not a move to courage from the other extreme, recklessness, nor did I consider a move to liberality from prodigality. These moves can be described in exactly the same way, though. Interestingly, showing this also covers the second point about motivation and enabling.

To start with recklessness, a reckless person is, one might say, imprudently brave, or 'too courageous'. A reckless S seeing a drowning child dives into the river without thinking, and is injured because the water is too shallow. One might think that for a reckless person to learn how to steer the middle course between cowardice and recklessness requires a form of 'disenabling'. On that count, S has acquired internal obstacles to the performance of reckless acts. A reckless S may well learn, however, to change preferences and acquire a motivation for more careful and considerate, but not cowardly, behaviour. Courage is a virtue that both enables and motivates. This is not true of all virtues. The move from the extreme of prodigality to the mean of liberality only constitutes a preference change (roughly, a change to give less and keep more). When an excessively generous person learns to acquire the right attitude to getting and giving, this does not mean disenabling certain prodigal actions but only demoting these actions in the preference ordering.

Even though I have not yet fully introduced the concept of epistemic virtue, this is the appropriate moment to say something about the way epistemic virtues motivate and enable their possessors to act in epistemically virtuous ways. I deal with the details in Chapter 3, but for now it is interesting to point out that research in behavioural economics has revealed a number of biases that human beings are prone to suffer when processing information. This research is increasingly also attracting the attention of ethicists.[14] A significant number of these biases have to do with belief formation. I take the confirmation bias as an example. People vulnerable to this bias stick to their beliefs too tightly even when they face significant counterevidence. They have difficulties abandoning their beliefs even when the available evidence gives reason to believe them to be wrong. What epistemic virtues do is decrease the influence of these biases by motivating and enabling people to do what it is epistemically virtuous to do. To continue the example, epistemic justice makes a person open-minded with respect to various sorts of evidence, and epistemic humility leads people to be aware of their own fallibility, helping them to realize that their beliefs may be wrong after all. These virtues motivate and enable people to take counterevidence seriously and not to stick to their beliefs too long.

Epistemic actions

Before exploring this issue in greater depth in Chapter 3, it is important to develop the concept of epistemic virtue in more detail, because at this stage of the argument the reader may wonder whether it makes any sense to speak of *virtue* in the context of epistemic activities. Courage, for instance, applies to the things soldiers do. How can it apply to belief formation or knowledge acquisition? Are inquiring,

---

[14]   Barberis and Thaler, 'Behavioral finance' introduces the topic. See, e.g., Bazerman and Tenbrunsel, *Blind spots* for applications to ethics.

believing, knowing and so on genuine activities one can perform more or less virtuously?

Doxastic voluntarism

Questions such as these land us, first, in a debate about *doxastic voluntarism*, which is the thesis that one is free to form any belief at will. Its strong form, *direct doxastic voluntarism*, implies that one can now decide to believe any proposition *p*, or at least a sufficiently large number of propositions. A weaker form, *indirect doxastic voluntarism*, maintains that one can bring it about that one believes any proposition *p* by soaking one's mind, say, with books supporting *p*, and by avoiding what refutes *p*, in the expectation that in the end one has formed the beliefs aimed at. It appears at first sight that both positions give us too much power actively to influence our beliefs. Both seem to go against the fact that in typical cases of belief formation we feel compelled by the evidence to believe what we believe rather than free to believe anything at will. How can one decide to adopt the belief that York is the capital of the United Kingdom or that water is poisonous? What sorts of web sites or brochures can one consult in order to form that belief? Will they be available, in the first place?

For a long time in the history of epistemology either form of doxastic voluntarism had few adherents. Under the influence of recent work in philosophy on epistemic agency and doxastic responsibility, however, the popularity of certain versions of doxastic voluntarism is on the rise. *Epistemic agency* here stands for the idea that believing and knowing are activities that share many features with ordinary actions such as walking or making investment decisions, and if plausible, this idea might lend support to the view that freedom applies to belief and knowledge in the same way as it applies to actions. *Doxastic responsibility*, moreover, is the idea that we bear responsibility for what we believe and know, and that our beliefs and knowledge are not things that merely 'happen' to us. Since responsibility implies freedom on many counts, this idea again supports the thesis of doxastic voluntarism.

It is important to stress that epistemic virtues would not be particularly interesting to ethicists if believing and knowing were not sufficiently similar to ordinary actions that we have some freedom to perform and for which it makes sense to ascribe some responsibility to us. Whenever one has no influence on one's beliefs at all, or cannot be held responsible for holding them, it is senseless to examine epistemic virtues from an ethical point of view. Although a thorough treatment of doxastic voluntarism is beyond the scope of the present chapter, it is important to see how belief formation and knowledge acquisition can be seen as forms of acting.

Investigation

Knowledge acquisition has to begin with what I call *investigative actions*. Prospective house owners visit web sites of banks to search for the best mortgage deals. Marketing researchers set up surveys and experiments. Rating agencies develop models to estimate the probability that a company cannot repay its debt. Surely these actions often do not lead to knowledge. Mortgagors may find out that they are borrowing money under different conditions than they initially assumed. Marketers may find that their results are not statistically significant. Rating agencies may fail to predict bankruptcy. These activities are not a sufficient condition for gaining knowledge, but they are certainly necessary.

Doxastic stance

On the whole, it is unproblematic to see these activities as genuine actions. They may require such commonplace things as going to the bank, handing out surveys, programming computers. What makes them special is that they are performed to provide evidence for or against adopting a belief. One might think that despite the fact that investigative actions themselves are quite ordinary types of actions, the need to include belief formation in the account dashes our hopes of viewing knowledge acquisition as an ordinary form of human action too. Yet it is relatively easy to see that belief formation is a form of acting. To approach the issue slightly formally, assume I want to gain knowledge about a proposition p. I carry out a number of investigative actions and now I ponder the belief to adopt. I can select one of three possible *doxastic actions*. I can, first, adopt the belief that p is true. I can, secondly, adopt the belief that p is false (*disbelieve* the proposition, as it is called). Thirdly, feeling that the investigative actions have not delivered sufficient evidence to justify either of these doxastic actions, I can perform a third sort of doxastic action and suspend belief. *Suspending belief* means that I neither believe that p is true nor believe that p is false. What exactly the attitudes of belief, disbelief and suspension of belief amount to psychologically is not essential to the analysis offered here. Believing a proposition may come down to giving full credence to it, but it may also mean accepting it, rather than its negation, for the sake of argument or for the sake of deliberation. This need not detain us here.

Justification

An extra condition has to be introduced. One performs investigative actions and subsequently selects a doxastic attitude *justified* by the outcomes of the investigative actions. Here things start getting tricky as normativity trickles into the argument. I approach these considerations from various angles. First, I consider the concept of justification from the perspective of the standard philosophical analysis of the concept of knowledge, which I very briefly introduce. Then, in the next section, I approach justification from the perspective of epistemic virtues. Together this leads to a defence of the view that epistemic virtues help people to perform investigative actions, and subsequent doxastic actions, in such a way that the latter are justified by the outcomes of the former. Moreover, I describe epistemically virtuous people as people whose goal it is to perform a third class of actions, epistemic actions, where an *epistemic action* is a combination of investigative actions and justified subsequent doxastic actions with the added condition that the doxastic actions are the right ones; this means that there is belief when the proposition is true, and disbelief when it is false.

The standard analysis of knowledge sees knowledge as a form of belief. A person knowing that Tegucigalpa is the capital of Honduras believes that Tegucigalpa is the capital of Honduras. Moreover, the belief has to be true. One cannot, for instance, know that Tegucigalpa is the capital town of Nicaragua, but one can hold that proposition as a belief. True beliefs are not necessarily knowledge. If, when quizzed about the capital of Honduras, one were to make a wild guess and answered Tegucigalpa, it would be wrong to claim knowledge; for to know it, one must have looked it up previously in an atlas, learned it from a geography teacher and so forth. One needs, that is, *evidence* that *justifies* the belief.[15] How justification should be analysed is beyond the scope of the present discussion. Suffice it to say that epistemologists, quarrelling about the exact specification of the justification condition, agree that a bit more is needed than the belief being merely justified.[16] Referring to what is needed in addition to mere justification with the symbol +, knowledge is thus sometimes characterized as true belief that is 'justi-fied+'. These technicalities are unimportant here, and in what follows I therefore use *justification* where others perhaps use *justification+*.

It is crucially important in the present context, however, to point out that both the truth condition and the justification condition contribute instrumental value. For truth this is plain. One is not helped much by the *false* belief that house prices will keep on rising if one considers buying a house that is excessively priced. For justification, however, it is less clear. In some sense, it even sounds totally counterintuitive. Assuming that a belief is true, why does it matter whether one adopted it on the basis of justifying evidence or just by sheer luck? The insight that justifi-cation does matter goes back to Plato. In the *Meno* Socrates considers the difference between a person S, who merely possesses a true belief about the way to the town of Larissa, and a person T, who possesses genuine knowledge about the way to Larissa. Suppose S embarks on a journey to Larissa, but after a while finds that the road is gradually going in what she believes to be the wrong direction. Then she will probably return. Moreover, imagine that T is going exactly the same way. Of course she too notices that the road is going in the wrong direction, but this does not cause her to give up her belief that she is going to Larissa. The evidence justifying T's belief allows her to see it as a small detour only and, unlike S, she knows she will ultimately arrive in Larissa. From this observation Socrates derives the famous claim that knowledge is more 'fastened' or 'secured' than true belief; knowledge is more stable in that it 'remains' longer. One does not lose knowledge as easily as one loses true belief, and as a result, knowledge is to be preferred over mere true belief, even from the instrumental point of view that sees it as a means to an end only.

Truth and justification are not part of the concepts of investigative and doxastic action. One can perform investigative actions that do not yield evidence justifying any particular doxastic action. Moreover, even

---

[15] See Pritchard, *Epistemic luck* for a discussion of what role luck still has to play in knowledge acquisition.

[16] The *locus classicus* is Gettier, 'Is justified true belief knowledge?'.

if inquiry provides evidence, one may still perform the wrong doxastic action. It is therefore useful to introduce a third concept to capture it all. An *epistemic action* is a combination of investigative and doxastic actions satisfying truth and justification conditions. The investigative part of the epistemic action may take the form of inquiry, observation, experimentation, asking questions and getting answers, and many other investigative actions. I use the plural here, but it may be convenient to speak about one large investigative action with respect to gaining knowledge about one single proposition p, where this large investigative action may contain many rather different sorts of inquiry. The doxastic part of the epistemic action is one of only two doxastic actions. Having researched p, one may decide one has not obtained sufficient evidence to support adopting a belief or disbelief; belief will then be suspended. This cannot be part of a genuine epistemic action, however, because the concept of epistemic action is intended to capture an action resulting in knowledge. As a result, the doxastic part of an epistemic action is either to believe the proposition or to believe its negation. Two conditions are in place, finally. The chosen doxastic action has to be the right one, because the belief or disbelief has to be true; and the chosen doxastic action has to be justified.

To the extent that philosophers disagree about the precise analysis of justification they may disagree about whether a particular person has performed an epistemic action in the sense in which I have introduced it here. This may look like a drawback of the concept, but the situation is no different from many other disciplines. Competent judges or legal scholars may disagree about whether a person has committed manslaughter or murder; competent accountants may disagree about whether to subsume an item under cost of sales in the profit and loss account, or to capitalize it on the balance sheet; and similar examples can be found in medicine, engineering and other fields. This does not make concepts of manslaughter, murder, cost of sales or capitalization meaningless or arbitrary.

In the context of a theory of epistemic virtues, however, an additional pressing issue arises, for some writers see the theory as entailing a *novel* view of justification. It all depends on how we read the following statement:

> An agent is justified in adopting a particular belief whenever epistemically virtuous agents would adopt that belief if they were in the same position as the agent.

One way to read the statement is that it *defines* justification. Virtue epistemology, then, provides a novel view of justification in competition with existing views. Advocates of this position have to argue that virtue epistemology offers a genuine concept of justification that, it is hoped, does better than the incumbents. Another way to read the statement is to see the statement as expressing a conceptual link between a theory of epistemic virtues and a particular theory of justification. To defend this second reading, one has to show that whenever epistemically virtuous behaviour results in beliefs, these beliefs are justified in the sense of the particular theory of justification. The difference between the two positions is that the former gives a new definition of justification whereas the latter leads to new insights about an existing definition or theory of justification. Both approaches may be attractive. A theory of epistemic virtues that is serviceable to genuine normative issues that people face in their everyday lives must, however, have a broader orientation than knowledge alone. Financial markets are full of situations where people have to form beliefs that fail to qualify as knowledge by any standard. People typically do not *know* whether one insurance policy is best suited to their situation, not to speak about investment and other decisions with even greater degrees of uncertainty and scarcity of evidence. Add to that, in the next section I argue that there are also more fundamental reasons why virtuous behaviour need not result in knowledge in all cases.

The alternative view of justification that I develop is sensitive to these concerns and sees justification as coming in degrees. It sees epistemic virtues as contributing to increased degrees of justification. They maximize the likelihood that their possessor ends up with knowledge, but they do not guarantee knowledge. Exploring that view further is part of the aim of the next section. The idea is that notwithstanding the fact that epistemically virtuous people *ceteris paribus* perform epistemic actions and adopt beliefs that are genuine knowledge, they may depart from this ideal for several reasons. One is that insufficient evidence is available; another is that carrying out the investigative actions leading to sufficient evidence takes too much time, given the other goals one may have.

Epistemic virtues

The view of epistemic virtues I defend here contrasts with the views of several other authors. Linda Zagzebski, for instance, espouses the view that epistemically virtuous behaviour and knowledge acquisition cannot but go together. She maintains that epistemic virtues require 'reliable success' in bringing about the epistemic goals, which means that we must not describe people as virtuous unless knowledge has resulted from their epistemic activities.[17] As I said, this puts a severe restriction on the applicability of the theory of epistemic virtues; but it is, in addition, unconvincing for more theoretical reasons. Soldiers with non-epistemic courage by definition have the disposition to act in fearless but not too fearless ways on the battlefield. This does not mean that they always succeed. Courageous soldiers can get caught in a trap; they can be betrayed by their comrades or navigation systems. Their weapons malfunction, and sometimes they die. But though they are unsuccessful in such cases, it is a gross misrepresentation to describe them as lacking courage. Virtues do not come with a 100 per cent guarantee of success.

Courageous soldiers and evil demons

Weakening the success condition somewhat, Julia Driver proposes that epistemic virtues are character traits that systematically produce true beliefs, which means that they tend to produce more true than false beliefs in the circumstances in which they are possessed.[18] This may help overcome the *courageous soldier objection*. Courage does not guarantee success, but across the board courageous people tend to be more successful than people who are not. Yet Jason Baehr has criticized consequentialist approaches to epistemic virtue such as Driver's on the grounds that they founder on another objection, the *evil demon objection*. Baehr invokes Descartes's evil demon manipulating the world in such a way that most of the beliefs we adopt are false, despite our using the highest standards of epistemic virtue. Baehr believes that the situation of the person manipulated by an evil demon can be described in only one of two ways. Either we must say that there is an 'intuitively and reasonably pretheoretical' view of epistemic virtue such that the person has 'satisfied only *one half* of its requirements'.[19] If we

---

[17] Zagzebski, *Virtues of the mind*, 137 (for a more detailed discussion, see 176–84).
[18] Driver, *Uneasy virtue* and Driver, 'Moral and epistemic virtue'.
[19] Baehr, *Inquiring mind*, 135.

accept this description the person does not possess the virtue. Or we must say that the person is virtuous 'in one legitimate sense' of virtue (i.e., Baehr's personal intellectual worth sense), but that in 'another distinct but still legitimate' sense (i.e., a consequentialist sense such as Driver's) the person is unvirtuous.[20] Baehr then states that the second description is the most plausible. In the presence of an evil demon, consequentialist approaches fail to see virtue where Baehr himself sees virtue.

It is undoubtedly true that Driver's approach fails to see virtue in the evil demon case; in a manipulated world epistemic virtue does not help people to produce more true than false beliefs. To state his case, Baehr could equally well have taken a real-life example (epistemic virtue does not inoculate consumers against deceptive marketing strategies) or have used Aristotle's own example of Priam, king of Troy during the Trojan wars and most unsuccessful because of great misfortune. Aristotle did not call Priam unvirtuous, however, nor should we necessarily call deceived consumers so.[21] Aristotle allowed for an empirical connection between *eudaimonia* and fortune. Good fortune may not be a necessary condition of the good life, but we do not describe as *happy* or *living well* a person stricken by serious setbacks.

This point can be adequately captured by a consequentialist approach to epistemic virtue. A simple model makes this clear. In order to gain knowledge about an issue, people select investigative actions. The best choice is to select activities that, given a number of constraints that I shall deal with shortly, maximize the probability of obtaining evidence concerning the proposition at stake. The likelihood of epistemic success depends on the likely consequences of the investigative actions. Suppose one has a choice either to make a phone call to a service desk or to consult a web site concerning information about, say, the departure of a bus. Given that the service desk is staffed with people getting real time information about delays and detours, the probability of epistemic success is greater if one calls the desk than if one consults the web site. But selecting investigative actions is only where things start. Having called the service desk, one can decide to perform a doxastic action and adopt a belief about the departure time, but all the same one can postpone this and also check the Internet, just in case.

---

[20] Baehr, *Inquiring mind*, 135.   [21] Aristotle, *Ethica Nicomachea*, I 9 1100a5–9.

A consequentialist might embrace the view that an epistemic virtue is an acquired disposition to select investigative and doxastic actions in ways that maximize the likelihood of obtaining knowledge. This definition will not do. To begin with, the investigative actions that people select depend, quite trivially, on what investigative actions they believe they can select. I may lack information about the availability of very good investigative actions. I am unlikely to call a service desk if I do not know I can call a service desk, in spite of this being the best way to gain knowledge about the bus. Or I may not have adequate beliefs about the likely consequences of investigative actions. I may have inaccurate beliefs about the 'informational' or 'evidential' value of investigative actions. I know I can call the service desk and check the web, but I do not know that the service desk is exquisitely staffed with friendly and competent people. That I do not select this action, however, is no indication of a lack of epistemic virtue. (At least, it is no such indication as long as the lack of knowledge about the availability of the investigative actions or their likely consequences is not a result of epistemic vice.) This is similar to the non-epistemic case. When soldiers lack knowledge about ways to access a building in which the enemy is hiding it is no indication of cowardice if they do not enter the building.

First improvement

A first improvement is to define epistemic virtue as an acquired disposition to select investigative actions (from the set of investigative actions of which the person is aware) and subsequently to perform doxastic actions (based on the outcomes of the investigative actions) in ways that maximize the likelihood of obtaining knowledge, where the likelihood has to be determined relative to what people believe about the likely outcomes of the investigative activities of which they are aware. But this is not sufficient. Suppose I am in a hurry to get home by bus. To do that I need to know when and where the bus departs. It does not foster my goal of getting home quickly to call the service desk several times and check the Internet in addition. Certainly doing so increases the likelihood of ending up with full-blooded knowledge, but I am probably going to miss the bus. The investigative actions I carry out and the amount of time I allow to pass before I decide which doxastic action to perform have to depend, for an epistemically virtuous person, on the goals that the knowledge is supposed to help realize.

This may seem to be a radical, perhaps undesired consequence of my adopting an instrumental view of epistemic value rather than Baehr's personal intellectual worth view. That I opt for an instrumental view of epistemic value is motivated by a desire to apply the theory of epistemic virtue to less intellectualist pursuits, and this view unmistakably entails a different view of the value of justification. But there are independent and more theoretical reasons why the degree of justification that epistemically virtuous people aim at must depend on the broader set of goals they want to realize. This is no different from the non-epistemic case. Take precision. This is an 'instrumental' virtue. Good bakers and pharmacists have to be precise because it allows them better to realize their goals. One could think that the more fine-grained their weighing instruments are the better they realize this virtue. What precision amounts to for a baker, however, is crucially different from what it means to a pharmacist. A baker using a pharmacist's tools to weigh ingredients is not precise, but overly precise, which is a vice.

Second improvement

What epistemic virtues help people to accomplish is, in my view, not so much to maximize the chance of obtaining knowledge; it is that they help people to select investigative actions and adopt beliefs in ways that maximize the likelihood of forming beliefs and gaining knowledge inasmuch as this is necessary for reaching other goals. This may seem a capitulation to lesser epistemic standards than most virtue epistemologists accept: for if knowledge is not needed, epistemic virtues do not force you to pursue it. This way of looking at things has two advantages, however. First, it offers a view of epistemic virtue that is more broadly normative than, for example, the personal intellectual worth view. It offers normative guidance in situations where a view that singles out knowledge as the sole epistemic ideal cannot. Unlike others, I defend a view that is sensitive to the fact that people often act on beliefs that are more or less justified, but are far from knowledge. One hardly ever knows the exact departure time of an aeroplane; things change too quickly there. Yet it makes a lot of sense to say that one can act more or less epistemically virtuously when it comes to acquiring information about departures. One might suspect that knowledge-centred virtue epistemologies will easily accommodate this objection and that recommendations for non-ideal circumstances can easily be derived; for instance, that in non-ideal circumstances one must do one's utmost to come as close as possible to gaining knowledge. This, however, is unpersuasive when coming as close as possible to knowledge stands in the way of realizing other goals. One can certainly get more reliable information about departure times by checking the screens in the waiting area more frequently, but one may also want to have lunch or read a book. The view I defend allows for a possibility where epistemically virtuous people do not carry out any further investigative actions, knowing full well that they have not reached certainty, yet knowing too that they are fully justified in doing so because getting more evidence would hamper the realization of other goals. Such situations are certainly less prominent than it may seem. This point constitutes a fundamental difference from other approaches, however.

Secondly, the view defended here sees epistemic and moral virtues in a much more unified way. Ultimately, in order to accomplish the goal of getting home in time, one has not only to select a mode of transportation (including a departure time), but also to select a way of *finding out* which modes of transportation one can choose. One confronts a large decision problem with actions that are partly epistemic and partly non-epistemic; and epistemic virtues and non-epistemic virtues both help to maximize expected utility.

This should not be taken to entail that I agree with the view that epistemic and non-epistemic virtues are more or less similar.[22] Aquinas, who had an intricate theory of epistemic virtues *avant la lettre*, observed that though the usual moral virtues aim at the good, epistemic virtues aim at the truth, even if aspiring to the truth is subservient to reaching the good.[23] This is not by itself a knockdown argument for a distinction between non-epistemic and epistemic virtues, particularly because following Aristotle, Aquinas's approach is still very much wedded to the idea that epistemic virtues are innate. It might have been the case that even if epistemic aims are categorically different from other aims, similar methods are suitable to reach these aims. A second distinction between non-epistemic and epistemic virtues, however, is that they apply to different kinds of *actions*. Performing investigative actions is performing ordinary activities, and because one needs motivation or enablement here, epistemic virtues are like non-epistemic virtues. The courage I need to work as a war reporter near the battlefields is the

---

[22] Zagzebski, *Virtues of the mind*, 218.   [23] Aquinas, *Summa theologiae*, I–II q.57.

courage the soldier needs too. It is, one could say, a form of non-epistemic courage set to use for epistemic purposes. Another form of courage is concerned with essentially epistemic issues. An example is the courage to 'face the truth', that is, to adopt a particular belief knowing that this is going to hurt one's self-image. Portfolio managers require such courage if they have long placed all their confidence and money on particular investments but gradually obtain increasingly strong information that their investments are not going to pay off. Take Thierry de la Villehuchet, CEO of Access International Advisors, a feeder fund in the Madoff scam, who stuck to his belief that Madoff was quite all right even though very close colleagues possessed overwhelming evidence to the contrary. He said:

> I'm comfortable with it ... I've got all my money in it. I've got most of my family's money in it. I've got all my friends – the wealthy families of Europe – they're all with Madoff. I've got every private banker I've ever dealt with in this damn thing.[24]

De la Villehuchet found it difficult to part company with his received views. Similarly, whereas non-epistemic temperance is typically concerned with tactile pleasures only, epistemically temperate people are sufficiently reticent not to adopt any belief on the basis of insufficient evidence. It is natural, I believe, to call these virtues (epistemic) *courage* or *temperance* rather than use a different terminology. They describe forms of courage and temperance after all.

Yet because they act on different sorts of actions, the way they motivate and enable is different from the case of the non-epistemic virtues. I tend to disagree therefore with virtue epistemologists putting too much stress on the similarity between epistemic and non-epistemic virtues. At the same time, the view defended here gives, I hope, a more convincing picture of how epistemic and non-epistemic virtues 'interact' when people make decisions, and in that sense my view stresses the unity of the virtues. To solve a decision problem, people need epistemic and non-epistemic virtues simultaneously. A view of epistemic virtue that requires too much from epistemically virtuous people risks being incompatible with the demands placed on decision makers by non-epistemic virtues. The risk is particularly present when the fact that epistemic virtues aim at the truth is seen as something that has non-instrumental

---

[24] Quoted by Markopolos, *No one would listen*, 91.

intellectual value that may more readily clash with other values. When aiming at the truth is seen as ancillary to realizing the good, epistemic and non-epistemic virtues are more likely to place consistent demands on people.

Courageous villains

Before I turn to an examination of individual epistemic virtues in the next chapter, one potential worry needs to be addressed. It concerns the problem of the *courageous villain*. A villain by definition has an unvirtuous character. All the same, he can display courageous behaviour, and perhaps we can even attribute courage to him. Courageous villains pose a problem to virtue theorists, in particular those embracing the view that virtues form a unity. Robert Adams, for instance, has argued that a person may possess courage and use it in the pursuit of some evil ends, but that such a person lacks what he calls 'capital V virtue'.[25] Jason Baehr rejects Adams's approach, and defends a view according to which a courageous villain displays courageous behaviour even though he is not courageous:

> Suppose, for instance, that we were to ask of a particular courageous villain: Why is he virtuous? Why do we have some admiration for this otherwise dubious character? I take it that it would not be very plausible to respond by saying, 'We admire this character because he has a trait which, if put in the service of the good, *would* enhance a person's overall orientation to the good.' Rather, to the extent that it is plausible to regard the courageous villain as virtuous or admirable at all, this is so, I would suggest, on account of the way courage is manifested in *him* or in *his* actions, attitudes, and the like (again, not on account of how it would be manifested, or the role it would play, within a psychological orientation that the villain himself lacks).[26]

Baehr, I believe, conflates here a question about whether the villain should be called *courageous* with a question about whether we should admire him for being courageous if he is. What matters for the villain to be called *courageous* is, first, whether he displays 'courageous looking' behaviour rather than, say, recklessness, rashness, faked fearlessness and so on; or in Baehr's words, what matters is whether courage rather than something else is 'manifested' in his actions and attitudes.

[25] Adams, *Theory of virtue*, 30.   [26] Baehr, *Inquiring mind*, 121.

For the villain to be courageous, it is not sufficient, however, that he manifest courageous behaviour only once. It has to be a stable disposition for him to act in courageous ways. To ascertain whether the villain should be called *courageous* consequently requires us to probe deeper into his character. As long as we know the villain only very superficially, we can only describe him as manifesting courageous behaviour, not as a courageous villain.

But suppose we are sufficiently familiar with the villain to know that he has a stable disposition to act courageously. Then, I claim, if we admire him for being courageous, we admire him not for the *actual* way in which courage is 'manifested' in him, as Baehr writes, because the way he makes use of his courage is by definition villainous. We admire him for possessing a character trait that would, *counterfactually*, enhance his overall virtue if he also possessed other virtues. This fits well with the fact that virtue theory accords considerable room to moral education and character improvement. A virtue is an acquired character trait. One learns to be courageous by acting in 'courageous looking' ways in circumstances that require courage, and despite the fact that this may initially require a lot of willpower, the idea is that after some time practising one will have acquired the trait, which thenceforth needs maintenance only.

Consider this argument. Some people, let us suppose, have more or less finished the acquisition of courage and a number of other virtues, but are still struggling with another virtue: generosity, say. Living extravagantly, they are prone to give away too much and exemplify one of the extremes of generosity: prodigality. Must we wait before admiring their courage until they have given up the wasteful life and learnt to be generous? That is not just unnecessarily harsh but highly artificial. We should rather say that we admire them for their courage, even if they sometimes use courage in the pursuit of extravagance. If we do that, then we admire them precisely because of a character trait that, 'if put in the service of the good, *would* enhance [their] overall orientation to the good'.[27]

This is important for courage and other moral virtues, but it is likely to be even more important for epistemic virtues. Many atrocities are committed because of ignorance, stupidity, gullibility and other epistemic bads and vices. But just as many would not have been committed

[27] Baehr, *Inquiring mind*, 121.

had the perpetrators been lesser epistemic agents. Cooking the books as creative accountants do, manipulating the bonuses as clever bankers do, money laundering, deceptive sales techniques, marketing products to vulnerable consumers, misleading the tax office: without epistemic virtues these forms of misconduct are less common. Does this mean that we should describe the perpetrators as epistemically unvirtuous? Not at all. As long as people lack certain virtues and possess certain vices, the virtues they do possess may be applied in ways that support the vices. Hardly anyone exudes all virtues, so being too rigid risks ascribing courage only to saints and angels. Everyone falling short of that ideal is a coward, then, because courage may be used in tandem with one or more vices. That makes for much too ethereal and esoteric a view of virtue to be applicable in real life.

Summary

The theory of epistemic virtues is developed fairly extensively within philosophy. A quick glance at a recent proposal by Jason Baehr revealed, however, that a degree of intellectualism makes applications to real-life situations quite hard. This is particularly so in business and finance, where knowledge almost always serves instrumental aims rather than contributing to personal intellectual worth. This is one issue discussed in this chapter. A second issue concerned the psychological mechanisms governing epistemic virtue. To address the issues of intellectualism and psychology, I proposed a view of epistemic virtue based on the notion of instrumental epistemic value: epistemic virtues are character traits that help people to gain instrumentally valuable bits of knowledge. I defended a view, for which I am indebted to Julia Driver, among others, according to which virtues motivate and enable their possessors to perform certain actions by affecting their preference ordering and by removing internal obstacles. When cowards become courageous, internal obstacles to the performance of courageous actions disappear; and when stingy people become generous, their preferences about giving change.

But what sort of actions – and what sort of obstacles – are epistemic virtues concerned with? Does it make sense to speak of *action* when we are concerned with knowledge and belief? I analysed epistemic actions as comprising three elements: inquiry, belief adoption and justification. Gaining knowledge starts with inquiry that, if all goes well, leads to evidence justifying the adoption of a belief. I argued that all three elements may be performed in more or less virtuous ways.

Epistemic actions are clearly instrumentally valuable to perform if they deliver instrumentally valuable knowledge. What role do epistemic virtues play here? I started considering Linda Zagzebski's claim that epistemic virtues are to guarantee epistemic success, and argued against it on the grounds that courageous soldiers ought not to count as lacking courage when they are defeated on the battlefield. I then turned to Jason Baehr's evil demon objection, which was meant to cast doubt on the prospects of making epistemic virtues entirely independent of epistemic success. To accommodate this objection, a first attempt was to define epistemic virtue as an acquired disposition to select investigative actions and subsequently to perform doxastic actions so that the likelihood of obtaining knowledge is maximized relative to the beliefs that the possessor of the virtue has concerning the outcomes of potential inquiry. This first attempt was discarded, however, because it was not consistent with the idea of instrumental epistemic value: the amount of inquiry that epistemically virtuous people devote to a particular issue depends on the reasons why they want the knowledge in the first place. Ultimately, epistemic virtues do not maximize the likelihood of gaining knowledge as such. Rather they motivate and enable people to perform investigative actions and adopt beliefs in ways that enlarge the likelihood of gaining knowledge to the extent that this is necessary for reaching other goals they have.

How do epistemic virtues do this? So far I have only dealt with the problem of psychological mechanism in the abstract. Looking at the psychological biases that epistemic virtues help overcome is part of the project of the next chapters. This will show what preferences epistemic virtues modify and what obstacles they remove.

3 | *Internalizing virtues: the clients*

The first 'pre-emptive' strike of the Financial Conduct Authority (FCA), the new British watchdog guarding the interests of consumers of financial services, was to attack interest-only mortgages.[1] Interest-only mortgages are mortgages where the borrower only pays interest – until the mortgage reaches maturity and the borrower has to pay back the entire principal at once; for there is of course no free lunch in finance.

Is it confusing to call something an *interest-only mortgage* if there is more to it than interest only? The FCA found that 13 per cent of UK borrowers with this type of mortgage did not understand the exact terms of their loans. In the Netherlands such loans are called *aflossingsvrije hypotheek*, of which the literal translation is *repayment-free mortgage*. With the English term confusing 13 per cent of the borrowers, it is unsurprising that compliance officers of Dutch banks have had a hard time dealing with complaints from borrowers believing that their mortgage did not require them to repay the mortgage at all.

Is it true that 'when people take a punt and get it wrong they have only themselves to blame', as one contributor to a *Financial Times* blog wrote? Is it true, as Eli Lehrer of the Competitive Enterprise Institute claimed in the Debate Room of *Bloomberg Businessweek*, that '[a] simple look at the blunt reality reveals that borrowers themselves should assume primary responsibility for the current subprime crisis'?[2] In Chapter 2, I introduced a powerful argument for liberty, or for free-market capitalism, based on the value of personal responsibility and desire satisfaction. Taking this argument at face value, it becomes easy to say that mortgage lenders should be free to sell any sorts of mortgages. Interest-only mortgages will be bought if they satisfy the needs of certain consumers, and if they do not they will not be bought. Let the market decide. We saw that this argument depends on an epistemic assumption holding that

---

[1] Powley and Masters, 'Interest-only mortgage crisis'.
[2] Lehrer, 'Willing customers'.

individual consumers know what they can choose; and apparently in the United Kingdom at least 13 per cent did not know what they chose.

A haphazard glance at the emerging literature on *financial literacy* shows that epistemic assumptions are essential. This literature establishes a correlation between people's level of knowledge about finance and various financial activities. People with lower levels of financial literacy are, for instance, less likely to plan for retirement.[3] Much financial literacy research is concerned with rather local samples, but it is instructive nonetheless to go through a number of examples. Small-scale farmers in India are less likely to adopt the innovative yet complex financial product of rainfall insurance if they have low levels of financial literacy.[4] UK households with lower degrees of financial literacy are more likely to have high-cost credit (mail order catalogue loans, payday loans, store cards, etc.).[5] Chileans are more likely to accumulate wealth the higher their level of financial literacy is.[6] US house owners with little financial literacy are more likely to be unable to repay their mortgages. This is not caused by their having selected an inappropriate mortgage, but by issues independent of loan selection.[7] Dutch households with low financial literacy participate less in the stock market.[8] German girls with little knowledge of finance are less likely to save.[9] Relatedly, American citizens with low levels of basic knowledge of health and health insurance tend to have higher medical bills and use inefficient combinations of medical services.[10] And an explanation offered for the fact that women take on more expensive mortgages than men is that women, on average, have lower levels of financial literacy.[11]

It is no surprise that policymakers and academics alike advocate programmes to improve financial literacy. It is difficult to improve financial literacy, though; and even if it were not so difficult, the success of financial literacy programmes depends quite significantly on the

---

[3] Van Rooij et al., 'Retirement planning'.
[4] Gaurav et al., 'Rainfall insurance'.
[5] Disney and Gathergood, 'Consumer credit portfolios'.
[6] Behrman et al., 'Household wealth accumulation'.
[7] Gerardi et al. 'Mortgage default'.
[8] Van Rooij et al., 'Stock market participation'.
[9] M. Lührmann, M. Serra-Garcia and J. Winter, 'The effects of financial literacy training: evidence from a field experiment with German high-school children', University of Munich Discussion Paper 2012-24 (2012).
[10] Howard et al., 'Health literacy'. McCormack, 'Health insurance literacy'.
[11] Cheng et al., 'Do women pay more?'

participants' motivation.[12] Some researchers even point to the potential negative effects of educational programmes. One study revealed that university students who have gone through a nineteen-hour financial literacy training programme were more likely to purchase less comprehensive health insurance policies, thereby taking a higher risk.[13] Reminiscent of Bernard Williams's startling claim that 'reflection might destroy knowledge', this phenomenon is serious enough to warn against inflated expectations.[14] Some interpretations of the beneficial effects of financial literacy, moreover, require much more detailed evaluation. It may be the case that a greater knowledge of finance is associated with greater equity participation. What should interest us, however, is whether financial literacy makes people invest in shares in a manner that helps them take personal responsibility for meeting their needs. A study using Swedish panel data showed that education, among other things, is associated with avoiding a number of investment mistakes such as under-diversification, unwillingness to take risk, and the disposition effect (the tendency to keep underperforming shares and to sell shares that do well).[15] Yet apart from the fact that this study did not measure financial literacy, these investment mistakes are not the only mistakes people make. Moreover, to date no study seems to have broached the topic of the correlation between financial literacy and *wise* investment. Whether people invest their money wisely depends on whether their financing decisions match their goals. For low-income households, investing in superbly diversified mutual funds may be inferior to depositing money in a savings account as long as the goal is to set aside money for emergency expenditure.

An alternative tack is to think that a lack of financial literacy is compensated by buying financial advice: after all, don't we buy medical services for want of medical knowledge? There are several reasons why that is implausible. Not only has trust in financial advisers diminished significantly over the past few years (so much so that the *Guardian* short-listed *trusted financial advisor* as the 'biggest oxymoron of the decade').[16] More than that, financial advice may not reach those needing it most because financially unsophisticated people take counsel less

---

[12] Mandell and Schmid Klein, 'Motivation'.
[13] Carlin and Robinson, 'Decision support'.
[14] Williams, *Limits of philosophy*, 167.
[15] Calvet et al., 'Financial sophistication'.
[16] McGee, 'Choosing a financial advisor'.

frequently than they should.[17] It is, by contrast, people with higher incomes or wealth or with higher levels of education that are more likely to seek advice.[18]

Financial consultants often view themselves as aspiring to the ideal of medical doctors.[19] It is questionable whether this is the right analogy. Medical services are indeed sometimes bought to substitute for ignorance, but visiting the GP in general results not in a changed state of knowledge, but in a state in which a particular condition has been treated by the medical professional. The analogue of the physician is not the financial adviser, but the financial majordomo actively managing the finances of a particular person or household. Such forms of financial stewardship are rare, though, and are often offered only to 'high net worth' customers. Add to that the observation that as soon as we move away from medical treatment and consider health *advice* as a more plausible exemplar we are confronted immediately with the infelicity that health advice is not very powerful. Many patients do not follow their GP's recommendations. This is mirrored in finance; many customers requesting advice do not follow the advice.[20]

The question addressed in this chapter is not what levels of knowledge about finance are sufficient for adequate financial planning. On the contrary, I investigate the epistemic virtues leading people to acquire the knowledge and the vices that result in their failing to do so. Doing this suggests ways to strengthen financial literacy. But financial literacy is not always accompanied by epistemic virtue, nor does financial illiteracy imply epistemic vice by necessity. As we have seen, one study of financial literacy suggests that low financial literacy is associated with low stock market participation.[21] We may deplore this on the grounds that adequate financial planning typically requires some exposure to the stock market, but we may also applaud it. People who know they do not grasp the difference between saving money in a deposit account and buying equity in a company must not deceive themselves into believing that their ignorance is no obstacle to mingling in the stock market.

This chapter features a number of epistemic virtues and links them to customer behaviour. First, love of knowledge. One may have one's

[17] Hackethal et al., 'Financial advisors'.   [18] Collins, 'Financial advice'.
[19] McGee, 'Choosing a financial advisor'.
[20] Bhattacharya et al., 'Retail investors'.
[21] Van Rooij et al., 'Stock market participation'.

reservations about the presence in business of this virtue. Rejecting an elitist reading of love of knowledge, however, I show that business-people need to have the curiosity to gain information and to learn about things novel in order to flourish and make a profit; and for similar self-directed reasons customers too require love of knowledge. Then I turn to epistemic courage, justice, temperance and humility, with a brief excursion into a particularly stubborn bias endangering epistemic justice: racism. I also discuss in more detail the concept of open-mindedness, which draws together aspects of various epistemic virtues, and I conclude with an admonitory case that has gained some notoriety in the United Kingdom and abroad showing that, despite contributing to the chance of epistemic success, internalizing and practising epistemic virtues does not guarantee success and that other epistemic agents have to cooperate as well.

Love

A very good place to start is the epistemic motivator par excellence: *love* of knowledge. This virtue is already present in Aquinas's writings about epistemic virtue. Aquinas distinguished a virtuous form of love of knowledge (*studiositas*) and an unvirtuous preoccupation with acquiring knowledge (*curiositas*).[22] Aquinas's terminology has not caught on. The word *curiosité* came into vogue when epistemic virtue gained traction among Enlightenment thinkers.[23] But despite the change in terminology, Aquinas's distinction is still with us. Contemporary authors such as Robert Roberts and Jay Wood define love of knowledge as a desire for (i) gaining true beliefs about worthy and relevant objects (ii) in ways ensuring these beliefs are adequately supported by available evidence (iii) using the acquired knowledge in the right circumstances. According to this view, reading tabloids as a way to find gossip, for example, is a form of unvirtuous love of knowledge, a form of nosiness or prurient curiosity that Aquinas called *curiositas*. Such a love of knowledge does not count towards virtue owing to both the unworthi-ness of the content and the fact that a significant amount of what the

---

[22] Aquinas, *Summa theologiae*, II–II q.166. See also, e.g., Trottmann, 'Studiositas et superstitio'.
[23] Blumenberg, 'Neugierde und Wissenstrieb'.

popular press writes is unsupported by evidence.[24] Or as Roberts and Wood write:

Individuals who are concerned about the truths they read in *Science* magazine, or the *Atlantic Monthly*, the *National Geographic*, the *New York Review of Books*, or *Books and Culture*, are in this respect more virtuous than people who are most interested in the truths they read in the *People* magazine or the gossip columns, because the truths that are found there are mostly trivial or even salacious.[25]

Avoiding elitism

If this sounds elitist, they write, 'this is an elitism we cannot avoid'.[26] As I explained in the previous chapter, such a form of elitism risks making knowledge acquisition too intellectualist to be sufficiently broadly applicable. Hardly any businessperson is interested, as a businessperson, in reading the periodicals Roberts and Wood recommend, nor can potential customers find much help in them for their purchasing choices. There may even be a grain of truth in Richard Posner's suggestion that the newspaper columns allegedly shunned by the elites, as long as they state truths, give people valuable information about how to live their lives – or how not to.[27] This is why I favour a view explaining epistemic value in purely instrumental terms according to which lovers of knowledge have a positive orientation towards true beliefs that are relevant to the realization of particular aims (which, if they have also internalized non-epistemic virtue, likely also contribute to *eudaimonia*); in addition to that, knowledge lovers have a positive orientation towards these beliefs being justified to a degree that is determined by the sorts of aims to which the knowledge is a means.

Some theorists may, as we have seen, suspect this view will lead to a lowering of standards. This is true in a sense. If viewing knowledge as primarily instrumentally valuable leads to a greater tolerance for various kinds of topics and evidence, what others call unvirtuous love of knowledge I may call virtuous. But this is the result not so much of leaving it to the individual to decide what to read or how to investigate

---

[24] Sparks and Tulloch, *Tabloid tales*.
[25] Roberts and Wood, *Intellectual virtues*, 159.
[26] Roberts and Wood, *Intellectual virtues*, 159.
[27] Posner, *Frontiers of legal theory*, 93.

but more of letting topics and evidence be dependent on the goals that knowledge acquisition is to serve. I do not see a reason why an instrumental view of epistemic value leads to less stringent requirements than a view based on personal intellectual worth, for instance, if we focus on a pre-eminently intellectualist endeavour: science. The difference between the views only appears when we direct our attention to more down-to-earth subjects such as business and finance.

Consumers, for a start, need a love of knowledge thus construed. Research on consumer behaviour has focused primarily on what sources of information consumers use when they make consumption choices, and how prominent these sources are. The most prominent source of information is dealers and consumer reports published by such organizations as the Consumers Union or Which? Experts and friends rank second, and advertisements and media third.[28] That independent sources rank highly may reveal a genuine love of knowledge. Yet the ranking says nothing about whether consumers are motivated and capable of estimating the trustworthiness of these sources. Consumer organizations may easily be identified, but whether salespeople, self-proclaimed experts, advertisements or friends should be trusted is an entirely different matter. There seems to be a considerable need to improve search behaviour, because psychologists have found that we generally overestimate our friends' knowledge and experience. It may even happen that we attribute knowledge to friends when we are in a position to know that they cannot possibly possess the knowledge, which probably has to be explained by our desire not to endanger our friendships.[29] Asking friends for advice is risky.

Financial planning

All this may lead cynics to expect that genuine inquisitiveness is fairly scarce in business. A casual glance at the popular literature on the global financial crisis reveals a careless disdain for investigation among consumers, finance practitioners, overseeing authorities, journalists and politicians. Few people bothered to read the prospectuses that came with mortgage-backed securities, to do the research that financial due diligence requires, or to engage in more than superficial search behaviour about suitable house loans. In these examples, what constitutes

---

[28] Babutsidze, 'Consumer choices'.   [29] Gershoff and Johar, 'Friends' knowledge'.

a lack of epistemic virtue is primarily the failure to start performing investigative activities in the first place; without a sufficient degree of curiosity, people lacked the motivation to search information. Failures to search or research may not be the most prominent form of a lack of love of knowledge in business. An easily overlooked aspect of love of knowledge is the requirement that one adopt a belief only if one has a justification to do so. Many businesses and government agencies use decidedly substandard justificatory methods. Consider, for instance, the paucity of so-called *evidence-based* procedures. Evidence-based procedures are developed on the basis of scientific evidence. A failure to establish evidence-based procedures is to be deplored, if not severely condemned, in medicine and fortunately rather seldom occurs these days. Evidence-based methods in marketing or management, by contrast, are frequently wanting. A recent study revealed that no item out of a convenience sample of nine textbooks and three practitioner books in the field of advertising contained one single reference to empirically backed advertising principles.[30] Another recent study showed that only 25 per cent of American business schools make use of evidence-based management principles 'in some form'.[31] Nor is the picture in finance much better. Highly specialized concepts and theories are used and not seldom developed by practitioners working in the higher echelons of the finance industry; they even quite frequently collaborate with colleagues in academia, which often leads to joint publications in top-ranked journals. Most of finance is different, though. More than twenty years have elapsed since financial planner Dick Wagner wrote a well-known accusatory feature article in the *Journal of Financial Planning* deploring the dearth of theory in the planning profession.[32] Wagner argued that, unlike law, finance had not developed into a serious profession over the course of its history. He looked to law for his inspiration. He observed that law students become acquainted with legal theories, concepts and arguments, and that they are immersed in a tradition that is a 'source of pride, of humor, of common bonds, of self-knowledge'.[33] Law students as a result adopt a common methodological and normative framework

---

[30] Armstrong, 'Evidence-based advertising'. Cf. commentaries to Armstrong's article in the same issue by Carlson et al., 'Comments' as well as Armstrong's response to the commentaries.
[31] Charlier et al., 'Teaching evidence-based management'.
[32] Wagner, 'To think ... like a CFP'.   [33] Wagner, 'To think ... like a CFP'.

and learn to 'think like a lawyer'. Reading publications in the same and other journals in financial planning cannot but leave the impression that little has changed since Wagner first voiced his concerns. The field is still rather underdeveloped methodologically, and when it comes to financial planning, theory does not seem to play a consistent and systematic role in the practitioners' work.[34]

Courage

But love of knowledge is not the only virtue. To increase the chances of epistemic success people need courage too. The traditional Aristotelian view locates courage between the extremes of cowardice and recklessness.[35] Seeing that performing a particular action is a way to realize some good, and noting that this action may have harmful consequences, the courageous person knows how to strike the right balance between risking harm and achieving the good. Harm is typically thought of as involving dangers to one's own or others' safety, physical integrity or personal wellbeing. The literature on epistemic virtues follows this view.[36] A war reporter working on the battlefields, a researcher working with dangerous chemicals, or a test driver testing a prototype of a new sports car all need courage. In the previous chapter, I used courage as an example of how virtues enable, so I can be rather brief here; it is important to stress again, though, that courage is not only needed to carry out the investigative part of an epistemic action. It is not only the inquiry, the actual travelling through war-torn areas at risk to one's own life, that epistemic courage supports. Epistemic courage also applies to the doxastic and justificatory part. This happens when evidence calls on us to revise beliefs that we have held on to for a long time, or when 'facing the truth' has highly unpleasant consequences.[37] As such, epistemic courage is often hard to distinguish from honesty.

A telling case is derived from Matthew Gill's study of epistemological and ethical aspects of accountancy, based on interviews with chartered accountants in the City of London. One of the insights of his study

[34] See, e.g., Buie and Yeske, 'Evidence-based financial planning'.
[35] Mills, 'ANDREIA'.
[36] E. Kraemer, 'Epistemic courage and epistemic virtue'. Paper presented at COURAGE, A Conference on the Cardinal Virtues, D.B. Reinhart Institute for Ethics in Leadership, Viterbo University, La Crosse, Wisconsin, 27–29 March 2008.
[37] Kaplan, 'What to ask'.

concerns the aversion to risk for which accountants are famous. Risk aversion makes accountants reluctant to give their real opinion. One accountant put it thus:

[i]t's a desire not to give an opinion; [accountants] are genuinely constrained about giving an opinion. It's risk management led, [*sic*] I think accountants are risk averse and therefore, it's probably the way they're trained, but it comes through in every accountant we work with.[38]

But a reluctance to opine may compromise honesty, the accountant went on to argue, because '[o]ne of the hardest things ... is standing up and, you know, challenging when you have to'.[39] Risk aversion surely is often a laudable character trait to possess, but when it leads to a lack of epistemic courage and people do not ask questions or express their opinions, it does not benefit the acquisition of knowledge. As the interviewed accountant suggests, in such a case it rather helps to sustain falsehoods.

Justice

Aristotle's concept of justice is a notoriously 'difficult notion to interpret', applying as it does to distributive and corrective or compensatory justice alike.[40] Yet the notion of the *fair* or *just man* translates rather straightforwardly to epistemic contexts. Most virtue epistemologists use terms such as *open-mindedness, fairness* or *impartiality* to describe the virtue, but nothing, I believe, prohibits us from staying closer to Aristotle's terminology and using the term *justice* here. Epistemically just people are motivated and enabled to give a fair hearing to opposing positions and they are open-minded and impartial when it comes to dealing with new information. Justice is relevant when people are undecided and have not yet adopted any beliefs or disbeliefs. Justice safeguards them, ensuring they are disposed carefully to sort and weigh evidence in favour of both positions before deciding which doxastic stance to adopt, and it motivates them to start investigating various positions in the first place. But the virtue is exhibited equally when people deal with conflicts arising out of their receiving counterevidence to beliefs they already possess.

---

[38] Gill, *Accountants' truth*, 63.   [39] Gill, *Accountants' truth*, 63.
[40] Rosen, 'Aristotle's categories of justice', 229.

Tax advice and functional food

Epistemic justice motivates and enables people to counter a number of biases studied in behavioural economics. One goes by the name of *confirmation bias*. Relevant studies of the confirmation bias among consumers of financial services are scarce, but work on tax professionals by Bryan Cloyd and Brian Spilker offers a nice illustration of the phenomenon.[41] The main task of tax professionals is to provide businesses with an estimate of the risks of particular ways of reporting company taxes. The professionals arrive at these estimates by researching judicial precedents. They have a strong incentive to give as accurate an estimate as possible, because companies want to minimize litigation costs. Even so, tax professionals favour cases confirming their client's desired position over cases that refute it. In other words, when they search the databases to find relevant court decisions, the likelihood that they will select a favourable case for further study is greater than the chance that they will select an unfavourable case. This is a failure of epistemic justice, with undesired consequences. By not giving an equal hearing to both sides (the two possible positions on the issue that courts can take), tax professionals arrive at suboptimal risk estimates, thereby leading them to make overly aggressive tax reporting recommendations to their clients.

Cloyd and Spilker's article attests to the value of epistemic justice when it comes to adopting a belief about a proposition about which one did not hitherto have a belief. The tax professionals start from a situation in which they suspend belief concerning the legality of the client's tax reporting, and wish to move to a state in which they have a justified belief concerning this issue. But epistemic justice also has value in situations where people start from a certain already formed belief. As I have said, relevant experimental studies on the confirmation bias among consumers of financial services are still awaited, but a study of how consumers choose what is called *functional food* nicely illustrates the effect. Functional food is food that is claimed to contribute to realizing particular health effects, such as lowering cholesterol or lowering the chances of particular forms of cancer. These claims, however, are ardently contested, and consequently the media (particularly the Internet) contain conflicting information. One might expect health-conscious

---

[41] Cloyd and Spilker, 'Tax professionals'.

consumers to search more for information about functional food than others, in particular if they are knowledge lovers. If they exhibit epistemic justice, they nevertheless have to remain undecided about the effectiveness of functional food as long as opposing and equally plausible or authoritative claims appear in the media. One study showed, however, that consumers with a high degree of health consciousness tend to set aside claims undermining the effectiveness of functional food.[42] These consumers do not show a concern for epistemic justice. They do not listen to both sides. Consumers with poor health consciousness, by contrast, tend to draw the epistemically just conclusion when confronted with conflicting evidence and suspend their beliefs about the effectiveness of functional food.

If confirmation bias were deeply rooted in human psychology one should object to considering it as a vice that the virtuous knower ought to overcome. How can consumers be motivated and enabled to care for different views about functional food or retirement plans if they have an innate tendency to pay attention only to what is in line with their own beliefs? Empirical research is still incipient, but it looks as though confirmation bias and other biases are far from innate and unchangeable tendencies. Explicitly discussing biases, for instance, may decrease their effects by making people aware of them, but there are other ways of *debiasing*, some of which I shall turn to later.[43]

Epistemic injustice

These reflections on epistemic injustice suggest that an important aspect of epistemic justice is the selection of sources of information. Falsely selecting sources of testimony is among the reasons why consumers of financial services may end up with suboptimal choices. Consumers who, for instance, form their beliefs about insurance on the basis of word of mouth or testimonials from friends and family are less well informed than those using more formal sources of information such as the Internet, independent experts or even insurance salespeople.[44] But the relevance of epistemic justice is broader. It is perhaps the epistemic virtue with the clearest moral and political consequences. From the fact that epistemically just people judge information only on the basis

[42] Walker Naylor et al., 'Eating with a purpose'.
[43] Misra, 'Conventional debriefing'.   [44] Tennyson, 'Insurance literacy'.

of epistemically relevant considerations it follows that in particular they do not discard information on such grounds as that it is provided by people of a particular race or ethnicity, or simply because the sources go against views that one holds dear.

Miranda Fricker has pioneered an account of epistemic *injustice*. She takes her cue from the case of Tom Robinson, the black defendant in Harper Lee's novel *To kill a mockingbird*.[45] Robinson is accused of raping a white girl, and despite the fact that the evidence is overwhelmingly and plainly on the side of Robinson's innocence, the jury refuses to trust his testimony due to racial prejudice against the general trustworthiness of people of colour, and convicts the defendant.

How could that be relevant to consumer behaviour? Not all consumers are paragons of epistemic justice. A recent study provided what the authors indeed call 'disturbing evidence' of racist and sexist biases among consumers.[46] They showed that when customers are asked to evaluate the quality of services rendered by salespeople, they favour white and male salespeople over non-white or female salespeople, despite the fact that the experiment ensured that all salespeople offer indistinguishable levels of service. An echo of this experiment may be heard in an oft-quoted sentence from a book by Steven Carter, *Reflections of an Affirmative Action Baby*: 'Our parents' advice was true: We really do have to work twice as hard to be considered half as good [as whites].'[47] In the next chapter I show that racist epistemic injustice can also be found among loan officers deciding whom to extend bank finance to.

Temperance

Aristotle's 'surprisingly neglected' virtue of temperance governs tactile pleasures only, with food, drink and sex as paradigmatic cases.[48] An epistemic analogue can be construed for all that, incorporating all three elements of epistemic actions encountered in the previous chapter.[49] Epistemic temperance is the disposition to choose the right amount of inquiry (this concerns the investigative part of the epistemic action), to

---

[45] Fricker, *Epistemic injustice*.
[46] Hekman et al., 'Racial and gender biases', 238.   [47] Carter, *Reflections*, 58.
[48] Curzer, 'The virtue of temperance', 5.
[49] For related proposals on how to develop epistemic temperance, see, e.g., Aikin and Clanton, 'Group-deliberative virtues' and Battaly, 'Epistemic self-indulgence'.

reach one's judgements and adopt one's beliefs at the right speed (this relates to the doxastic part) and to strive for the right degree of warrant for one's views (this is associated with justification). What temperance requires of people depends on the ends that knowledge acquisition is supposed to help realize. A consumer buying a house and taking out a mortgage ought to spend more time searching for information than, say, someone buying a vacuum cleaner. In the former case the stakes are much higher and it is more important to avoid drawing conclusions hastily and to demand a higher degree of warrant for the beliefs espoused.

Efficiency

The contribution that temperance makes to realizing one's goals is partly one of efficiency. Overly temperate people maximize the chances of gaining knowledge, but only by wasting time and resources. Spending a whole day reading consumer reports and web sites before buying a vacuum cleaner is senseless for most people. But there is more to temperance than fending off epistemic waste. It strengthens the chances that one will reach one's goals. The epistemic activities of epistemic self-indulgers (self-indulgence is a lack of temperance) are so meagre that they seriously compromise the likelihood of reaching their goals. For most people, taking out a mortgage without having clear and sufficiently reliable expectations about their future cash flows is foolish because of the unacceptable risk that they cannot afford to repay their mortgage.

Temperance is what financial markets require from consumers lest they be saddled with shoddy services. It has been argued that markets are not particularly favourable to non-epistemic temperance, so one may wonder if this also applies to epistemic temperance.[50] Empirical research indicates that consumers tend to stop searching for product information too early in that they would have reached outcomes with higher expected utility had they investigated longer. Had they continued for some further time searching the Internet, making phone calls or soliciting information from trustworthy advisers, they would have reached superior results. A study of consumer behaviour, which I deal with in more detail in the next chapter, shows that house owners with prime mortgages are twice as likely as subprime borrowers to have searched extensively to find the best mortgage deal. What is more, the

[50] Graafland, 'Do markets crowd out virtues?'.

study suggests that subprime borrowers who search better decrease the chance of their getting a subprime deal.[51] On the other hand, research on consumer choice also suggests that increased search behaviour may cause decreased feelings of satisfaction; the more we know, the more we regret.[52] If the vacuum cleaner, carefully chosen after a day of reading reports, is still noisier than expected, one's resentment is certainly greater than if one had bought it unmethodically.

Temperance thus not only sets a minimum on knowledge acquisition, but also a maximum. An epistemically temperate person strikes the right balance, is motivated to go on when necessary and stops when going on is no longer any use. This applies to all three parts of epistemic actions. What doxastic stance to adopt and whether the adoption of the doxastic stance is warranted given the evidence depend on the aims to which the knowledge is subservient. Suppose I carry out a lot of investigation, but I never draw the conclusion and keep my judgement suspended. Or suppose that I increase my level of investigation, and become persuaded that thanks to the increase rather than the results of the investigation I must draw the conclusion now and cease suspending judgement. That is not a failure of amount of investigation; the failure has to do with doxastic stance and justification, the other parts of the epistemic action. I am too reticent (in the first case) or too eager (in the second) to adopt the doxastic stance that is justified by the outcomes of the investigative action.

Online investing

These admittedly abstract points are highly relevant to practice. They connect well to behavioural economics research on consumer investment decisions. Brad Barber and Terrance Odean examined a sample of private investors some of whom had switched from telephone trading to online trading in the 1990s.[53] Before they switched they had beaten the market by 2 per cent on average, but after they switched they fell behind the market by 3 per cent. Barber and Odean explain this by the switchers being overly confident about the information they use for

---

[51] Courchane et al., 'Subprime borrowers'.
[52] Schwartz, *Paradox of choice*. Cf. Scheibehenne et al., 'Choice overload', a recent meta-analysis showing mixed findings on information overload.
[53] Barber and Odean, 'Online investors'.

their investment decisions. The amount they searched may have remained the same as before the switch. It is likely, however, that the switchers increased the amount they searched, because many online brokerage firms offer private consumers access to databases that used to be the preserve of professional investors before online trading became fashionable. This makes it likely, Barber and Odean posit, that the switchers increased the amount they searched: the switchers explored these newly available web resources. Following this interpretation, many of the switchers deceived themselves into thinking that once they investigate more, they have to adopt more beliefs; the more one searches, the less attractive suspending belief seems to be. The switchers did not realize that they were being epistemically self-indulgent and that they ought to have, as Barber and Odean write, 'more than a glimmer of additional insight to profit from trading'.[54] Epistemically temperate people, on the other hand, may invest more time in research, but this does not necessarily lead them to adopt more beliefs. As long as they consider the information they find inaccurate or irrelevant they will keep suspending their beliefs.

Humility

Aristotle's 'much-maligned' *megalopsuchia*, which I translate as *humility*, contrasts with vanity and arrogance.[55] Vain people are exaggeratedly preoccupied with themselves and the way others think of them. They crave the attention of others and are continually obsessed with showing off their accomplishments, talents and luxuries.[56] As an epistemic vice, vanity makes people draw attention to themselves and their knowledge, giving more importance to what the recipients of their information think about them than what their audiences may learn from them. Vanity is not arrogance. Arrogance is the disposition to claim a right to certain things on behalf of one's perceived superiority or authority, where the right does not follow from the superiority or authority, or where the superiority or authority is absent.[57] These observations apply to epistemic and non-epistemic actions alike. Pension fund managers presuming to be better placed than their subordinates to judge the risks

---

[54] Barber and Odean, 'Online investors', 460.
[55] Curzer, 'Aristotle's *megalopsychos*'.   [56] Nuyen, 'Vanity'.
[57] Tiberius and Walker, 'Arrogance'.

of particular investment decisions are indeed epistemically arrogant if they think that their mere position as managers makes them a valuable source of information about such risks. Their position is of no effect, from an epistemic point of view, if they have not undergone the necessary training or if they have forgotten the essence of risk management. Their epistemic authority ought to depend on their knowledge, not their status as managers. As opposed to the vain, people espousing epistemic humility are ultimately driven by a desire to gain knowledge rather than how others think of them. Furthermore, as opposed to the arrogant, people practising epistemic humility acknowledge that they may in reality fail to know what they believe they know, and that when someone disagrees with them the other may be right and they may be wrong. They continuously have their eyes on their fallibility and potential limits in their knowledge and intellectual capacities. But no one should be self-effacing. Giving way to others all the time may lead one to follow the crowd uncritically. The virtuous knower consequently strikes the right balance and stays away from *hubris* as well as from *groupthink*.[58]

CEO hubris

Starting with the one extreme, hubris finds expression in many domains, capturing, for example, the alleged arrogance underlying the imperialist tendencies of economists attempting to mould all social sciences into the form of economics, a theme more important than ever after the dubious role professional economists played in the global financial crisis.[59] But the most lively literature on hubris is concerned with *corporate* finance. A starting point of this line of research was work on mergers and acquisitions, more specifically the initial observation that directors, knowing that the majority of mergers and acquisitions do not end happily, fail to incorporate that insight into their own decision making. A seminal paper explained this failure in terms of directors being so arrogant as to set aside important information obtained from capital markets.[60] Valérie Petit and Helen Bollaert give a graphic illustration of this phenomenon. When Jean-Marie Messier, then CEO of

[58] Solomon, '*Groupthink*'.
[59] See, e.g., Mäki, 'Economics imperialism' and DeMartino, *Economist's oath*, and for hubris in different contexts, e.g., Baertschi, 'The argument from hubris' and Gert, 'Moral arrogance'.
[60] Roll, 'The hubris hypothesis'.

Vivendi Universal, was confronted in 2002 with a spectacular fall in his firm's value, he was reported as saying that '[w]e must understand that even though the market is always right, it is not right every day', and as claiming a month later that 'Vivendi is in better than good shape.'[61] Less than six months later, however, Vivendi ended up as a junk investment and Messier had to leave the company.

Whereas vanity has, in Hume's words, no 'pernicious consequence' in society, arrogance in business may lead to disastrous results.[62] Apart from the fact that hubris theories are invoked to explain unsuccessful mergers and acquisitions, they account for failing ventures; moreover, hubris has been associated with excessively aggressive approaches to banking.[63] Arrogant leaders are found to inhibit knowledge sharing between the people they manage, whereas humility increases the amount of information sought.[64]

Long-Term Capital Management

Perhaps the most notorious example of epistemic arrogance is Long-Term Capital Management (LTCM).[65] This hedge fund was founded by John Meriwether of Salomon Brothers, and Robert Merton and Myron Scholes, two economists wishing to apply in practice the novel option pricing theory that they had developed with Fisher Black. It looked very promising, and during its first years the fund boasted returns of over 40 per cent. Merton and Scholes gained the Nobel Prize in economics in 1997 'for a new method to determine the value of derivatives' that is applied by '[b]anks and investment banks regularly ... to value new financial instruments and to offer instruments tailored to their customers' specific risks'.[66] But not even one year after the ceremony in Stockholm, probably initiated by Russia's default at the time, the hedge fund was hit hard, incurring losses of around 50 per cent. When both Warren Buffett and George Soros declined to help, LTCM had to be bailed out by fourteen Wall Street banks.

---

[61] Petit and Bollaert, 'Flying too close to the sun?', 265.
[62] Hume, *Treatise*, 3.2.2.12.
[63] Hayward et al., 'Entrepreneurship'. Lawrence et al., 'The risks of hubris'.
[64] Nevicka et al., 'Narcissistic leaders and group performance'. Weiss and Knight, 'The utility of humility'.
[65] Ferguson, *The ascent of money*. Stein, 'Organizational narcissism'.
[66] www.nobelprize.org/nobel_prizes/economic-sciences/laureates/1997/press.html.

Niall Ferguson observes that at the bottom of LTCM's failure lies its reliance on historical data of only the previous five years. The fund's managers had not even included the crash of 1987 in the models. This reveals the epistemic arrogance that had taken hold of the managers. With tremendous creativity they had developed a theory of option pricing later crowned with a Nobel Prize. Their ingenuity was to develop a model of option pricing that obviated the need to calculate the risk premium by containing it in the price of the underlying asset. To calculate the price of the option, the only significant variable to be plugged in is the asset's volatility; this, as I explain in greater detail in the next chapter, is a measure of how great the expected deviation from the mean is. The theory does not provide any help in estimating the volatility, however, and its authors arrogantly assumed that developing the theory gave them the authority also to *apply* the theory in real life. Using historical data of only the five previous years proved insufficient. Ferguson maintains that 'the Nobel prize winners had known plenty of mathematics, but not enough history … and that was why Long-Term Capital Management ended up being Short-Term Capital Mismanagement'.[67] Epistemically virtuous cobblers stick to their lasts.

Talking about retirement

Love of knowledge, epistemic courage, justice, temperance, humility and their cognates such as inquisitiveness, attentiveness, fair-mindedness, self-awareness, creativity and tenacity, are all essential for gaining knowledge. Behavioural biases may stand in the way of internalizing and realizing virtue, but I suggested that strategies for debiasing are increasingly presenting themselves. Even if biases can be overcome, however, epistemically virtuous people cannot be entirely sure that they will end up gaining knowledge successfully whenever they act virtuously. They also need others.

To show this let me return to the argument for liberty and its implicit epistemic assumptions. As I noted earlier, this argument inspired, among many other things, the deregulation of the pension system in the United Kingdom and other countries; retirement is therefore a good case to examine the role of epistemic virtue in more detail. One fairly obvious implication is that policymakers extolling the virtues of liberalization

---

[67] Ferguson, *The ascent of money*, 330.

because of its contribution to personal responsibility and preference satisfaction must be aware of the fact that the argument breaks down if the epistemic preconditions do not hold. Policymakers embracing the argument must either develop policy to make the conditions hold, or demonstrate that they hold without additional measures. So far I have considered the epistemic assumptions from the point of view of the client. As a matter of fact, most people face increasingly great responsibilities to organize things that used to be organized for them, including financial planning; and it is quite clear that internalizing epistemic virtue enlarges their chances of success. Without epistemic virtue, the epistemic presuppositions of the argument for liberty are scarcely satisfied. This is something that regulators have to acknowledge. In particular, they have to acknowledge that the mere provision of information concerning freedom is only partly going to address the needs of people facing financing decisions. A brief excursion into a case that has acquired some fame in the United Kingdom and abroad concludes this chapter by illustrating this point.

The meaning of guarantee

In order to help British citizens make an informed pension choice in the late 1980s and early 1990s, the Financial Services Authority (FSA), the main financial regulator at the time, published several guides for the general public. Some of these leaflets suggested that employer pensions were often preferable to alternative schemes because they 'guarantee' the pension. These guides did not, however, mention the risk that if the employer fails or the scheme is wound up, members may lose some or all of their pension. This happened to more than 150,000 UK citizens. The pensions were *not* 'guaranteed' after all.[68]

Ros Altmann, a British pension expert, suggests that the FSA misled the citizens.[69] An alternative explanation more plausibly blames the FSA for failing to be sufficiently sensitive to what they should have expected the readers of these brochures to know about finance. Rather than deceiving citizens, which may suggest the regulator *intended* to mislead the citizens, the FSA failed to track whether the readers of the brochures understood the meaning of *guarantee*. The FSA used the word to distinguish *defined-benefit* schemes (final-salary schemes in

---

[68] Osborne, 'Pension victims accuse government'.   [69] Cohen, 'FSA rejects call'.

which people get a specific sum of money) from *defined-contribution* schemes (in which people invest a specific sum of money). This becomes clear when we examine the context in which the guides use the word *guarantee*. Consider some quotes from the brochures:

> Some types of employer's schemes (the ones called 'final salary' or 'defined benefit' scheme) give you a guaranteed pension.

> The amount of pension you get from a personal pension is unpredictable.

> In a final salary scheme you know broadly how much pension you'll get.[70]

From these quotes it becomes clear, I think, that the FSA uses the word *guarantee* in what one could call a *conditional* way. Suppose this interpretation is correct. Then the idea these three sentences are meant to express is that under the condition that a pension fund remains solvent, a defined-benefit plan guarantees a fixed amount of pension and a defined-contribution plan does not.

Minding your audience

The authors of the FSA brochures are finance professionals who are acutely aware of the insolvency risk (the risk that a pension fund will go bankrupt); they know very well that they use the word *guarantee* to explain the difference between two kinds of schemes without wanting to suggest that insolvency risk is absent. The readers of the guides, however, do not have that depth of financial understanding. A person without knowledge of the difference between an occupational and a personal scheme or between a defined-benefit and a defined-contribution plan is highly unlikely to be aware of insolvency risks. But such a person is the guide's intended user. The typical reader of the guide consequently gives *guarantee* an *unconditional* interpretation.

This is true even if the reader is fully epistemically virtuous. Even a reader with vague recollections of the concept of insolvency and the possibility that some fund may fail will probably give *guarantee* an unconditional interpretation. Nothing in the guide makes it inconsistent for such a reader to take defined-benefit schemes to be schemes without insolvency risk, and defined-contribution schemes as schemes with such risk. As I said, however, the whole idea of insolvency crossing the mind

---

[70] The first two quotes are from *FSA guide to the risks of opting out of your employer's pension scheme*; the last is from *FSA guide to pensions*.

of a typical reader of the brochure is already quite arcane. What went wrong here was that the FSA failed to communicate in a way that had any chance of being correctly interpreted, even with sufficient epistemic virtue. That some readers show little regard for epistemic virtue is not something for which the FSA can be blamed; that readers practising epistemic virtue do not necessarily arrive at the right interpretation is something that the FSA could and should have foreseen. The FSA's writers should have put themselves more into the perspective of the financially illiterate yet epistemically virtuous reader. In fairness it should be noted that reprints of the guides after 2002 started to do exactly this; yet this came too late for the roughly 150,000 early victims.

Summary

A great many people have little knowledge about finance, lacking what is called *financial literacy*, making sometimes disastrous financial decisions as a result. Financial illiteracy may stem from meagre quantitative skills or low IQ. But it is surely exacerbated by a lack of interest in finance. In this chapter, I defended the claim that for consumers to reach levels of financial literacy that enable them to make reasonable financial decisions epistemic virtues are needed. I also showed that the value of epistemic virtues lies, among other things, in mitigating behavioural biases that stand in the way of adequate belief formation. Thus I provided an illustration of a phenomenon uncovered in the previous chapter: virtues motivate and enable people to do things by changing their preferences and removing internal obstacles. Of course, the connection between epistemic virtues and behavioural research remains tentative, and more empirical work ought to be carried out; however, the bits of research mentioned in this chapter do lend initial support to the hypothesis, and more is to follow in the next chapters.

One aim of this chapter was also to introduce a number of key epistemic virtues: love of knowledge, courage, justice, temperance and humility. Without love of knowledge (or its cognates of inquisitiveness, curiosity, etc.) hardly any knowledge will be gained. Love of knowledge refers not only to an obvious appetite for investigation, but also to a sense of urgency to find adequate and sufficient justification for one's beliefs. The eager consumer of gossip investigates a lot, listening to whatever source of rumours is available, but shows little interest in the reliability of the information. We found a similar lack of genuine love of knowledge in consumer search behaviour, where people tend to listen to friends and acquaintances rather than to more trustworthy consumer organizations.

Love of knowledge motivates people to investigate and to be concerned about justification. Courage and a number of other virtues enable them to do the necessary epistemic work. Without asking questions it is hard to find information and update or revise your beliefs. If you are too shy to approach a potential informant or if you are afraid to reveal your ignorance about a particular subject matter, you will not ask any questions. Then what you need is epistemic courage. Justice, moreover, is needed to counter the confirmation bias and to enable you to be open-minded enough also to pay attention to evidence that may run counter to what you think. A brief excursion to epistemic injustice showed how prejudices against particular social groups may have a negative impact on the quality of one's beliefs, and on actions springing from these beliefs.

Love of knowledge, courage and justice motivate and enable people to inquire and search for evidence. Another virtue is meant to constrain people in what they do with the evidence: temperance. Sometimes the evidence that investigative actions have led to is insufficient to adopt a belief. A study of private investors switching from telephone to online trading showed that the sheer increase in available information made them adopt beliefs that were ultimately not supported by the information. Temperance is the virtue that adjusts the amount of investigation and evidence to a person's needs. There is not only a downward limit to investigation. One can also search too much, as the sceptic shows to an extreme degree. Humility, moreover, helps people to turn to experts whenever needed and justified. Its contraries are arrogance and vanity, and we saw that it is in particular the vice of arrogance or hubris that has done much damage in finance. The demise of Long-Term Capital Management offered an example.

Retirement planning brought the chapter to a practicable close, encouraging as it did people to spend more time on thinking about the intended audience of their utterances. One may be epistemically virtuous through and through, but if one's informants do not communicate accurately, one will not gain knowledge. This topic will be taken up again in Chapter 7, where I come to speak about other-regarding virtues. The next chapter, on the other hand, will deepen our understanding of self-regarding virtues, particularly in the context of the market for mortgages.

4 | *Case study I: primes and subprimes*

The tale has become only too familiar. A mortgage broker offers customers a choice among several different kinds of mortgage. The broker highlights loans with exceedingly low *teaser rates* of, say, 1.25 per cent, but does not stress the fine print. The customers fail to query these rates; they accept the mortgage without knowing what it entails, only to learn later that in reality they obtained a mortgage with a normal rate of 5 per cent, that they have been borrowing the difference of 3.75 per cent from the mortgage lender and that they have to pay back this difference in only a few years – with interest.[1] Such is the plight of many subprime mortgage borrowers, highly educated people among them, as *New York Times* economics journalist Edmund Andrews has vividly shown.[2]

All this may be rather unsurprising given the fact that, as we have seen, research into financial literacy reveals that many people do not grasp such financial concepts as compound interest or the difference between real and nominal value.[3] A 2009 White Paper, 'Reforming Financial Markets', outlining the British government's plans and policy on financial supervision, therefore stated that steps should be taken to ensure that 'simple and transparent products are available for those who need or want them'.[4] US President Barack Obama voiced similar concerns when he announced that he wished government to take action to guarantee that the financial services industry offers 'products that consumers actually want – and actually understand'.[5]

It probably does not matter much if certain financial products were discontinued. There is quite a lot of room for pruning if only 20 per cent of a bank's products provide some 90 per cent of its sales volume.

---

[1] Bar-Gill, 'Subprime mortgage contracts'.   [2] Andrews, *Busted.*
[3] Lusardi, 'An essential tool?'
[4] HM Treasury, 'Reforming financial markets', 104.
[5] White House, 'Remarks by the President on 21st century financial regulatory reform', 17 June 2009, www.whitehouse.gov/the_press_office/Remarks-of-the-President-on-Regulatory-Reform.

Furthermore, it is certainly a matter for regret that only relatively few players in the financial industry have decided to focus more on offering *plain-vanilla* products, simple products designed to meet the everyday concerns of typical households. Most retail banks have gone through a measure of reform here already. Yet the mere fact that certain people do not understand the details of a financial product does not imply that they do not benefit from obtaining that product. Financial products such as the continuous-workout mortgage are more difficult to understand than interest-only mortgages, but many customers may be better off with them. Robert Shiller has convincingly argued that, more generally, a ban on the sale of complex financial products forgoes an important opportunity to prepare customers for harsh economic circumstances, especially customers with low levels of financial literacy.[6]

Another relevant issue is that consumers face increasing personal responsibility for organizing their financial planning. This was captured by the argument for liberty, which, as we have seen, has become popular among politicians and policymakers of divergent ideological stripes. The roots of this development may be found in governments having appeared rather impotent when confronted with a number of challenges that traditionally lay firmly within the province of the state. States seem fairly powerless in the face of climate change, worldwide poverty, public health and financial turbulence. At the same time, the power of corporations has increased, despite significant disagreement about the magnitude of this phenomenon.[7] In the wake of liberalization and government failure, citizens have in sum turned into mere consumers to some extent. Whether this is something to applaud or lament, the fact is that when people have to assume responsibilities that they have hitherto trusted others to assume, they may turn out to be rather unprepared. I argued in the previous chapter that internalizing epistemic virtue is part of preparing for increased personal responsibility. The present case study of subprime lending continues this argument.

Costly and complex contracts

Prime and subprime mortgages differ in several important respects. Oren Bar-Gill's analysis of subprime mortgage contracts is very enlightening

---

[6] Shiller, 'Crisis and innovation'.
[7] See, e.g., Crane and Matten, *Business ethics*, 67–73 for a rapid survey of the debate.

here.[8] According to Bar-Gill, the characteristics of subprime mortgages can be subsumed under two rubrics. One is that subprime mortgages defer costs by way of three contractual mechanisms. First, unlike most prime mortgages, which require down payments on the house of at least 20 per cent of its purchase price, subprime mortgages require little or no down payment. In 2005 and 2006, just before the subprime melt-down started, the median subprime borrower made no down payment and obtained finance for 100 per cent of the price.[9] Secondly, in contrast to the interest rates of most prime mortgages, which are fixed for the entire loan period, subprime mortgages have interest rates that change several times, particularly after an introductory period of two or three years. This means that subprime borrowers are confronted with increasing monthly payments, sometimes amounting to a rise of more than 100 per cent. Thirdly, subprime mortgages come with high prepayment penalties. This is partly a consequence of offering borrowers enticingly low rates during the introductory period. Without severe prepayment penalties, borrowers would hop from one subprime mortgage to another, refinancing their loan by the end of the introductory period; and compared to prime borrowers, subprime mortgage hoppers would pay low rates during the entire loan period and pocket the difference between the initial subprime rate and the rate that prime borrowers pay. Or so it might seem. This is one of the reasons why subprime mortgage contracts stipulate that paying off the mortgage during the introductory period may lead to penalties of up to 5 per cent of the loan.[10]

The second feature of subprime mortgages is their complexity. The different interest rates (initial rate, subsequent rate, etc.) are one source of complexity, not only in the sense that several borrowers failed to realize the actual consequences, but also because rates are often determined as a function of a particular index, typically the six-month Libor, which is difficult for most borrowers to grasp. Potentially more daunting is, however, the array of fees that are included in a subprime mortgage contract. Bar-Gill mentions credit check fees, appraisal fees, pest inspection fees, title examination fees, flood certification fees, tax certification fees, escrow analysis fees, underwriting fees, document preparation fees, document notarizing fees, email fees, fax fees, courier

---

[8] Bar-Gill, 'Subprime mortgage contracts'.
[9] Mayer et al., 'Rise in mortgage defaults'.
[10] Bar-Gill, 'Subprime mortgage contracts'.

mail fees, late fees, foreclosure fees, prepayment fees, dispute-resolution fees, arbitration fees, fees for credit insurance, title insurance and private mortgage insurance as well as for origination, loan processing, signing documents and closing the loan.[11] 'It's big business', *New York Times* contributor Gretchen Morgenson wrote in 2007, noting the fact that 'during the last 12 months, Countrywide did 2.5 million flood certifications, conducted 10.8 million credit checks and 1.3 million appraisals'.[12] From the appraisals alone Countrywide, the largest mortgage lender in the United States, generated an income of $137 million in 2006. As a result of all this, prospective borrowers are by and large incapable of comparing various subprime mortgages. Bar-Gill claims that the option of prepayment makes it difficult even for finance professionals to attach a value to a mortgage and that only 'sophisticated numeric algorithms' can do the job.[13] All in all, there is no hope for consumers searching for the best subprime mortgage. The epistemic assumptions underlying the argument for liberty fail to hold.

Behavioural biases

Bar-Gill's own diagnosis is that a significant share of mis-selling can be explained by the borrowers' behavioural biases. He explains the terms of subprime mortgage loans by way of the lenders answering demands arising from biased borrowers, which in my terminology may amount to nothing less than exploiting epistemic vice. Subprime mortgages are by their very nature meant to cater to the demands of borrowers who do not qualify for prime mortgages. Lack of career prospects, little capital or a bad credit score may form too high a risk to lend money on prime terms. Subprime lenders assume these higher risks, but in return they demand a higher price. Bar-Gill argues that the basic problem is that behavioural biases deter borrowers from fully realizing the higher price. Owing to what he calls *myopia* borrowers do not take the long-term consequences of the mortgage sufficiently seriously in their decision and have an overly optimistic view of their ability to estimate the influence of the mortgage on future cash flows, if they have any clue about finance in the first place. In focusing only on a few 'salient' or easily discernible

[11] Bar-Gill, 'Subprime mortgage contracts'.
[12] Morgenson, 'Countrywide lending spree'.
[13] Bar-Gill, 'Subprime mortgage contracts', 1106.

elements of the contract, clients, moreover, miss numerous important features, including the fee structure and the prepayment penalties.

Epistemic injustice

Granting that Bar-Gill is right and that behavioural biases are an important determinant of mortgage selection, epistemic virtues seem to have much to recommend themselves. The idea is that customers with internalized epistemic virtues are closer to satisfying the epistemic preconditions of the argument for liberty than those without. Support for this suggestion can be gathered from research into consumer search behaviour. One line of research studies *gender disparity* among mortgage borrowers. This is the phenomenon that on average women pay interest rates that are 40 basis points higher than rates paid by men. One explanation might be that lenders use implicit or explicit discriminatory lending practices that disadvantage women. This would not be very surprising given the prominence of *racial disparity* arising out of *redlining* practices. These practices amount to charging higher interest rates for mortgages on houses in areas with a majority of people of colour, 'redlined' areas on maps used by lenders. In a Pulitzer Prize winning series of articles on 'The Color of Money' in the *Atlanta Journal Constitution* in 1988, journalist Bill Dedman famously demonstrated that banks in Atlanta that had been lending money to people in the poorest white neighbourhoods of the city largely refused to lend to people in affluent black neighbourhoods.

A similar prejudice seems on the face of it to lie at the bottom of gender disparity. Ping Cheng, Zhenguo Lin and Yingchun Liu have recently argued, however, that gender disparity has to be explained in terms of a difference between the search techniques used by men and women.[14] As a point of departure the study's authors take two observations about search behaviour. The first is that men search more intensely and inquisitively for the lowest available rate. Around 40 per cent of men but only 20 per cent of women actively attempt to find the lowest available rate. The second is that women rely more than men for their decisions on recommendations obtained from other people. Around 40 per cent of women but only 25 per cent of men choose lenders recommended by

---

[14] Cheng et al., 'Do women pay more?'

others.[15] Based on survey data including answers to questions about search behaviour, Cheng and his colleagues claim to be able to show that gender as such becomes insignificant when search techniques are included in a regression analysis besides such traditional explanatory variables as gender, race or income. That gender becomes insignificant is very important because the difference between decisions based on one's own searching, and decisions based on recommendations of others amounts to almost 25 basis points on average. This means that to the degree that men and women differ with respect to the rates they are charged, the difference has to be explained in terms of search behaviour rather than discriminatory lending practices.

It is important to stress that evidence is still rather scant here. Only a handful of papers address gender disparity in relation to subprime mortgages. The findings of Cheng and his co-workers, however, do not seem to have been rejected by other researchers as yet. These findings are important to our purposes for several reasons. Inspired by the discussion of redlining above, one hypothesis is that gender disparity arises because the mortgage broker lacks epistemic justice. The plausibility of this hypothesis derives, for lack of more readily applicable research, from existing research on corporate loans and racial disparity. One study examined bank finance for small enterprises headed by black and non-black women and established a stunning effect of university education on the probability of obtaining loan approval.[16] For a firm headed by a black woman, not having a university degree decreases the likelihood of loan approval by more than 80 per cent; for firms headed by non-black women, the figure is negligible: only 0.4 per cent.

One interpretation of these findings is in terms of the loan officers being epistemically unjust towards applications from firms headed by black women. It is quite clear that the applicant's knowledge and skills are factors that loan officers must take seriously. It also seems quite clear that if the knowledge and skills of two applicants are the same, a rational loan officer either approves both of them, or rejects both of them, unless the applications are different in some other respects. But if that is true, the fact that college education has a huge impact on loan approval for black applicants and no impact on loan approval for non-black applicants suggests that loan officers do not consider black and

[15] Cheng et al., 'Do women pay more?'
[16] Gray, 'Education and loans to businesses'.

white applicants as equally knowledgeable. Loan officers do not treat similar evidence of knowledge and skills similarly across race. To show that they have the appropriate level of knowledge and skills to deserve the loan, proof of secondary, not university, education is enough for non-blacks. Blacks, by contrast, need to show proof of a university degree. Alternative explanations are possible, and more research is needed here. Yet I believe it is plausible to take the study as still another echo of Steven Carter's statement: '[w]e really have to work twice as hard to be considered half as good' as whites.[17]

Love

Certainly what I say about epistemic injustice and loan approval rates should be tested first. I venture these hypotheses here not to defend a claim about racial disparity but rather to show that epistemic injustice may equally well be among the causes of another form of disparity: gender disparity. The study by Cheng and his colleagues gives initial evidence that, unlike racial disparity, gender disparity is caused by a lack of epistemic virtue among consumers, not among the financial industry. This is backed by a study by Marsha Courchane, Brian Surette and Peter Zorn, which was conducted and published prior to the subprime meltdown, which started around 2006.[18] Courchane and her colleagues examine the differences between prime and subprime borrowers via a Freddie Mac survey of borrowers from 2001. The survey contains questions to assess borrowers' financial literacy and search behaviour. Respondents were asked whether they searched for the best rates and whether they had opportunities for choice (possible answers: 'not at all', 'a little', 'some', 'a lot') and whether they were familiar with the terms of their house loans ('not at all familiar', 'somewhat unfamiliar', 'somewhat familiar', 'very familiar'). Since the mid-range answers lay close to each other, the most interesting observations are primarily drawn from the extremes. The researchers found that only 26 per cent of subprime borrowers are 'very familiar' with the various types of mortgages that are offered on the market, in contrast to 43 per cent of prime borrowers. They found similar figures for familiarity with mortgage interest rates and costs (35 and 57 per cent, respectively), and with loan qualification requirements (39 and 57 per cent, respectively). With respect to search

---

[17] Carter, *Reflections*, 58.   [18] Courchane et al., 'Subprime borrowers'.

behaviour they found that around 32 per cent of subprime borrowers and 49 per cent of prime borrowers search 'a lot', whereas 15 per cent prime borrowers and 27 per cent subprime borrowers do not search at all. Subprime borrowers, the suggestion is, are less likely to love knowledge.

A finding that Courchane and her colleagues do not emphasize is the even stronger dissimilarity between the room for choice that prime and subprime borrowers perceive there to be. Almost 80 per cent of prime borrowers say they have had 'some' or 'a lot' of opportunity to choose the terms of the mortgage, as opposed to not even 55 per cent of subprime borrowers. Given Bar-Gill's description of the multifarious terms of subprime mortgage contracts compared to those of the fairly uniform prime mortgage contracts, it is not implausible to interpret these findings as corroborating the impression that subprime borrowers have not generally been able to attach a value to the various possible mortgages. They do not even seem to have realized that many different subprime mortgages were available, which again is a failure to satisfy the epistemic conditions of the argument for liberty.

The reader might mount the objection that the study assumes that subprime mortgages are bad in all cases and prime mortgages good. To meet that objection, Courchane and her co-authors also developed a measure of the quality of the borrower's choice. This does not change the figures. Looking at epistemic determinants, the contrast is even starker between good and bad outcomes than between prime and subprime borrowers. Borrowers whose decisions end well have more knowledge of mortgage terms, they show more extensive search behaviour and see more room to choose terms. Love of knowledge, one could say, pays off.

A possible policy response to protect citizens applying for house loans is to introduce legal requirements concerning mortgage advice. Here, though, I must caution against overly optimistic expectations about the efficacy of such measures. An implicit assumption of such policy proposals is that financial advisers are adequately endowed with the knowledge, skills and experience necessary to provide bespoke advice to clients with often very specific financial situations. Anecdotal evidence as well as more thorough empirical research suggests, however, that this assumption is unsubstantiated. The FSA inspected 252 mortgage providers in 2006 and found that the level of their advisers' training was unsatisfactory and that, in particular, the advisers had little experience in forming adequate estimations of the repayment capacities of prospective borrowers.[19] It might be objected that these advisers were not independent, working as they did for mortgage brokers or lenders. Independence may indeed increase the quality of financial advice. Most empirical research in economics to date has examined the potential added value of investment advice, primarily by stock market analysts. However, even if consistently following stock market recommendations helps beat the market – which is doubtful – this sort of advice is unlikely to be of any relevance to consumers with little interest in finance.

Anecdotal evidence about mortgage advice confirms some of these suspicions. Analysing a number of relevant books and web sites for the consumer mortgage market, Sumit Agarwal, John Driscoll and David Laibson showed that the advice these sources provide on mortgage refinancing is suboptimal.[20] To decide whether I should get rid of my current loan and get a new one (of a different size or with a different interest rate) partly depends on the influence this has on my future cash flow. To estimate this, the books and web sites examined in the study only recommend using a simple break-even rule: refinance whenever the refinance costs (prepayment penalty, fees for new mortgage contract, etc.) are lower than what one saves by paying less interest on the new mortgage. Agarwal and his colleagues, however, point out that this ignores the fact that people may gain more by waiting – namely, if mortgage interest rates decline even further. They estimate that discarding this option leads on average to losses of almost $10,000 for a mortgage of $250,000. Take financial advice with a grain of salt, in other words.

An alternative view of the function of financial advice is emerging. A recent stream of research, of which I shall give an example shortly, zooms in on advisers playing a different role that is very interesting from the point of view of epistemic virtue. The idea is that rather than seeing financial advisers as a source of privileged knowledge about the future value of securities people consider buying, the adviser's primary function is to shield people from falling into the traps of their behavioural biases. Epistemic virtue is in part outsourced to financial advisers instead of internalized and practised by the customers. So far the literature has mostly investigated whether professionals are less vulnerable to behavioural biases than laypeople; the answer seems to be a qualified

[19] Goff, 'Lenders' advice to borrowers'.
[20] Agarwal et al., 'Optimal mortgage refinancing'.

yes. Less attention has been devoted to the effects of professional advice on the actual financial health of households seeking advice and on whether it is bought most frequently by those needing it most urgently.

A paper by Andreas Hackethal, Michael Haliassos and Tullio Jappelli offers support for a call upon consumers to cultivate these virtues themselves as it gives us some initial evidence to doubt whether financial advice can limit the influence of behavioural biases. Based on data from a German brokerage firm and a large German bank, the study's authors argue that the impact of advice on financial health is minimal or negative, partly owing to the additional cost of advice. Moreover, they observe that people turning to advisers often have significant financial experience themselves. The study suggests, in the authors' own forceful words, that

advisors are matched with richer, older, more experienced, self-employed, female investors rather than with poorer, younger, inexperienced and male ones. In this respect, advisors are similar to babysitters: babysitters are matched with well-to-do parents, they perform a service that parents themselves could do better, they charge for it, but observed child achievement is not boosted by babysitters but by positive characteristics of the family.[21]

We should be careful when seeking to generalize these findings to the entire sector. Needless to say, however, financial advice is not the unequivocal panacea some policymakers imagine.

To summarize, financial advisers, even if they are independent, provide at best unreliable information about strategies to beat the market; they are often so expensive as to make a do-it-yourself strategy more profitable; and they are typically hired by people who do not need them. But suppose people who do need them are legally obliged to obtain their services. Does that lead to better outcomes? Is that a way to circumvent biases and beat epistemic vices? Here too research is fairly thin, but a unique natural experiment by Sumit Agarwal, Gene Amromin, Itzhak Ben-David, Souphala Chomsisengphet and Douglas Evanoff suggests that the questions have to be answered in the negative.[22] A pilot programme in Cook County, Illinois, in 2006 and 2007,

---

[21] Hackethal et al., 'Financial advisors', 510.
[22] S. Agarwal, G. Amromin, I. Ben-David, S. Chomsisengphet and D. Evanoff, 'Do financial counseling mandates improve mortgage choice and performance? Evidence from a legislative experiment', Federal Reserve Bank of Chicago, WP 2009–07, www.chicagofed.org/digital_assets/publications/working_papers/2009/wp2009_07.pdf.

required 'high-risk' people applying for new or refinancing house loans to consult an adviser certified by the US Department of Housing and Urban Development. The adviser's task was to explain to the client, during a session of one to two hours, the terms and conditions of the various loan offers as well as to check that the information about the borrower set down in the loan application was correct. At the end of the session advisers were required to give a recommendation to the client about the reasonableness of the fees charged and the interest rates, and also to form a judgement about whether the client actually understood the consequences of the loan and whether the client could afford it.

Agarwal and his co-authors convincingly argue that the pilot programme had a number of desired effects. Confining their attention to borrowers with low credit scores, the rates of delinquency and default decreased significantly. This sounds all very nice as a new form of policy. The study suggests, however, that the actual causal mechanism accounting for the positive consequences arises not so much out of the informational content of the advice, but rather out of threats, to lenders and borrowers alike, made by the regulatory regime. In order to avoid having to consult an adviser, some borrowers actively shunned mortgage contracts that would qualify them as 'high-risk'. In addition, the authors found that, in response to the pilot scheme, lenders increasingly came to reject prospective borrowers. Lenders affected by the regulation witness an increase of rejection rates of around 8 per cent, contrasting with other lenders that increased rejection by 2 per cent only.

Lack of knowledge about finance evidently accounts for a significant amount of low-quality financial planning. I have focused here on mortgaging decisions, but I see little reason to assume that other domains (retirement planning, insurance, etc.) would present a very different picture. The upshot of the present case study, however, is not merely that it has shown that the epistemic assumptions of the argument for liberty fail to be generally satisfied. It has also demonstrated the need to foster epistemic virtue. Mandatory financial advice may seem attractive to policymakers as a way to keep behavioural biases and other epistemic errors and irrationalities at arm's length. Yet the reality is that such policies hardly obviate the need to internalize epistemic virtue if at the same time citizens see the government's sphere of influence shrinking. Mandatory financial advice is, as we have seen, not a reliable instrument. Scattered throughout the present book I have included observation supporting the view that promoting epistemic virtue is feasible, but I do not have a fully developed theory, nor do I think that the empirical literature provides sufficiently secure answers to the questions that should be asked first. One thing is clear. If financial products exploit the behavioural biases of potential clients and epistemic virtues counter such biases, epistemic virtues are worth developing.

5 | *Incorporating virtue: the banks*

An important Wiley publication entitled *European retail banks: an endangered species?* noticed in 2003, well before the crisis hit, that 'very few banks know their customers well'.[1] It lamented, moreover, the lack of product development, harshly commenting that

'Banking R&D', if you could ever call it that, has focused on process innovation, new distribution channels (for example on-line banking), or complex corporate banking products. The standard product spectrum of retail banking has remained largely unchanged over the years.[2]

Banks use Procrustean methods when they 'try to fit the client's problem to [the banks'] products rather than their products to the client's problem'.[3] Not a great signal of epistemic virtue. Six years later, the debate over financial innovation was taken to another level when Paul Volcker, former chairman of the US Federal Reserve, described the automated teller machine or cash dispenser as the best thing that had come out of financial innovation in the past twenty-five years.[4]

Is the paucity of research and development in retail banking an indication of a lack of curiosity and other epistemic virtues among bankers? This is not too clear. Most customers do not seem to be very interested in making their purchasing decisions dependent on the true differences between products; they select on brands, prefer customer satisfaction delivered by suave salespeople, and choose convenience and comfort. Ethicists often rebuke companies for exacerbating consumer culture by creating demands through innovative but useless new products.[5] Here, however, it may be the other way around. For want of demand banks do not innovate.

---

[1] Dombret and Kern, *European retail banks*, 50.
[2] Dombret and Kern, *European retail banks*, 31.
[3] Dombret and Kern, *European retail banks*, 51.
[4] Atkins, 'Financial innovations'.   [5] Galbraith, *The new industrial state*.

So far I have dealt with individual virtues only. They are important, particularly as they may save customers from the pitfalls of financial planning, but I should avoid giving the impression that epistemic virtue is solely the business of customers of finance, because corporate virtues matter too. A literature on corporate virtues and a literature on collective epistemology are developing, but research combining the two and treating corporate *epistemic* virtues is well-nigh non-existent.[6] The work of Reza Lahroodi is an exception, and the present chapter starts with a critical introduction to his approach.[7] I then give some background on Margaret Gilbert's plural subject theory, which underlies Lahroodi's approach but is also relevant in its own right.[8] I subsequently examine and extend Todd Jones's criticism of Lahroodi.[9] Jones suggests that we should take a look at the internal structure of the organization. His suggestions are still rather abstract, and I turn to the writings of Peter French and Seumas Miller to make things more concrete and pave the way for an investigation of corporate epistemic virtue in finance.[10]

Corporate entities

Lahroodi first introduces the distinction between *individualist* and *holist* accounts of collective virtue.[11] Individualism is the idea that when we speak about corporate entities embodying virtues we are in reality ascribing virtues to the people who make up the collective. Holism, on the other hand, goes against this view, maintaining that corporate entities can have virtues that are irreducible to individual virtues. When, for example, a *Financial Times* journalist calls ETF Securities 'a courageous company' because it has been 'brave enough' to issue exchange-traded products, individualists hold to the view that what the journalist attempts

---

[6] Business ethics publications on corporate virtue include Gowri, 'On corporate virtue' and Moore, 'Corporate character'. Schmid et al., *Collective epistemology* is a recent collection of articles on collective epistemology.

[7] Lahroodi, 'Collective epistemic virtues'. Related work includes Fricker, 'Group testimony?' and Aikin and Clanton, 'Group-deliberative virtues'.

[8] Gilbert, *On social facts.*   [9] Jones, 'Open-minded organization'.

[10] French, *Corporate ethics.* Miller, *Moral foundations.* Miller, 'Korruption' is more directly concerned with the financial services industry.

[11] Lahroodi, 'Collective epistemic virtues' uses a different terminology. He calls individualism *correlativism* and holism *anti-correlativism*. This makes sense in the context of his discussion, but I prefer to use the less technical, more evocative terms of *individualism* and *holism* here.

to do is praise the company's directors, managers and employees (or a majority of them) for their courage.[12] According to holists, by contrast, the journalist irreducibly praises the company as whole.

Lahroodi provides an argument against the individualist view of corporate epistemic virtues by developing a case in which a group of people lack a particular epistemic virtue, even though they possess the virtue as individuals. His example is highly abstract, but the phenomenon he is engaged with can be witnessed in business contexts too. For example, a study of non-executive directors of financial services firms in America revealed that they feel curtailed by structural, organizational and legal limits such as the very limited number of opportunities for genuine interaction with the company, despite the fact that they often personally express a great desire to carry out investigations they deem important to accurately monitor the firm.[13] In other words, as a collective of directors, the board lacks inquisitiveness, even if board members individually possess this epistemic virtue.

Yet this observation is not a vindication of holism, Lahroodi thinks. To argue his case he presents a puzzle based on an influential theory of collective entities by Margaret Gilbert.[14] Her *plural subject theory* views corporate entities as collections of people all having jointly and openly committed themselves to an attempt to realize certain specific goals. The theory is gaining a lot of traction in social philosophy and beyond, and has been successfully applied to such themes as political obligation, social roles and collective emotions, and it is not surprising that the first attempt in the literature to develop a theory of collective epistemic virtues uses plural subject theory as its point of departure.[15] Before dealing with Lahroodi's puzzle, I briefly introduce Gilbert's theory.[16]

Plural subjects and a puzzle

The core of Gilbert's theory is formed by her idea that when a collective is performing a joint action, it has to be a *plural subject*. Gilbert

[12] Stevenson, 'New UK listed ETFs'.   [13] Lorsch, 'Board challenges'.
[14] Gilbert, *On social facts*.
[15] Sheehy, 'On plural subject theory' is an introduction to plural subject theory. Also see Gilbert, *Sociality and responsibility* and Gilbert, *Political obligation*.
[16] See De Bruin, 'We and the plural subject' for a critical discussion of Gilbert's linguistic argument for plural subjects.

defines a plural subject as a set of human beings among whom there is common knowledge that each of its members has openly manifested to all other members a quasi-readiness to perform some joint action. Let me explain Gilbert's technical terminology. First of all, the members have to be *quasi-ready* to perform the joint action. This means that if you are a member, then you are individually willing to perform your individual share of the joint action, provided the other members also perform their shares. Quasi-readiness is a kind of conditional willingness in the sense that, for example, you are quasi-ready to go to the opera with someone else if you go to the opera on the condition that the other person joins you. Secondly, the members of the collective must have *expressed* their quasi-readiness in such a way that all other members notice this (unless they do not pay attention, fail to interpret the utterances in the right way or fail to draw standard logical inferences). You could express your quasi-readiness to go to the opera with someone by saying such things as 'Let's go to the opera tonight.' And if the response is positive – 'Yes, let's. *Parsifal* had a rave review in the *Guardian* last week!' – the other person reveals quasi-readiness to go to the opera as well, and you have established a plural subject with respect to going to the opera. *Common knowledge* refers here to the fact that not only do you know about the other person's quasi-readiness, but also that you know that the other person knows about your quasi-readiness, and so on. It is, in other words, completely open to the two of you that you are both quasi-ready to go.

This is an admittedly rough sketch of plural subject theory, but no more details are needed to understand Lahroodi's puzzle. To recall, Lahroodi discredited individualism about corporate epistemic virtues, arguing that individual epistemic virtues are not always sufficient to obtain corporate epistemic virtue. Rather than defending holism about corporate epistemic virtue, he promised a puzzle about holism, based on plural subject theory. He considers a group of people incorporating open-mindedness. For the group to possess this virtue, it must have the disposition to perform open-minded group activities. Now for activities to count as genuine group activities they have to result from the group's members having expressed their quasi-readiness to perform their parts of these activities. This, Lahroodi seems to claim, means that the ultimate requirement is that the group's members are individually ready to perform activities that result from their individual disposition to proceed in an open-minded manner.

Suppose this were right. Then plural subject theory, which Lahroodi considers to be a holist theory par excellence, would lead us to conclude that corporate epistemic virtues reduce to individual epistemic virtues. Holism would paradoxically support individualism. The plausibility of this puzzling conclusion, however, depends on the assumption that the only view of corporate epistemic virtues consistent with holist theories is one according to which a corporate entity possesses an epistemic virtue V precisely when its members are jointly committed to acting according to virtue V. In a reply to Lahroodi, Todd Jones casts some doubt on this assumption, claiming that corporate entities can derive their epistemic virtues from their members instantiating what he calls 'knowledge-enhancing tools' and from their 'simulating' epistemic virtues.[17] Jones hints at a number of ways in which collectives accomplish such simulation. The gist of his contribution lies, however, in exploring the conceptual space between individualism and holism, without offering hands-on tools enlarging our understanding of corporate epistemic virtues in business. This is not to diminish the importance of the problems Jones hints at. Quite the contrary, it is when we home in on collective entities as we know them in business that Lahroodi's puzzle and Jones's critique become pressing. Were organizations to possess epistemic virtues only to the degree that management and employees possess them, the relevance of individual virtues would be overrated and the value of the precise structure of the organization undervalued. Individual virtues are important, but if they are a precondition for corporate virtue, hardly any virtuous corporation exists.

Corporate internal decision structures

Where Jones speaks about the *simulation* of virtue this can be taken as a suggestion to pay more attention to the internal organizational structure of the company. Plural subject theory provides little in the way of explaining a corporate entity's internal workings; we have to consider alternative views. It is only natural to turn our attention to the highly influential theory of corporate entities developed by Peter French.[18] This theory, which is part of a view of corporate moral agency that need not detain us here, holds that, unlike people, corporate entities

---

[17] Jones, 'Open-minded organization', 441.
[18] French, 'The corporation as a moral person'.

have *corporate internal decision structures*. These structures consist of two elements. First of all, a *responsibility flowchart*. This flowchart sketches a hierarchical command structure in the organization as well as positions and levels of management. The corporate internal decision structures also determine the relationships of subordination and authority between these positions and levels. Secondly, there are *corporate decision recognition rules* allowing us to distinguish between genuinely corporate decisions and individual ones. Even though very different sorts of corporate entities fall within French's definition, one may suspect that it owes much of its inspiration to the concept of the public limited company or corporation that we encountered in Chapter 1. Despite fundamental disagreements with Ronald Coase and other economists working on the theory of the firm, French's concept of responsibility flowchart may be seen as reflecting insights on the efficiency of hierarchical corporate governance structures, whereas the recognition rules offer mechanisms tailored to allowing corporate entities to conform to corporate law and become legal persons with limited liability.[19]

The responsibility flowchart of a corporation is described in such things as the memorandum and articles of association or the certificate of incorporation and bylaws, in the terms of employment of directors, managers and employees, and in many other official and internal documents. They determine the rights and duties of directors, management and employees, the hierarchical structures of authority and command among them, and the principles and methods of operation. Typically, these documents also contain provisions about the way the board and its members represent the company, and how these powers of representation can be delegated to a corporation's employees. Such provisions function as corporate decision recognition rules determining the conditions under which an employee's actions are to be conceived as corporate decisions. A loan officer sending an email to a client with an offer for a particular loan performs a corporate action; a loan officer using a corporate email account to send an email to a friend does not.

How does French's theory of collective entities allow us to develop a view of corporate epistemic virtues that steers clear of Lahroodi's puzzle? The problem was to develop a view of epistemic virtue that

---

[19] French, 'The corporation as a moral person' does not speak warmly about the view of Jensen and Meckling, 'Theory of the firm'. To my knowledge, French has not expressed himself on Coase's contributions.

is sensitive to the fact that for a firm to have the virtue of open-mindedness, say, not all employees need to be open-minded individually. What makes a firm open-minded is whether as a firm it displays open-minded behaviour springing from a stable acquired disposition towards open-mindedness.

Describing the hierarchical command structure of a firm, corporate internal decision structures clearly suggest themselves as a locus of corporate virtue. Or so I argue. A firm is open-minded whenever its responsibility flowchart and corporate decision recognition rules together lead to a tendency to make open-minded decisions. Decision structures have to ensure that evidence from different sides is weighed, that the firm's own preconceptions are not unduly privileged and so on. This requires a hierarchical command structure in which open-minded people are assigned to specific tasks and allocated specific powers. More generally, for a firm to incorporate epistemic virtue its employees have to possess the epistemic virtues that are necessary to fulfil the particular functions they occupy within the firm. Open-minded people, for example, have to be employed in positions that require open-mindedness, or current employees occupying such positions have to acquire open-mindedness. Management has to safeguard what I call *virtue-to-function matching*. Incorporation also requires employees to be in a position to act on virtues they possess. The firm must warrant that whenever open-mindedness is required, employees can act open-mindedly without obstruction. Management structures of command and control must, more generally, encourage and support virtue instead of frustrating it. There has to be *organizational support for virtue*. Furthermore, wherever open-mindedness is absent, responsibility flowcharts and recognition rules must help to counter epistemically unvirtuous behaviour. There have to be *organizational remedies against vice*.

Structures, functions, cultures and sanctions

To make this more precise, I turn to a third view of collective entities that looks into the internal workings of collective entities with an even sharper eye for detail than French's, and with closer connections to some of the Aristotelian themes of epistemic virtue theory. Subsequently, I discuss virtue-to-function matching, organizational support and organizational remedies. Seumas Miller analyses organizations as systems of interdependent roles determined by four characteristic elements:

structure, function, culture and a system of sanctions.[20] To begin with, Miller views an organization as an institution in which individual human beings play roles defined in terms of the specific tasks they have to carry out and the specific rules and procedures determining the performance of these tasks; in his own words, this is an 'embodied [structure] of roles and associated rules'.[21] Roles are typically interdependent. Performing tasks requires cooperation between various roles, and the way roles interrelate is generally one of hierarchical command. The *structure* of the organization, for Miller, comprises the roles that constitute the organization as well as the relationships between them, and is quite similar to French's responsibility flowchart. In a business context, the Cadbury Committee offers a good illustration of this point. The Cadbury Committee was set up in 1991 in response to a number of accountancy scandals in the United Kingdom. It promoted the separation of the positions of chairman and managing director as well as the placing of independent directors on the board, and its description of the role of non-executive board members is still influential: 'Non-executive directors should bring an independent judgement to bear on issues of strategy, performance, resources, including key appointments, and standards of conduct.'[22] This is a clear element of a responsibility flowchart determining the structure of public limited companies.

This description, however, depends on the role that directors are meant to play, which in turn depends on the corporation's aims. Unlike French, Miller therefore devotes a significant part of his theory to the *function* of organizations. Functions give rise to the tasks associated with the roles of an organization's individual members. For Miller, the maximization of shareholder wealth is only one of the many goals a corporation can have. Short-term financial self-interest may be what inspires most shareholders, but markets and firms are there to satisfy more fundamental societal goals, Miller believes, such as increasing material wellbeing. Coming close to Robert Solomon's virtue ethical position, which I dealt with briefly in Chapter 1, Miller defends the claim with the example of privatized jails, the goal of which is to contribute to retribution, rehabilitation, security and deterrence, even though as a for-profit organization they also aim to maximize gains. Similarly, Miller hints at the idea that

[20] Miller, 'Social institutions'.   [21] Miller, 'Social institutions', 5.
[22] Cadbury Report, 4.11.

finance firms operating on the capital market have as a goal the provision of finance to enterprises in the production industry.

But more is needed. Structure and function together determine the formal tasks and rules that characterize the organization. The third element, institutional *culture*, captures the norms, values, beliefs and attitudes that informally run through the organization. Culture may conflict with the rules and procedures determined by an organization's structure and function; see, for instance, the frequently mentioned case of Enron, the American energy company that collapsed under the weight of ethical misconduct to which a culture of dishonesty and epistemic vice had significantly contributed.[23] Miller's view entails that subgroups within an organization, however, may have significantly different, possibly competing subcultures. The last ingredient of an organization is, finally, a system of formal and informal *sanctions*. Informal sanctions are an immediate consequence of an organization's culture inasmuch as organizations (or parts of organizations) have ways to express disapproval with nonconforming members. Particularly in business, however, formal sanctions are an important part of the organization, incorporated in internal disciplinary measures, dismissal procedures, incentive schemes and so on.

Back to the puzzle

Recall that Lahroodi observed that there may be a group of individually open-minded people who as a group lack open-mindedness. A real-world example of this phenomenon was a situation in which a firm's directors individually possess love of knowledge, but not as a group. This shows that mere individual epistemic virtues are not sufficient to incorporate epistemic virtue. We have also seen that individual epistemic virtues are not even always necessary for group epistemic virtue. The argument here was the feasibility constraint that if corporate entities are to be open-minded only if all of their members are, then hardly any corporate entity would count as open-minded.

That individual epistemic virtues are neither necessary nor sufficient is not altogether to deny the correlation between individual and corporate

---

[23] Sims and Brinkmann, 'Enron ethics'. The phrase 'culture of dishonesty' originates in a discussion of this paper by Crane and Matten, *Business ethics*, 173. O'Connor, 'The Enron board', attributes the Enron collapse to groupthink, an epistemic vice.

virtue; rather, the correlation is more complex than has been described above. To understand the complexities it is useful to look at the concept of function as it occurs in Aristotle's derivation of *eudaimonia* and virtue.[24] A textbook example to explain the concept of function considers the function of a tool – a hammer, say. A hammer has a function for a carpenter to drive nails into wooden objects to join them. For the hammer to fulfil this function well, it should be made of the right materials and be of the right size and weight. This is what sets it apart from a pair of tongs or a croquet mallet. A carpenter's hammer that optimally meets these requirements can be called an *excellent* hammer, or a *virtuous* one, because it fulfils its function excellently.

Aristotle famously extends functions to natural phenomena, animals and human beings, defining the function of human beings as an activity of the soul that conforms with or not – 'unconforms', he writes – with reason.[25] This extension of function to human beings has prompted the response that function presupposes a form of design that, the objection goes, is absent in everything not man-made.[26] Neither Aristotle's cryptic formulation nor the critique should detain us here, however, because it is my intention to consider roles and functions in the context of business only; and these are paradigmatic cases of human design, for what a company should aim at, or what an employee should do, is up to human beings to determine.

The idea of exploiting Aristotle's concept of function as a tool to gain a deeper understanding of corporate virtues is not entirely novel. One line derives corporate virtues from the function of the firm. Assuming it is the function of a firm to generate sustainable profit, this line considers such corporate virtues as efficient production, resource management and correct pricing.[27] Another line derives *individual* virtues from the function of the firm, holding to the view that for a firm to fulfil its function well, its employees, managers and directors also have to fulfil particular functions, and from these particular functions particular virtues follow. This view is defended by Robert Solomon, among others.[28] My derivation of epistemic virtues follows Solomon's line. The idea is that just as the different functions of hammer and tongs

---

[24] Gomez-Lobo, 'The ergon inference'.
[25] Aristotle, *Ethica Nicomachea*, I 7 1098a.   [26] Fitzpatrick, *Norms of nature*.
[27] Schudt, 'Corporate monster'.   [28] Solomon, 'Corporate roles'.

within the carpenter's workshop give rise to different 'virtues' for these tools, so too do directors, managers and employees require different *epistemic* virtues within the firm.

Matching virtues to functions

It is now time to look at the three elements of corporate epistemic virtue. Virtue-to-function matching is dealt with in this section; organizational support and remedies come in the following two. Every firm faces considerable epistemic challenges, irrespective of whether its function is narrowly defined in terms of profit maximization only or includes such things as the creation of sustainable societal value. Every firm has to gain knowledge about the quality of its products and services, about the vagaries of its consumers' tastes and its suppliers' tactics, and about the skills and character traits of prospective employees. It has to obtain estimates about the real and perceived value of its operations, its opportunities and challenges on the capital market, and a host of other accountancy, taxation and legal data. Apart from collecting information, information has to be sorted, stored, tested, converted, evaluated, generalized, extended, criticized, rejected, corroborated, disseminated, taught or learnt, translated into practice and adapted to policies or products, and much more.

These disparate activities require different epistemic virtues.[29] Collection requires inquisitiveness, reflectiveness, wonder and other forms of love of knowledge. Sorting and storing require attentiveness, care, perceptiveness, fair-mindedness, consistency and other cognates of epistemic justice. Testing, evaluation, criticism, rejection and corroboration require intellectual integrity, honesty, courage, transparency and epistemic humility. Application and translation of information require imaginativeness, creativity, adaptability, but also temperance. Dissemination, finally, requires generosity.

A firm acquiring, processing and applying knowledge in excellent ways need not demand every epistemic virtue of every individual member, but it must see to it that particular epistemic virtues are present in its members when their roles require them. The firm has to ensure that virtues are matched to functions and the person with the right epistemic virtues sits in the right place. People hired as employees (or existing

[29] The following is based on Baehr's taxonomy, *Inquiring mind*, 21.

employees placed on committees or work teams, or assigned other duties) should possess the epistemic virtues required for their roles.

Board roles

To get a better understanding of how virtue-to-function matching works, let us look at the roles and functions of members of the board of directors of a firm. As a rough point of departure, the function of the chief executive officer (CEO) is that of the managing director, determining the company's strategy and acting as an agent for its owners, to whom fiduciary obligations are owed. The chief financial officer (CFO) acts as a controller and financial director of the firm. CFOs are in charge of a firm's financial reporting, they interact with the capital markets and they play an increasingly significant role in strategic decision making. Besides these two directors, boards may feature chief development officers, chief governance officers, chief information officers, chief internal control officers, chief operating officers, chief risk officers and chief technology officers, not to forget the non-executive directors, sometimes collected in continental-style supervisory boards, whose function it is to monitor and oversee management.[30]

That virtues have to match functions becomes clear if we contrast the CEO and the chief risk officer (CRO). Unlike the CEO, whose appetite for risk is sometimes necessary to realize long-term innovative projects, the CRO has to safeguard the company from risks, but not excessively, for that could endanger the firm's expected profits. In a telling statement, Stefan Schmittmann, CRO of Commerzbank, Germany's second-largest bank, explains that this requires not only that CROs have actively to strive to uncover hitherto hidden risks, but also to be open to discussion and disagreement.[31] Explorativeness, temperance and justice are the primary epistemic virtues for the CRO. This contrasts with CEO virtues in many ways. The CEO is the firm's main decision maker and communicator, bearing the main responsibility for the company's strategic decisions and management. Embodied in the recognition rules of the firm, CEOs represent the company to shareholders and other stakeholders and are the main source of information to investors, journalists, consumer organizations, employee representatives, suppliers, governments

[30] Huse, *Boards, governance and value creation*.
[31] Schmittman, 'Chief risk officer'.

and non-governmental organizations. The ensuing epistemic virtues form a diverse group. CEOs need epistemic generosity because they are an important source of information to the company's stakeholders. They need humility and justice because they must pick up signals from the market and the employees, from suppliers and customers, even though they may consider these sources of information to be subordinate. They also need courage to admit that in many cases they are much less knowledgeable on particular company details than their subordinates.

Which particular epistemic virtues are required of particular functions is often a *relational* matter. Epistemic virtues are required of particular roles in their dealings with other particular roles. Consider another example. For a company to function well and remain profitable, it is important that no trade secrets and other sensitive information leaks to competitors, and as a result of this, epistemic generosity towards competitors is a vice. Equally it is a virtue towards non-executive directors, who have to supervise the company. Non-executive directors depend for their knowledge of the company on the willingness of executive directors to provide sufficient, adequate and understandable information about the company.[32] That non-executive directors increasingly turn to other sources of information reflects the fact that terse, even reticent CEOs form important obstacles to adequate monitoring of the firm.[33] CEOs often limit the amount of information they provide and it is often impossible for non-executives to discover whether what they receive has any value to them.[34] One director put it thus:

[M]anagement basically provides the material at a board meeting and if you don't live day to day in the company, you're not going to know whether in fact you are hearing all the relevant aspects of it, the good, the bad and the ugly.[35]

Virtues of overconfidence

CEOs should share information more generously with non-executives, but one thing should not be demanded from them: epistemic temperance. Or so it might seem. Empirical and theoretical research suggests that some functions and some relationships require not so much epistemic

---

[32] Stiles and Taylor, *Boards at work*.   [33] Zhang, 'Board information'.
[34] Rutherford and Buchholtz, 'Board characteristics and information'.
[35] Quoted by Lorsch, 'Board challenges', 175.

virtue but rather epistemic vice. A recent article by David Hirshleifer, Angie Low and Siew Hong Teoh, for example, addresses what they call the '[t]he biggest puzzle raised by existing research on managerial beliefs and corporate policy', namely, that companies frequently hire overconfident managers, allowing them to 'follow their beliefs in making major investment and financing decisions'.[36] Companies should hire managers who lack epistemic temperance.

Or should they? Hirshleifer and his co-authors complete their puzzle by showing that overconfident managing directors are better innovators, which they think is a good reason to hire them; their prime example is the late Steve Jobs, former CEO of Apple. The connections between epistemic virtue theory and these forms of behavioural research are worth investigating because, as I indicate at several junctures in this book, such research helps reveal where epistemic virtues are needed and why realizing epistemic virtues is difficult, and also what forms of education or training may assist people to acquire virtue. If CEO overconfidence is instrumental in realizing corporate aims such as innovation, epistemic virtues may not be as relevant as I claim.

But matters are not entirely as they may appear. First of all, we have to pay close attention to the way behavioural researchers measure or 'operationalize' overconfidence and other epistemic vices. We cannot measure people's overconfidence in the same way we measure their height, and that is why researchers attempt to develop proxies for overconfidence. An approach in behavioural finance pioneered by Ulrike Malmendier and Geoffrey Tate is to consider *options exercise* as a proxy.[37] CEOs typically receive large allocations of options on shares in their own company as part of their compensation package, often surpassing their base salaries several times over. In 2012, for instance, Jamie Dimon, CEO of JPMorgan Chase, the US multinational bank, received options worth $5 million (with a base salary of $1.5 million and $12 million in shares). Only after what is called a *vesting period*, and only if various predetermined performance criteria are met, will Dimon be able to exercise these options, in conformity with general rules of corporate governance. It is this feature that Malmendier and Tate exploit to define a measure of overconfidence. CEOs are overconfident when, very roughly, they hold these options even after the vesting period has expired.

---

[36] Hirshleifer et al., 'Overconfident CEOs', 1459.
[37] Malmendier and Tate, 'CEO overconfidence'.

Why does this make initial sense as a measure of overconfidence? The next chapter explains how diversification removes a certain sort of risk from a portfolio of assets: it is better to have shares in different companies and different sectors than in one only (except if the company in which one invests is going to do better than the diversified portfolio). A CEO who does not act in line with the tenets of diversification, sticking to the options after the vesting period, is markedly irrational unless, for sure, the CEO holds the belief that the company is going to beat the market. Malmendier and Tate assume that this belief betrays overconfidence. If you think that your company is going to do better than a diversified portfolio, then you are overconfident.

In another article, Malmendier and Tate put forward an alternative measure of overconfidence, based on *press coverage*.[38] They scanned newspaper articles in the *New York Times* and a handful of finance periodicals for the company name and the word *CEO* and for the following words that, the researchers believed, relate to overconfidence and its contraries: *confident, confidence, optimistic, optimism, reliable, cautious, conservative, practical, frugal* and *steady*. CEOs using the first four words more often than the last six count as overconfident, according to this alternative measure.

The exercise of options and press coverage may have their use as proxies in finance; it is rather less clear whether they adequately capture the concept of epistemic vice and virtue. It may be the case that the decisions of CEOs to retain their options stem from beliefs about the prospects of the company that they gained in epistemically unvirtuous ways. It may also be the case that journalists use the word *confident* to describe what is more accurately called an *overly confident* director. But optimistic beliefs about the company are not necessarily the result of epistemic vices, and journalists do not always use understatement (probably quite the opposite). Behavioural researchers readily admit that a subtler measure of overconfidence has to capture the way CEOs use information, interact with other directors, management, employees and others; significant progress may be expected here as behavioural finance is a rapidly growing field. My remarks, then, are meant to caution against deriving hasty conclusions about epistemic virtues from empirical research, rather than to criticize the research itself.

---

[38] Malmendier and Tate, 'Who makes acquisitions?'

Secondly, what behavioural economists call *overconfident* may in reality be a virtue that matches a function. If CEOs are expected to spur innovation and if this requires a certain form of bold confidence, then overconfidence may be a virtue for them. Consider again the difference between the chief risk officer (CRO) and the CEO. Epistemic temperance is, as we have seen, typically required of the CRO, but it is not particularly a character trait that follows from the job description of a CEO. What we condemn as *excessively* confident or *overly* optimistic in a CRO we may praise as adequately risk-loving in the CEO. (Just as we call *overly precise* the baker working like a research chemist.) This observation is backed by empirical work showing that boards are more likely to fire not only CEOs embodying the one extreme of temperance, *diffidence*, but also those showing the other extreme, clumsily called 'excessively overconfident' in the literature.[39]

This brings me to a third point. The view I defend in this chapter is that specific epistemic virtues that employees ought to possess should originate from the firm's corporate aims. Given such a point of view, only research that relates virtues or vices to the realization of corporate aims is relevant to an evaluation of the empirical plausibility of epistemic virtue theory. Innovation is absolutely essential to almost all firms, but it cannot be the ultimate goal of any firm. Innovation for its own sake is senseless. For our purposes, it is perhaps more relevant than the work of Hirshleifer and his co-workers to consider research on overconfidence and the generation of shareholder value. To begin with, firms run by overconfident CEOs are thought to pay out smaller dividends.[40] This is an obvious negative side effect to the owners of the firm (except perhaps if it is offset by capital gains). Moreover, when overconfident CEOs engage in mergers and acquisitions they are more likely to fail due to the fact that, for example, they have inflated ideas of their own capacity to generate profit.[41] Overconfidence is, more generally, claimed to have an adverse impact on corporate investment decisions.[42] These are plain disadvantages to the shareholders, but other authors again claim that managerial overconfidence contributes to the solution of coordination problems and that it mitigates moral hazard, which is

[39] Goel and Thakor, 'CEO selection', 2740.
[40] Deshmukh et al., 'Overconfidence and dividend'.
[41] See Malmendier and Tate, 'Who makes acquisitions?'
[42] Malmendier and Tate, 'Corporate investment'. Heaton, 'Managerial optimism' uses an older methodology.

good for shareholders.[43] Yet all in all, though the results are mixed, little evidence shores up the claim that overconfidence is an essential epistemic character trait that CEOs ought to possess to fulfil their function as the prime steward of the firm and its owners.

This critical excursion into behavioural finance is intended as an example of the sort of empirical and conceptual argumentation that we should engage in when it comes to applying epistemic virtue theory to business, finance in particular. But it also points to a number of methodological hurdles that any such application encounters. Instead of stressing these difficulties even more, I return now to the question of how organizations can acquire epistemic virtues at the corporate level, in particular by providing organizational support for virtue.

Organizational support for virtue

A firm hires a consultant to study a particular issue, say, the safety of certain procedures. The consultant writes a report and receives a handsome fee. The report disappears in the firm's archives, the contents ignored, the knowledge unapplied. This phenomenon is amply documented, and reveals that epistemic virtue has not been adequately incorporated.[44]

Until now I have focused on one prerequisite for corporate epistemic virtue, namely, that the functions in the firms be adequately matched by virtues. But when reports go unused there is no failure at the level of virtue-to-function matching; the failure has to do with organizational support. A second condition for corporate epistemic virtue is that exercising these function-matched virtues be enabled and encouraged by the firm's internal decision structure, its culture and its system of sanctions. One of the first examples in this chapter cited a study among non-executive directors of finance firms in the United States. To do their job as independent judges or supervisors of the firm, they need love of knowledge. We saw that even though individually they possessed the virtue, the firm's structure inhibited their practising it.[45] The directors were prohibited from speaking to particular people, they often lacked a

---

[43] See Bolton et al., 'Leadership' for coordination, and see Gervais et al., 'Overconfidence' for moral hazard. Both articles also show that too much overconfidence is not desirable.

[44] Messick and Bazerman, 'Ethical leadership'.   [45] Lorsch, 'Board challenges'.

decent office, they were not paid sufficiently well, or they were confronted with executive *omertà*. In such a situation, there is insufficient *organizational support for virtue*. Organizational support is not to be seen as remedying a lack of virtue among employees (although it may help overcome certain misconceptions about knowledge within the firm that may make epistemically virtuous behaviour difficult). Remedies against vice exist, and they can be used effectively to invigorate corporate virtue, as we shall see in the next section, but they are conceptually different from organizational support. Organizational support only makes sense when employees possess epistemic virtues; remedial strategies are needed only when they do not.

Organizational support takes many forms. It always pays off, for example, to have the right 'tone at the top'. Alfred Sloan, former chairman and CEO of General Motors, is said to have actively solicited contrary opinions among managers.[46] Jack Welch, between 1981 and 2001 chairman and CEO of General Electric, typically required managers to share ideas of business proposals with as many people as they thought relevant.[47] These are certainly no more than anecdotes, but it is plain that if these directors mean what they say, they signal their acknowledgement of the value of epistemic justice and generosity. Of course, organizational support does not spring from the top of the firm only. Things as simple as schedules may influence the input received on strategy proposals, and consequently the quality of decision making. Meetings scheduled early in the morning, for instance, exclude employees with children whom they have to drop off at school first.

To see how firms fare in terms of supporting epistemic virtue, they could ask the following questions. Do employees capture, codify and retrieve information by themselves or assisted by librarians or 'knowledge journalists', or is information wasted? Does the organization use corporate yellow pages allowing employees to approach colleagues with particular expertise when they face challenges or questions, or are employees left in the dark about where to go with their queries? Does management have a coherent view about innovation and knowledge infrastructures, and does it assign work groups to knowledge management issues? Do employees regularly discuss and review best practices and lessons learnt, and does the organization encourage employees to

[46] Grandori, *Epistemic economics*, 89.   [47] Dalkir, *Knowledge management*.

internalize them? Are there mechanisms or procedures whereby disparate bits of knowledge are combined and synthesized in reports or data-bases or otherwise, by means of brainstorming sessions, problem-solving meetings or reflective interviews with experts? Do cooperating teams graft their respective bodies of knowledge in order to synthesize them? Does the organization make efficient use of data mining, exper-tise profiling, blogs, email, wikis, intranets, repositories and other knowledge management tools? Has it set up communities of practice focusing on particular issues and themes? And also: Do employees listen to what others say in respectful ways? Do they pay attention and ask questions? Do they revise their beliefs when new evidence becomes available and do they try to recall and store important infor-mation? Do they make notes?

Structure

Seumas Miller's four-pronged analysis of organizations in terms of structure, function, culture and sanctions helps to introduce a certain systematization in the various forms of organizational support. I start with structure. Relevant here is research on knowledge management. The useful concept of *knowledge management cycle* sees firms start by creating and capturing knowledge, continue with sharing and dissem-inating knowledge, and finally applying the knowledge.[48] Knowledge management research provides insights in ways that, at any of the three stages of the cycle, help or hinder employees to proceed in epistemically virtuous ways.

Consider epistemic generosity. This virtue can make or break a busi-ness. Robert Grant and others have pioneered what could be called an *epistemic theory of the firm*, advocating the view that firms are means by which managers coordinate and integrate the knowledge that resides in the individual employees with the end of developing certain products or services.[49] Knowledge sharing is found to increase a firm's competi-tive advantage, to help firms turn abstract ideas into concrete products and services, and to improve problem-solving capacities.[50] The need

---

[48] Dalkir, *Knowledge management.*   [49] Grant, 'Knowledge-based theory'.
[50] Argote and Ingram, 'Knowledge transfer'. Nonaka and Takeuchi, *Knowledge-creating company.* Grant, 'Knowledge-based theory'.

for epistemic generosity is further underlined by the estimate that around half of the knowledge within a company resides 'in employees' brains', only leaving those brains if they share.[51] This is reinforced by the following estimates, derived from a study by the International Data Corporation.[52] Knowledge workers spend around 15 to 35 per cent of their time seeking information, but they are successful in less than half of that time. Most of the information employees search for is readily available from colleagues; but the searchers do not know that. The explanation is not that the colleagues lack epistemic generosity. Knowledge sharing does not happen because there is no effective organizational support. Many firms have set up an intranet, which employees can use to post messages and requests for information. As Don Cohen and Laurence Prusak observe, however, knowledge sharing may work much better around the coffee machine than on an intranet.[53] This has led knowledge management scholars to stress the importance of endowing employees with sufficient time for knowledge sharing as well as a physical location for face-to-face meetings. It also shows that the optimism concerning the *New World of Work* or the *officeless* company may be misplaced.[54]

Another example of structural support for generosity is this. LabMorgan, a business unit of JPMorgan Chase, invested in web-based financial services.[55] Using Intraspect Software it created in 2001 a knowledge management site called Deep Thought. Deep Thought is a form of cloud computing, consisting as it does of nothing more than a set of web-based folders in which employees store business plans received from customers. It contains the fairly intriguing trick, novel at the time, that the folders have email addresses; users can upload documents by sending the document as an attachment to an email message. While the idea of Deep Thought is simple, it drastically changed the way employees shared information about business plans. It allowed users to go through all previous business plans, feedback and decisions, and to hold up new proposals against them. The system did not make employees more epistemically generous; rather it offered organizational support to epistemically generous employees to act on the virtue.

---

[51] Liebowitz and Chen, 'Knowledge sharing proficiencies'.
[52] Feldman, 'Cost of information'.   [53] Cohen and Prusak, *In good company*.
[54] Silverman, 'Office-less company'.   [55] Pflaging, *Enterprise communication*.

Culture

Culture being roughly a set of beliefs and values characterizing a corporation (or part of it), it impacts negatively on epistemic generosity if
a corporation is infused with the idea, for instance, that knowledge
belongs to particular employees rather than to the entire organization,
or in organizations where employees receive recognition primarily for
the knowledge they possess instead of for their knowledge sharing. If
teamwork is almost entirely absent, if only particular people are accepted as authoritative sources of information, if employees feel that they
are not allowed to make mistakes and reveal ignorance, or if they do not
speak the same language, sharing knowledge will not get off the ground
even if all employees are individually epistemically generous.[56]

How can organizations support generosity? Sometimes a change in
culture works. People tend to consider knowledge as personal property,
in particular when they have played a significant role in acquiring the
knowledge. In many business enterprises, however, knowledge is rather
seen as the property of the organization; knowledge in such organizations remains anonymous, not attributed to individual employees or
work groups. The combination of the individual private property view
of knowledge and the organizational anonymity view clash, with the
result that employees keep their knowledge to themselves rather than
generously sharing it with others. It is rather difficult to change individual views of property. Organizational support for generosity, however,
can be gained when we slightly change the culture in the organization
and attribute knowledge to particular employees and start making
authorship of knowledge explicit. An example can be found at Xerox,
the American document management multinational. Xerox engineers
help customers by developing innovative solutions for technical problems of printers and other devices. Ideally, when all engineers share their
solutions freely, no engineer has to reinvent the wheel. At Xerox, however, knowledge sharing was found to be relatively poor. The company
implemented a knowledge management strategy and set up a database to
which engineers could contribute their solutions. An important incentive
for the engineers to contribute to the database turned out to be the fact
that the names of the engineers figured prominently in the entries they

---

[56] Dalkir, *Knowledge management*.

contributed. A minimal change in culture was sufficient to obtain the desired result: Xerox acknowledges authorship of knowledge.[57]

Sanctions

Knowledge may not only be hoarded as private property; employees may also think of knowledge primarily as a means to increase their power. To support generosity here a change in sanctions may be needed, that is, a change in systems of punishment and reward. Knowledge-as-power views are exacerbated by a stick-and-carrot system praising people for the knowledge they possess rather than for the knowledge they share. Epistemically virtuous organizations have alternative systems of sanctions in place. As I have already noted, under CEO Jack Welch of General Electric, knowledge sharing became an important target for the firm. A *knowledge sharing warehouse* was, for example, developed for information and experiences with customer complaints about quality issues, which employees could access from the intranet. This was part of a larger move towards an epistemically generous culture. Kimiz Dalkir, from whose monograph on knowledge management this case is taken, describes the importance of knowledge sharing at General Electric thus:

If you are a CEO at GE and you mention that you have developed a great new business procedure, the first question the chairman will ask is, 'Whom have you shared this with?' People who hoard an idea for personal glory simply do not do well at GE.[58]

The knowledge management literature is awash with examples of companies rewarding employees for their knowledge sharing with shares or options or with gift cards they can redeem in online stores. Consider an example from Hill and Knowlton, a global public relations company. It takes a very unadorned approach against hoarding knowledge and for sharing it. Realizing that employee performance reviews, due to their low frequency, are unsuited to providing employees with effective feedback on their contributions to knowledge sharing, this company decided to give employees immediate gratification. It changed the sanction system and decided to award employees sharing their knowledge with coins in an electronic currency they could redeem for cash when

---

shopping at participating online stores.[59] Organizational support does not need to be difficult.

By rewarding some behaviours and sanctioning others, compensation schemes can influence epistemic virtue in other ways as well. Bonuses are an example. They have been criticized by the popular press, attacked on account of their having provided employees with perverse incentives that led them to work not with the customer's but with their own interests in mind. Some scholars have also pointed out that incentive schemes can be 'gamed' in such a way that it looks as though the employee has done a lot of work, but in reality has not. Here I show that they also have an epistemic side, the main claim being that it is very hard to set up performance-based remuneration contracts with employees working as portfolio managers in the financial services industry in such a way that senior management is able to find out whether the employees have done their job, or gamed the system.

An article by Thomas Noe and Peyton Young makes this more concrete.[60] Noe and Young invite us to imagine a trader in an investment bank whose remuneration package includes the following bonus. His investments will be compared to the S&P 500 index, and if he does better his bonus will amount to 20 per cent of the difference between his investments and the index. The trader controls $500 million in assets, which he chooses to invest in the S&P 500, gaining some dividends, and in addition selling *asset-or-nothing* put options to a third party. Such options are to the effect that if at the end of the month the S&P 500 is below a certain price, the option holder receives all shares in the trader's fund. Noe and Young specify the option in such a way that the likelihood of this event is 5 per cent. Consequently the trader can sell them for 5 per cent of the price of the total number of shares in his portfolio; after selling the options the trader can buy new shares in the S&P 500 for 5 per cent of $500 million. In the words of the authors, he then awaits the end of the month, 'keeping his fingers crossed'.[61] The probability that the trader will not lose is 95 per cent, and if that happens he can sit still for the rest of the year, claiming a bonus of 20 per cent of the 5 per cent of $500 million by which he has outperformed the index.

---

[59] Dalkir, *Knowledge management*.
[60] Noe and Young, 'Limits to compensation'. See also Foster and Young, 'Gaming performance fees'.
[61] Noe and Young, 'Limits to compensation', 67.

His personal gains in that case amount to $5 million. No doubt, the options will be called with a probability of 5 per cent, but Noe and Young emphasize that this

does not place him in legal jeopardy provided that he does not try to cover up what he is doing. After the fact he can always claim that the outcome was unfortunate and that in his judgment it had only a 'tiny' chance of occurring.[62]

A trader calling the options loses the shares. But this only happens with 5 per cent probability. An epistemically virtuous manager wants to know whether the trader's success in beating the index should be ascribed to brute luck or to skills and talent. Firms do not want to dole out lavish bonuses to employees whose success is merely a matter of luck. What the authors point out, however, is that performance-based compensation schemes make it very difficult for managers to distinguish talented from lucky traders. In the example, the trader's investments may collapse in the first year, and management may fire him; but management may also blame the collapse on 'bad luck'. The trader may, on the other hand, beat the market during the first year; but then it is difficult for management to find out if his success is due to skill. The trader's books contain information about the positions and thereby allow the firm to uncover the underlying investment strategies, but though this is relatively easy in the case above, traders can design highly complex strategies, which it will be very difficult and costly to discover.

The literature on incentive schemes has primarily investigated the effects of bonuses on individual behaviour, and has in particular defended the claim that they distract professionals from paying sufficient attention to their customers' interests. We have now seen that bonuses also make it more difficult for management to act virtuously. Even managers with high levels of inquisitiveness, attentiveness and perceptiveness likely miss manipulation where it occurs. Performance-based compensation contracts such as the one above erect smokescreen inhibiting epistemic virtue.

Organizational remedies against vice

An organization incorporating epistemic virtue provides organizational support and removes obstacles to virtuous action. Organizational

---

[62] Noe and Young, 'Limits to compensation', 67.

support and adequate virtue-to-function matching are not together a sufficient condition for corporate virtue, however, because no organization is populated solely by epistemically virtuous employees. What do epistemically virtuous organizations do when particular individual virtues are rare and virtue-to-function matching difficult? What do they do when organizational support is hard to provide? It is useful to set apart two sorts of *organizational remedies against vice* that they can apply, one at a macro- and one at a micro-level.

Macro-level remedies

Suppose a bank develops a new product. Knowledge about the product may originate from a product design team, but also from marketing, risk management, compliance, or even from the corporate social responsibility, sustainability or ethics department. Suppose that ultimately the board decides whether the product will be marketed. The decision is an easy one when all units agree about the product's potential. Generally, however, boards are confronted with conflicting views before making the final decision. They have to weigh more 'optimistic' product design and marketing views and more 'pessimistic' risk management, compliance or sustainability views.

Research on *judgement aggregation* makes abundantly clear that the order in which boards or other bodies deal with particular items on an agenda radically influences the ultimate decision. To take one striking example, had the German parliament in 1991 changed the order of proceedings during the voting that determined the future capital of unified Germany, Bonn not Berlin would likely have come out the winner.[63] Research in psychology has shown, moreover, that the mere order in which one receives information influences the beliefs one ultimately forms. This effect is an interplay of confirmation bias, the sunk cost fallacy and other phenomena. People pondering which doxastic attitude to adopt towards some proposition p, on the basis of available evidence, are rather likely to interpret the evidence as emphasizing their prior belief about p, thereby displaying the confirmation bias. Suppose that at t_0 I am neutral with respect to whether a product should be marketed, and that at t_1 I receive 'optimistic' information concerning the product. Then I am on the whole more likely to disregard 'negative'

---

[63] Pauly, 'Rules of play'. Pauly's argument is based on Leininger, 'The fatal vote'.

information about the product obtained at a later point in time t_2, or to misconstrue such negative information by interpreting it as *support* – this is the most striking aspect of the confirmation bias – rather than counterevidence for the optimistic views I adopted at t_1. The conclusion is that 'pessimistic' risk management, compliance and sustainability views are set at an epistemic disadvantage when they are deferred to the end of the epistemic decision procedure, which they usually are.

This is exacerbated by the *sunk cost fallacy*.[64] When a firm has so far spent £1 million on designing a new product, these costs are *sunk*, owing to the fact that they have been incurred and cannot be recouped. To determine whether the product shall be put on the market it is rational only to consider the future cash flows and other future costs and benefits of the project. The decision should not depend on how much money has already been spent on the project, but only on what we can expect the project to deliver in the future.[65] Human beings, however, find it hard to do this; they find it hard to ignore sunk costs. One readily spends £200 on a ticket for a concert, realizes that the concert is dreadful, but one does not leave because the money has been spent, as the traditional textbook example has it.[66] Similarly, if after spending £1 million on the design of a product, risk management, compliance or sustainability gives a more 'pessimistic' evaluation of the product, the 'pessimists' are down 1–0 at halftime. A risk manager contributing to *The Economist* in 2008 explained:

At the root of it all, however, was – and still is – a deeply ingrained flaw in the decision making process. In contrast to the law, where two sides make an equal-and-opposite argument that is fairly judged, in banks there is always a bias towards one side of the argument. The business line was more focused on getting a transaction approved than on identifying the risks in what it was proposing. The risk factors were a small part of the presentation and always 'mitigated'. This made it hard to discourage transactions. If a risk manager said no, he was immediately on a collision course with the business line. The risk thinking therefore leaned towards giving the benefit of the doubt to the risk-takers.[67]

Obviously much research remains to be done to find ways to remedy confirmation bias, sunk cost fallacy and similar psychological effects. Much can be gained from fairly simple procedural adjustments, though.

---

[64] Staw, 'Knee deep'.   [65] Garland, 'Throwing good money after bad'.
[66] Friedman et al., 'Searching for the sunk cost fallacy'.
[67] Anonymous, 'Confessions of a risk manager'.

One example is to avoid unnecessary temporal divisions. Risk management, compliance and sustainability, for instance, should participate actively in the design process from the very start, rather than at the end.[68] Boards should actively solicit not only evidence in favour of a prospective project, but also against it. It may well be the case that Goldman Sachs came through the crisis relatively unscathed because it was permeated with organized opposition. Simplifying somewhat, the idea was that instead of asking the authors of a business proposal to investigate not only the advantages but also the disadvantages, a proposal was, at Goldman Sachs, critically examined by a different team, independently of its authors. It should not come as a surprise that independent critics are better positioned to detect potential flaws than a project's advocates.[69]

Micro-level remedies

Organizing opposition in order to counter groupthink or sunk cost fallacies is a proven strategy for remedying epistemic vice at the macro-level of the organization. I now turn to micro-level remedies, which are probably useful more frequently because they require a lesser degree of intervention with organizational structures, cultures or sanctionary systems of reward and punishment. To defend this claim, I discuss a topic that has attracted a great deal of attention in academia and elsewhere: *rotation policies*. This is also a fine example of micro-level design that is interesting in its own right. For the purpose of introduction, consider the accountancy profession. If accountants and their clients develop too close a relationship, the objectivity and independence of the accountants' views of their clients' financial positions may decrease. Hence mandatory rotation policies have been suggested in which firms must change their accounting house after three, six or eight years.[70] Accountancy is not alone here. For similar reasons, the rotation of non-executive directors has been proposed in Britain and South Africa, requiring such things as that a third of all non-executives retire every year. Mandatory rotation has been recommended for tax officials in Bulgaria, and a widely publicized suggestion of a rotation policy was made by Michel Barnier, the

---

[68] A survey article is Van der Hoven and Manders-Huits, 'Value-sensitive design'. The paradigm comes from Friedman, *Human values*.
[69] Cohan, *Money and power*.   [70] Francis, 'Audit quality'.

European Commissioner for Internal Market and Services, when in 2011 he proposed that issuers of securities should be required to change their credit rating agencies every three years. The idea is simple. When accountants, non-executive directors, tax officials and credit rating agencies are swapped from time to time, their views about the firm, its products, its taxes or its debt come closer to the truth.

I defend the claim that rotation policies are micro-level remedies for epistemic vice. I focus on epistemic justice; other policies remedy other vices. I should tread carefully here. Most of the research on mandatory rotation has focused on accountancy, and even then, the results are mixed. They reveal an increase of independence, but one may fear that will be accompanied by a loss of knowledge and information. A long term relationship with a client risks an accountant's independence, but the knowledge an accountant gradually gains about the firm is greater than what a fresh accountant knows; and the increased depth of knowledge may well outweigh the decrease of independence.[71] I do believe, though, that effective rotation policies help incorporate epistemic justice. The mechanism by which rotation policies accomplish this feat is not that of virtue-to-function matching ensuring that individual employees possess this virtue, nor is it that of providing organizational support for already epistemically just employees. Rather, rotation policies are ways to guarantee epistemically just belief formation practices in an organization populated by employees lacking epistemic virtue or only possessing it to a slight degree. Though an individual accountant or firm may not be a gem of virtue, interchanging them guarantees objectivity and independence at a macro-level.

With the exception of director rotation, the policies mentioned above do not concern employees within one firm, but rather relationships between firms. To defend the claim that rotation policies help firms incorporate epistemic virtue, I use an example from banking examined by Andrew Hertzberg, Jose Liberti and Daniel Paravisini.[72] This is a rotation scheme at an Argentinian branch of a large US multinational bank among loan officers dealing with small and medium-sized enterprises. The function of loan officers is to screen loan applicants by determining the risks attached to the projects for which they request

[71] S. Sunder, 'Rethinking the structure of accounting and auditing', Yale ICF Working Paper 03–17 (2003), ssrn.com/abstract=413581.
[72] Hertzberg et al., 'Loan officer rotation'.

finance. In addition, loan officers have to monitor the loans, both actively and passively. *Active monitoring* is a prospective form of monitoring that starts right after the loan has originated. Its aim is to raise the net present value of the project, that is, to exert a positive effect on the future cash flows or value of the borrower's project. This requires various means to diminish the probability that borrowers will encounter problems with repaying their loans, ranging from the recommendation of adjusted conditions for new lending to downright interference in the borrower's affairs. *Passive monitoring*, by contrast, is retrospective and aims to measure rather than affect the project's value. It provides continuously updated estimates of the probability that the borrower will pay back in time.[73]

Why is monitoring a possible site of epistemic injustice? A problem may arise when one loan officer monitors a borrower both actively and passively. A dismal picture generated by passive monitoring reveals that the borrower's project is in bad health, but may also expose the loan officer's inadequate active monitoring because the officer had not been able to intervene constructively in the borrower's project. A loan officer downgrading the probability estimate of a borrower's repaying the loan therefore endangers her reputation, which often results in demotion or a cut in the number of assigned clients. This gives the loan officer an incentive to withhold bad news about the project and provide dishonest, or at least deceptive, reports.

The aggregate result of individual dishonesty and deception is corporate epistemic vice. It affects love of knowledge in the first place. As we saw in Chapter 3, love of knowledge motivates one to search for information; it also leads one to adopt beliefs only if one possesses sufficient evidence to justify the adoption of the beliefs; evidence-based practices in marketing provided an example. It is crucial to note that individual dishonesty and deception do not lead to corporate lack of information search; information is searched after all. The problem rather is lack of justification. If individual retrospective judgements concerning the net present value of a borrower's project are upwardly biased, the aggregate corporate judgement is based on what looks like justifying evidence (evidence obtained from individual loan officers) but in reality is not. The corporate view is skewed in the same way as

[73] Tirole, 'Corporate governance'.

individual views are skewed when they are based on biased evidence. There is a lack of justification.

It may be argued that as long as the problem lies in the loan officers' failure to pass on sufficient information to other positions in the firm, the corporate problem arises due to lack of individual epistemic *generosity*; and in the light of the above, two solutions may suggest themselves. One is to match function and virtue by hiring more epistemically generous loan officers; the other is to provide organizational support for generosity. From a theoretical point of view, the first solution is plain. Let me therefore focus on the second. Organizational support for generosity may result when management separates active and passive monitoring and makes loan officers responsible for one only. Yet this change in the structure of the organization is likely to go against business economic considerations. Banks want to stick to combining active and passive monitoring on the grounds that this exploits economies of scale. Because information garnered from active monitoring benefits passive monitoring (and conversely), separating these roles leads to inefficiencies, which banks want to avoid. The suggested form of organizational support is, then, theoretically very elegant and simple, but it is too expensive to catch on. Hence banks ought to consider other ways to incorporate virtue.

The rotation policy studied by Hertzberg and his colleagues is an example here. According to the policy they examine, a loan officer may at any time be withdrawn from a particular client (borrower), but the chance that this happens will change over time. During the first thirty-three months of a relationship with the client, the probability that the officer is replaced is below 5 per cent. As soon as the relationship has survived the thirty-fourth month, it is terminated with a probability of 58 per cent during the next three months, after which the termination rate decreases again. The details may sound arbitrary. The precise design of the policy, however, is of considerable importance because it ensures that loan officers know that they are very likely to be withdrawn from the project after around three years; the rub is, they are unable to predict precisely when.[74]

---

[74] The rotation policy turns the loan officer's decision situation into what game theorists call an *infinite horizon game*. Hertzberg et al., 'Loan officer rotation', does not give a game theoretical reading of the policy, though.

All this would not be an effective way to encourage corporate epistemic justice were it not for a very important finding about loan officer reputation that Hertzberg and his co-authors uncover. Identifying a loan officer's *reputation* with the volume of assets she has under management (as measured by the number of firms and amount of debt managed), the authors first stipulate that absent a regime of rotation one should expect loan officers who downgrade a firm always to suffer a loss of reputation. Confirming these expectations, the study subsequently shows that with the three-year probabilistic rotation policy such effects can only be seen in the third year. No reputational effects occur during the first two years. The cause of this difference is important. The authors suggest that during the first two years the loan officer's superiors believe that it is not the loan officer who should receive the blame for inadequate active monitoring, but her predecessor. Officers reporting bad news about a firm they have actively monitored for more than two years, however, typically suffer a significant change in assets managed.

This is all fine, but it is in the most significant reputational damage a loan officer may face that we can find an explanation of why the rotation policy is an effective way to increase corporate epistemic justice. If a loan officer's successor reports bad news about a client, the loan officer is confronted with a decrease in managed assets that may be up to four times as large as had the loan officer reported the bad news herself. Though bad news about a firm one has managed for more than two years never benefits one's reputation, it is, in other words, much more preferable to do the reporting oneself than to let one's successor be the bearer of the news.

To summarize, the rotation policy examined here increases epistemic justice at the corporate level along two lines. Loan officers report bad news during the first two years of their relationship with a client because they do not face any reputational damage; and they report bad news during the third year because, although they incur reputation loss, the loss is greater if they leave it to their successor to report. It is important to underscore that this is a phenomenon of corporate rather than individual epistemic justice. The loan officers display no epistemic *injustice* themselves; they lack epistemic *generosity*, as we saw, and may be *dishonest*, but I see no indication that in the process of passive monitoring they disregard particular items of information, fail to engage in particular forms of inquiry or otherwise act in epistemically unjust ways. Individual lack of one virtue entails the lack of another virtue at the aggregate corporate level. Absent rotation policies, the bank has too optimistic a picture of the health of its borrowers' projects, and proceeds to act on this mistaken picture. Though the individual loan officers have adequate views of the value of their projects, they do not communicate them truthfully. Remedying these vices, the rotation policy helps to incorporate epistemic justice.

Summary

Even if our understanding of corporate entities and corporate virtues has significantly grown in the past decade or two, the territory of corporate *epistemic* virtues is largely left unexamined so far. Building on work by Reza Lahroodi, Peter French, Margaret Gilbert and Seamus Miller, among others, this chapter has shown how one can think of business enterprises as possessing exactly this type of virtue. To ascribe a virtue to a thing, one has to ascribe a function to it: something has virtue to the extent it fulfils its function excellently. In Chapter 1, I explained my methodological reluctance to talk about the function of a bank – or any other company, for that matter. As a result of this reluctance, corporate epistemic virtues in business have to come from somewhere else, at least in the context of the argument proffered in this book.

The origin of corporate epistemic virtue I single out is the function that individual employees and groups of employees have within an organization. It is hard to deny that such functions exist. Law is often an obvious source here, determining such things as that it is the task of the CEO to serve the interests of the firm's shareholders; and within companies, job contracts typically do the same thing. It is out of these functions that virtues arise. To return to an earlier example, the tasks and responsibilities of a chemist working in the research and development branch of a pharmaceutical company are very different from those of a salesperson selling the drugs, and the extent to which the two employees need love of knowledge and open-mindedness is consequently different.

Three elements of corporate epistemic virtue were set apart: virtue-to-function matching, organizational support for virtue and organizational remedies against vice. A detailed investigation of the roles of directors was used to illustrate the first element. Recall the chief risk officer (CRO), the director bearing the main responsibility for a firm's risk management. While a certain degree of overconfidence may be desirable in CEOs, especially if it is their task to encourage innovation, crucial virtues for CROs are temperance, open-mindedness and a great amount of curiosity.

A firm may be highly successful in hiring people with virtues matching functions, but still fail to exhibit virtue at a corporate level. This happens, for instance, when the firm's structure or culture, or its system of punishment and reward, discourages or prohibits people from practising virtues. An example of this that has gained more attention during the global financial crisis concerns non-executive directors of finance firms. Their primary task is that of supervision, and this requires a great amount of inquisitiveness and other epistemic virtues. Yet as long as they only have a few meetings with only a limited number of people representing only a small part of the company, love of knowledge does not guarantee that in the end they know all they ought to know. More interaction with the workforce is needed, for instance: there has to be more effective organizational support for epistemic virtue.

It would be carelessly unrealistic to assume that virtue-to-function matching and organizational support can always be completely guaranteed. No employee is fully virtuous; no organization is fully supportive; and epistemically virtuous companies must design clever ways to cope with these facts of life. This is captured by the third element of corporate epistemic virtue: organizational remedies against vice. I gave examples of such remedies at a macro-level and micro-level, but I should stress that every firm aspiring to epistemic virtue must do its best to find novel and appropriate remedies itself. The economics and business literature contains a number of interesting suggestions. We examined, for instance, several strategies from knowledge management as well as the efficacy of rotation policies. But no manual with prefab solutions is available.

Chapter 3 and Chapter 5 have introduced individual and corporate epistemic virtues. Conceptual and empirical arguments have played an important role, but I have only very rarely touched on the normative question of when, if ever, epistemic virtues are morally mandatory. Consumers and corporations may benefit from epistemic virtue, but that does not make them into something that we can normatively expect them to possess. What reasons, if any, could we have to complain about someone's lack of open-mindedness, for instance? The next chapter looks at these questions from a very practical point of view. It shows how firms managing the money of other people are bound to do accurate financial due diligence. This in turn requires adequate virtue-to-function matching. That a great many investment firms failed to see through Madoff's Ponzi scheme owes much, I argue, to a lack of corporate epistemic virtue. And they are blameworthy for this. In Chapter 7 I examine the role of the government, arguing for the potentially surprising claim that the apparent lack of epistemic virtue among credit rating agencies is not the most serious moral issue in the scandal of misrated structured securities. Rather we should turn our attention to the dubious role of governments and regulators. But first we look at the virtues of nerds and quants.

6 | *Case study II: nerds and quants*

The greatest fraud in the history of the United States, the biggest Ponzi scheme ever, a stunning $65 billion lost to some 5,000 clients, a maximum prison sentence of 150 years: Bernard Madoff has found a safe place in the history of finance. In 1960 he established Bernard L. Madoff Investment Securities with $5,000 he had saved when he was working as a sprinkler installer, plus a loan from his father-in-law. The firm soon became a frontrunner in computer technology that considerably helped the establishment of NASDAQ, the world's first electronic stock market. Madoff went on to gain a reputation on Wall Street as one of the biggest market makers, and was among the first to use computer technology for automated trading. He became chairman of the National Association of Securities Dealers, maintaining close connections with the overseeing authorities, donating generously to various charities and political campaigns and enjoying great respect among the Jewish community in New York City – which he was ruthlessly to defraud.[1] Several people on Wall Street had their suspicions, and it is beyond doubt that some of the funds feeding money to Madoff performed some kind of financial due diligence on him. It was not until Harry Markopolos, a *quant* or financial mathematician working for a finance firm, started examining Madoff's investment strategies that the exact form of the fraud became evident.

In the previous chapter we saw that there are three ways to incorporate epistemic virtue: virtue-to-function matching, organizational support for virtue and organizational remedies against vice. The present case study illustrates the first form, defending as it does the view that accurate matching of virtues to functions encourages employees to work more effectively and efficiently on financial due diligence, the function of

---

[1] Berkowitz, 'The Madoff paradox'. Recent discussions of Madoff in relation to business ethics can be found in Eenkhoorn and Graafland, 'Lying in business', Freeman et al., 'Teaching business ethics' and Nielsen, 'Whistle-blowing methods'.

which is to ascertain the risks of particular investment decisions by means of qualitative and quantitative methods. The case shows how particularly temperance and justice are needed for financial due diligence analysts to do their qualitative and quantitative research.

Split strikes and Ponzi schemes

What Madoff claimed to be offering his clients was purportedly the result of a *split strike conversion* approach, based on buying shares in S&P 100 companies and simultaneously selling and buying particular options on the index.[2] A *call option* on XYZ shares is the option to buy, at or before a particular moment in time (the *expiration date*), a specified number of XYZ shares at a predetermined price (the *exercise* or *strike price*). A *put option* is conversely an option to sell particular shares. Suppose one has a call option to buy one hundred XYZ shares for £20 on or before 31 January 2014. Suppose, moreover, that today XYZ shares trade at £10. It is senseless for a person desiring to purchase XYZ shares to exercise the right granted by the option. The call option, in the jargon, is *out of the money*. Similarly, a put option is out of the money if the strike price is lower than the market price of the underlying shares.

A split strike conversion approach much like the one that Madoff used can now be illustrated by means of the following example. A person S buys one hundred shares at £10 per share. To person A, S sells a call with a strike price of £20, and from person B, S buys a put with a strike price of £5. Now there are three scenarios. As soon as the price of the shares rises above the strike price of the call, A wants to exercise the right to buy them from S at £20; and because S bought them at £10 S earns £10 per share for a total of £1,000 minus the fees, the price of the option and other expenses. Similarly, when the price of the shares sinks below the strike price of the put option, B wants to sell them at £5, and S loses £5 per share for a total loss of £500 plus fees and so on. In case the share price remains between the strike price of the call and put options, neither A nor B wants to deal with S, and S neither loses nor gains. This example graphically shows a relevant characteristic of a split strike. S can never gain more than £1,000 and can never lose more than £500. By choosing

[2] See, e.g., Bernard and Boyle, 'Mr. Madoff's amazing returns', Culp and Heaton, 'Financial due diligence' and Schneeweis and Szado, 'A returns-based analysis'.

the strike prices differently S can determine any other interval within which gains and losses remain. Split strikes are therefore unlikely to lead to spectacular results.

Madoff claimed to be engaged in a variant of this strategy. He claimed to hold a basket of thirty to thirty-five securities from the S&P 100 index. He claimed to sell an out-of-the-money call option on the index and buy an out-of-the-money put option, and, if the option prices were too high, to switch to holding a portfolio of 100 per cent treasury bills, the alleged epitome of risklessness. Moreover, Madoff claimed, he only traded once a month. As we should expect from a split strike strategy, Madoff's returns were not particularly spectacular if each month was considered in isolation. Very much unlike a split strike approach, however, Madoff claimed to reach returns of more than 10 per cent per annum consistently over almost twenty years, with a volatility of only 3 per cent on average.[3] This is very improbable for split strikes. Madoff's returns did not come from split strike conversion. They were fake. They were the result of a Ponzi scheme.

Named after the Italian-American Charles Ponzi, such a scheme is a very simple mechanism in which the money that investors pay into the scheme is not genuinely invested but rather used to pay returns to the investors in the scheme. In other terms, one offers investors, say, 20 per cent per annum on their investments, but instead of investing the money that they bring in, one uses the money to pay out the 20 per cent. The risk certainly is that the money will dry up, which makes it imperative for the fraudster to attract new investors. These new investors, however, also have to be paid 20 per cent, which spirals into an increasingly pressing demand to raise new capital. Ponzi schemes are highly unsustainable.[4]

Madoff's fundraising capacities were unequalled. Somewhere in the 1990s, perhaps even much earlier, he had stopped genuinely investing the money from his clients. He used his respectability, status and apparent trustworthiness to attract enormous sums of money to his scheme. Part of his strategy, and unlike that of many other Ponzi schemers, was precisely to offer rather unspectacular returns, to require absolute confidentiality from his investors, and to give a decidedly exclusive feel to his investments by making people feel privileged to be accepted into his fund. Many succumbed to his charms.

---

[3] Culp and Heaton, 'Financial due diligence'.
[4] Artzrouni, 'The mathematics of Ponzi schemes'.

Uncovering the fraud

Harry Markopolos is generally credited with having discovered the fraud.[5] Certainly many people in the finance industry had their suspicions about Madoff's operations, but their usual response was that he was probably engaged in illegal activities on the verge of insider trading and frontrunning, and that as long as Madoff paid his clients when they wanted, they should not care. Working for Rampart Investment Management, an options trader, Markopolos was asked by his employer to investigate Madoff's investment strategies in order that Rampart could emulate them. Rampart had heard from a partner, Access International Advisors, that it was dealing with a hedge fund claiming returns of 2 per cent per month on the basis of split strike conversion strategies. This fund was managed by Madoff. Markopolos analysed information about the fund's revenues obtained from Access co-founder René-Thierry Magon de la Villehuchet, and this started a lengthy investigation that ultimately led Markopolos to the conclusion that Madoff was indeed running a large Ponzi scheme. Warnings that Markopolos and a few people working with him on the investigation started to issue from 1999 onwards to Access and other funds working with Madoff, to journalists and to the Securities and Exchange Commission, the main American regulatory agency, were ignored. Madoff's fund did not start to wind up before the end of 2008.

How did Markopolos find out? He used models from mathematical finance that are part of the usual financial due diligence that Access and other Madoff clients should have carried out. The mere use of these models cannot explain why Markopolos succeeded, however, because it is highly unlikely that he was the only person ever to have done the maths on Madoff. Rather, I argue, Markopolos succeeded where others failed because he complemented the financial due diligence methods with epistemic virtue. He had, in other words, the epistemic virtues matching the function of financial due diligence. One way to put the difference is that Markopolos just did his job whereas others did not. When some do their jobs and others do not, however, many factors may explain the difference, including such things as lack of knowledge and skills, dysfunctional management, desire to frustrate one's superiors

---

[5] Recent popular accounts of the Madoff scam include Arvedlund, *Madoff*, Henriques, *The wizard of lies* and Sarna, *History of greed*.

and so on. The claim I seek to defend is that the difference between Markopolos and other financial analysts, due diligence analysts among them, is a difference of virtue-to-function matching.

When Markopolos's employer first heard about Madoff's fund, he requested that Markopolos imitate Madoff's split strike conversion strategy. Markopolos responded to the challenge with vigour. Describing himself as a 'research geek', he saw it as a purely mathematical challenge that it was 'only logical' to see 'as an academic exercise, and not as the largest fraud in Wall Street history'.[6] Writing about himself and a few colleagues whom he engaged in the project, he said 'we weren't looking for crime; we simply wanted to see how [Madoff] made his numbers dance'.[7] Strictly speaking, Markopolos's work started therefore as a form of reverse engineering rather than financial due diligence, but the methods he applied were exactly the methods that financial due diligence analysts use. As soon as the maths suggested that it was fraud instead of financial genius that made the numbers 'dance', Markopolos turned to genuine financial due diligence and abandoned the ambition to emulate Madoff.

Volatility and diversification

To defend a claim about virtue-to-function matching, I first need to consider the purpose of financial due diligence. *Financial due diligence* is the process by which one ascertains the risks and returns of prospective investment decisions. I give a sketch of what financial due diligence agents do, indebted to a recent article by Christopher Culp and James Heaton containing a treatment of the Madoff case that is very similar to the work that Markopolos carried out.[8] Financial due diligence uses both qualitative and quantitative methods. Examples of qualitative methods are scrutinizing the reputation of the fund manager, the quality of internal control in the investment firm, the adequacy of their reporting, and their regulatory compliance. Quantitative methods are primarily drawn from mathematical finance and are more specifically used to gauge risks and returns.

The first thing Markopolos was interested in was Madoff's returns. The concept of *return* is the analogue of interest received on money

---

[6] Markopolos, *No one would listen.*   [7] Markopolos, *No one would listen*, 20.
[8] Culp and Heaton, 'Financial due diligence'.

saved in a deposit account. Earning 5 per cent interest per annum, the return is 5 per cent per annum. Return on equity is similar, but because company shares may pay out dividend and change in value, calculations are unlike compound interest. If shares of, say, £100 pay a dividend of 5 per cent after the first year and appreciate to £120, the return is 25 per cent. The concept of return on equity is simply a generalization of interest on deposits. Yet investing in equities is very different from saving money in a deposit account. The difference is an epistemic one. One knows the interest rate, but one does not know the returns on equity in advance. This is why financial due diligence analysts desire to develop methods to estimate returns.

The premise on which the methods from mathematical finance are built is that the riskier the investment the higher the expected return investors demand on their investments. But what is *risk* in finance? The conception of risk used in finance is rather different from the decision-theoretic way to think of risk. In the formal study of rational behaviour, decision theory, people face choice situations with risk if they attach subjective or objective probabilities to all possible outcomes of all actions they can perform. Roughly speaking, risk is probability. In finance, by contrast, risk is not captured by probability but by the concept of *volatility*. To illustrate this concept, suppose one considers buying shares in a company. To get some idea of what the return might be, one first calculates the empirical mean of the returns based on historical data from, say, the past twenty years. This gives some idea of what to expect, but it does not show how *risky* the investment is; for it does not show how much the asset may deviate from the empirical mean. It is the standard deviation which estimates this, the square root of the mean of the squares of the differences between mean and the twenty yearly returns each. This is the asset's volatility. (The mathematical details are not important to understand the rest of this chapter.)

Yet it is misleading to claim that volatility is the only concept that financial due diligence analysts can use to ascertain the risks of an investment. To understand why, I must discuss the idea of *diversification*. An investment portfolio that contains shares in only one company bears risks that may partly be eliminated by buying shares in other companies. It is better, so to speak, to buy shares in five different food companies than in one; and it is better yet to buy shares in companies in five different industries than in one. The risk eliminated from one particular asset when one holds that asset in a diversified portfolio is called *unsystematic* or *idiosyncratic* risk.

Some risk remains attached to that asset. This sort of risk is called *systematic* risk. Why should one be particularly interested in this sort of risk? The assumption that underlies the finance theory of risk is that if markets are functioning efficiently, one may expect that the unsystematic risks of an asset, which can be eliminated by diversification, will *not* be reflected in the asset's price. Were a buyer to demand a reduction in the price of one asset because of its unsystematic risk, competing buyers would accept a lower price on account of their being able to remove that risk by diversification.

Risk that cannot be removed by diversification remains reflected in the price, however, and therefore it is an asset's systematic risk that financial due diligence analysts are typically interested in knowing. Several measures of systematic risk exist, but I focus here on the measures most frequently used by financial due diligence analysts; they are the concepts of *alpha* and *beta*. Roughly, an asset's beta captures the systematic risk of that particular asset in that it measures the extent to which its volatility is correlated with the volatility of the market. An asset's alpha, on the other hand, describes whether the investment offers investors enough to compensate for the risks they run. One of the models for estimating alpha and beta is the capital asset pricing model (CAPM) developed by William Sharpe and John Lintner.[9] A brief explanation of this model is appropriate, but by no means necessary for following the remainder of the chapter. Suppose one invests a proportion x of one's assets in a market portfolio (i.e., invests it in shares reflecting the market such as the S&P 100 index), and invests a proportion $1 - x$ in risk-free securities (Madoff opted for treasury bills). The market proportion of one's portfolio p is by definition perfectly correlated with the market and therefore has a beta of 1. The risk-free proportion, moreover, has a beta of 0 because it has by definition no correlation with the market at all. Betas are linear, and therefore the beta of the portfolio is $\beta_p = x \cdot 1 + (1 - x) \cdot 0 = x$. Let us denote the return we can expect from the entire portfolio $E(R_p)$. The expected return can be analysed entirely in terms of the expected returns of its two parts, namely, the market share (which following the same notation is $E(R_m)$) and the risk-free share (of which, because it has no risk, $E(R_f) = R_f$). This

[9] Sharpe, 'Capital asset prices'. Lintner, 'The valuation of risk assets'.

gives $E(R_p) = (1 - x)R_f + xE(R_m)$. Substituting β_p for x we easily obtain from this equation the CAPM formula:

$$E(R_p) - R_f = \beta_p(E(R_m) - R_f).$$

Epistemic virtue

Back to Markopolos. Seeing the challenge to mimic Madoff's success as a purely 'academic exercise' at first, Markopolos had to study historical time series of Madoff's returns on investment. As a proxy Markopolos used return streams he had obtained from Access, the company's trading partner. Closely scrutinizing the data, Markopolos soon ventured the hypothesis that the returns were fake: 'There's no way this is real. This is bogus.'[10] In order to confirm his suspicions, he developed a model to estimate alpha and beta. The model attempted to copy Madoff's alleged split strike conversion approach. Were Madoff applying this approach to baskets of thirty to thirty-five securities from the S&P 100 index, a reasonably strong correlation with the index should be expected, a high beta, because a basket picking around a third of a market is going to co-vary with the market quite significantly. When the market moves in one direction, the basket roughly moves in the same direction too. Because Madoff claimed to be dealing only once a month, this is largely true even if for whatever reason – insider trading or astrology – he always selected the best from among the one hundred shares available.

Markopolos does not provide information on how he estimated the risks on the basis of the data available to him around 1999, when he started his investigations. He does give details of a study involving the years 1990–2005.[11] For those years, he estimated alpha and beta by applying such models as CAPM to data from Fairfield Sentry, a *feeder fund* so called for its doing little more than feeding its clients' money into Madoff's scheme. Culp and Heaton's abovementioned article provides a similar analysis on the basis of an unnamed feeder fund for the period 1989–2001.[12] The differences between these data and the data from Markopolos's study (ranging over the period 1990–2005) are minimal, and anyone familiar with CAPM must be perplexed. Culp

---

[10] Markopolos, *No one would listen*, 30.
[11] Markopolos, 'Largest hedge fund is a fraud', Attachment 1, reprinted in *No one would listen*.
[12] Culp and Heaton, 'Financial due diligence'.

and Heaton find alpha and beta of 0.007 and 0.05, and Markopolos finds alpha and beta of 0.009 and 0.06. This means that for practical purposes these securities are entirely risk free. Markopolos writes that he expected the beta

to be around 50 per cent, but it could have been anywhere between 30 and 80 per cent. Instead Madoff was coming in at about [0.06]. Six per cent! That was impossible. That number was much too low. It meant there was almost no relationship between those stocks and the entire [S&P 100] index. I was so startled that the legendary Bernie Madoff was running a hedge fund that supposedly produced these crazy numbers that I didn't trust my math. *Maybe I'm missing something.*[13]

As I said, Markopolos cannot have been the only one doing the maths. Numerous people on Wall Street may have had their suspicions about Madoff, some based on quantitative financial due diligence.[14] Moreover, despite the fact that Markopolos describes his modelling strategy as 'complex' because it had 'a lot of moving parts', from a mathematical point of view the model is simple.[15] Dan DiBartolomeo, a mathematician from whom Markopolos learned the maths and whom he later approached to check it, described the methods as 'textbook simple quant methods of due diligence' that yield conclusions 'in a few hours'.[16] The mathematics of asset pricing appears indeed in most undergraduate economics curricula. It is hard to believe therefore that no one else had done the same financial due diligence and run the same regressions at the time.

Take Fairfield Greenwich Group (FGG), the investment firm offering feeder funds such as Fairfield Sentry. FGG had a detailed description of its financial due diligence practices on its web site, removed during the Madoff windup, stating that

[a] core area for further analysis is to attempt to dissect and further understand investment performance, how a manager generates alpha, and what risks are taken in doing so. As portfolio management and risk management

---

[13] Markopolos, *No one would listen*, 35.
[14] Arvedlund, *Madoff*, 77–8, 121–2.
[15] Markopolos, *No one would listen*, 34.
[16] D. diBartolomeo, 'Risk and attribution in the post-Madoff era', lecture CFA Institute, 25 February 2010, www.cfainstitute.org/Multimedia%20Documents/dibartolomeo_2010.pdf.

incorporate elements of both art and science, FGG applies both qualitative and quantitative measures.[17]

FGG even went so far as to claim that 'the nature of FGG's manager transparency model employs a significantly higher level of due diligence work than typically performed by most fund of funds and consulting firms'.[18]

This is surely very doubtful; it is more likely that due diligence was carried out at a fairly low level. This is not to say, however, that had FGG indeed run the regressions and estimated alpha and beta, as their financial due diligence statement claims they did, they would have come to the conclusions Markopolos had arrived at. Like many others, FGG's financial due diligence analysts would probably have blamed the maths rather than a person with a longstanding and unrivalled reputation, Bernard Madoff. Other feeders indeed simply admitted that they had not gone beyond investigating Madoff's reputation, which was, of course, spotless at the time. Villehuchet, co-founder of Access, told Markopolos that he was 'totally committed' to Madoff and that he had done his 'own form of due diligence'. He told Markopolos:

I'm comfortable with it. He comes with an impeccable reputation. I mean, my God, he's one of the biggest market makers in the US.[19]

To return to FGG's financial due diligence analysts, it cannot be excluded that it found a beta of 5 or 6 per cent. But if one is estimating the beta of a man with, as Villehuchet thought, an 'impeccable reputation', who has held important positions in the financial services industry, who is highly respected in society with close connections in politics and elsewhere, and who is praised for investor ingenuity and technological innovation – then one might indeed have doubted the maths and the beta rather than the man and his fund.

Markopolos, however, using similar methods of financial due diligence, went much further; and that he went further is to be explained because epistemic virtues motivated and enabled him. To begin with, Markopolos persistently showed great love of knowledge. Several people with whom he talked about Madoff admitted that Madoff's returns

[17] Quoted by Blodget, 'Fairfield Greenwich'.
[18] Quoted by Blodget, 'Fairfield Greenwich'.
[19] Markopolos, *No one would listen*, 91.

were 'unreal', but they did not care to investigate how to explain the lack of 'realism', only speculating about the possibilities of illegal insider dealing or frontrunning. Markopolos, on the other hand, employed a great diversity of methods to confirm his hypothesis. A report entitled 'The world's largest hedge fund is a fraud', which he sent to the Securities and Exchange Commission on 22 December 2005, contained no fewer than thirty red flags uncovered by a great diversity of qualitative and quantitative methods.[20]

Markopolos also showed epistemic humility when he had his mathematical models checked by various others inside and outside the firm and when he invoked the assistance of many other people. One such person was Michael Ocrant, a journalist with a record of unmasking several Ponzi schemes. After Markopolos had explained his suspicions to him, Ocrant simply decided to ring Madoff. He was invited over to Madoff's office the same day. Madoff made a tremendous impression on Ocrant, showing him around the office, allowing him to ask any question he might fancy and answering them in consistent and plausible ways. Ocrant concluded that if Madoff were indeed running a Ponzi scheme, 'he's either the best actor I've ever seen or a total sociopath'.[21] To Markopolos and his colleagues Ocrant reported back that

[t]his guy was as cool as can be. I mean, I didn't see the slightest indication that anything was wrong. In fact, rather than worrying about the story I was writing, he acted like he was inviting me over for Sunday tea. He doesn't act like he's got something to hide. He spent more than two hours with me. He showed me around the whole operation. He even offered to answer any other questions. Guilty people usually don't act this way.[22]

Markopolos retorted that '[t]he numbers don't lie'. But Ocrant doubted that: 'Is it possible we're missing something?'[23] Markopolos was soberminded enough to have asked that question himself after he had done his initial mathematical modelling and had concluded that the Fairfield Sentry feeder fund had a beta of 6 per cent. He had gradually discarded alternative explanations for the beta, however, and accepted his mathematical knowledge as a firm basis to conclude that Madoff was operating a Ponzi scheme. Another virtue that benefited Markopolos was

---

[20] Markopolos, 'Largest hedge fund is a fraud'.
[21] Quoted by Markopolos, *No one would listen*, 82.
[22] Quoted by Markopolos, *No one would listen*, 83.
[23] Quoted by Markopolos, *No one would listen*, 83.

epistemic courage. Markopolos courageously voiced suspicions about investments that many clients of Rampart, the business Markopolos worked for, firmly believed in, thereby risking the firm's relationship with the clients. He risked his own position in the firm when he made clear that he was unable to emulate Madoff's success, and he endangered his status as a quant when he admitted that he had even failed to develop mathematical models explaining Madoff's successes.

The most important epistemic virtues that contributed to Markopolos's success and that are essential for financial due diligence analysts are temperance and justice. Markopolos had started to entertain doubts about the legality or reality of Madoff's strategy as soon as he had seen the revenue streams. But he did not rush to a conclusion. He developed mathematical models that he had checked by others. He used a great range of methodologies to examine the issue. He used qualitative methodologies when he worked with Ocrant, the journalist, and he relentlessly discussed his findings with colleagues. Most importantly, even though quite early on he voiced the hypothesis that Madoff was running a Ponzi scheme, he gave careful consideration to alternative explanations provided by colleagues and clients. One alternative was that Madoff obtained his results from insider trading. Villehuchet had explained Madoff's competitive advantage as that Madoff's decision on what shares to buy or sell was 'based upon his knowledge of the market and his order flow', a form of insider knowledge.[24] A colleague of Markopolos accused Madoff of frontrunning, that is, of using knowledge obtained as a market maker about customers' upcoming trades. Then there was the third hypothesis that Madoff was in reality borrowing the money at an interest rate of around 15 per cent from his clients for him to use in his work as a market maker. Markopolos paid attention to all these hypotheses, and many others, and refuted all of them.

---

[24] Markopolos, *No one would listen*, 27.

7 | *Communicating virtues: the raters*

Credit rating agencies publish assessment (*ratings*) of the creditworthiness of issuers of corporate and government bonds and structured debt securities. Many investors use their services. If you visit the web site of Moody's, one of the big three credit rating agencies in the world, you acknowledge that you agree with its terms of use, which include the condition that you will

make your own study and evaluation of each credit decision or security, and of each issuer and guarantor of, and each provider of credit support for, each security or credit that you may consider purchasing, holding, selling, or providing.

You also agree that

any tools or information made available on [Moody's web site] are not a substitute for the exercise of independent judgment and expertise. You should always seek the assistance of a professional for advice on investments, tax, the law, or other professional matters.[1]

Could Moody's be any clearer in encouraging you to be inquisitive? Their statements would probably fail to persuade most commentators. In an interview with *Guardian* journalist Joris Luyendijk, a senior analyst who had worked for Moody's described raters as the 'all-purpose bogeymen' for the global financial crisis.[2] Paul Krugman, the Nobel-winning economist and *New York Times* columnist, called their judgements 'literally worse than useless'.[3] Other commentators certainly do not mince their words either when they compare the agencies to alchemists or astrologers, as we shall shortly see. The two quotes from

---

[1] www.moodys.com/termsofuseinfo.aspx.
[2] www.theguardian.com/commentisfree/joris-luyendijk-banking-blog/2012/dec/17/rating-agencies-bogeymen-william-j-harrington.
[3] krugman.blogs.nytimes.com/2013/02/23/little-statesmen-and-philosophers/.

Moody's terms of use may suggest, however, that if raters are astrologers they are considerably more explicit about the limits of their predictions than most of their star-gazing colleagues; for horoscopes generally do not come with disclaimers as detailed as those that Moody's provides.

More scholarly sides have fervidly criticized the rating agencies too. The most prominent criticism concerns misratings of structured finance. While in 2007 the bulk of mortgage-backed securities received top ratings, most of them are now considered junk bonds. The agencies are also blamed for their inordinately slow revisions. A day before Lehman Brothers blew up in September 2008, the bank still had good ratings from the big three credit rating agencies: Standard and Poor's, Moody's, and Fitch. In addition, the agencies have been accused of exacerbating the European government bond crisis; the increased costs of borrowing that Greece incurred after Moody's downgraded the country in June 2010 caused significant additional problems to an economy that was already in serious trouble. Raters have also failed to predict disastrous defaults (WorldCom, Tyco, Enron are only a few examples); they have been unwilling to disclose the methodological assumptions that underlie their judgements (methods are considered trade secrets); they have been accused of dubious sales techniques such as *tying* (threatening to downgrade an issuer if no additional services are bought from the agency), *notching* (only offering a rating of a security if other assets are rated as well), and helping issuers to design securities with a particular intended rating by providing them with the software they themselves use in their rating process. In addition, some authors decry the alleged conflicts of interest that arise when issuers instead of investors pay the agencies for rating (the *issuer-pays* compensation scheme), or when issuers solicit ratings from many credit rating agencies and decide to publish only the best (a phenomenon called *ratings shopping*). A plain fact of enormous ethical relevance, moreover, is that the market for credit rating is highly concentrated. Around 95 per cent of the market is in the hands of the big three American credit rating agencies. The Herfindahl-Hirschman index, a standard measure of market concentration, edges over 3,000, which is higher than for almost any other sector.[4]

Implicit in most of these criticisms is the claim that rating agencies do not do their work well enough. Moody's calls its ratings mere 'opinions' about the credit quality of debt obligations, which must not be viewed

[4] www.gao.gov/products/GAO-10-782.

as 'statements of fact' or 'recommendations to purchase, sell or hold any securities'.[5] But most commentators find this purely underhand and uncandid. It is as though one were to sell toys with the disclaimer that determining the risk to children is the buyer's responsibility. More should be done to guarantee that the toys are not hazardous. In one of the few publications devoted to the ethics of credit rating agencies, Steven Scalet and Thomas Kelly even argue that

> reasonably accessible investing information is not merely a public good ... but an important component for creating conditions of justice in a capitalist society, akin to making voting reasonably accessible to all in a democratic society.[6]

If they are right, rating agencies do not even resemble toy manufacturers very much. What agencies do comes close to realizing human rights. Such an important function, it seems, requires a high level of epistemic virtue, not only in the *production* of the ratings, but also in their *communication*. What dishonest disclaimers about 'opinions' seem to be motivated by is little more than a desire to evade liability. Consequently, the rating agencies need other-regarding epistemic virtues such as honesty and generosity; they need an ethics of communication. Or so it would seem.

The distinction between self-regarding and other-regarding virtues is not new. Primary examples of self-regarding virtues are courage and patience, because they are directed at ensuring our personal wellbeing; other-regarding virtues, by contrast, further the good life of others, and include benevolence, justice and honesty.[7] Virtue epistemologists do have a view of other-regarding virtues, although most authors have only discussed them fairly briefly. Jason Kawall, and Robert Roberts and Jay Wood are the authors of quite elaborate accounts of other-regarding virtue, to which I turn shortly. Linda Zagzebski lists the 'teaching virtues' among the intellectual virtues, defining them as 'the social virtues of being communicative, including intellectual candor and knowing your audience and how they respond'.[8] Jason Baehr spends some time on generosity.[9] Heather Battaly examines ways in

---

[5] www.moodys.com/termsofuseinfo.aspx.
[6] Scalet and Kelly, 'Ethics of credit rating', 489.
[7] See, e.g., Taylor and Wolfram, 'Self-regarding and other-regarding virtues', which critically examines the way self-regarding virtues have been appraised.
[8] Zagzebski, *Virtues of the mind*, 114.   [9] Baehr, *Inquiring mind*, 110–11.

which teachers may encourage students to show concern for epistemic virtue.[10]

In this chapter I discuss other-regarding epistemic virtues in more detail. One reason is that I have already referred to them before when, for instance, I showed why CEOs should be epistemically generous. Another reason is perhaps more surprising. Unlike most commentators I do not think that accusing the credit rating agencies of disingenuous communication is so straightforwardly plausible; rather, I believe, the problems surrounding them are to be seen in the light of a form of regulation that has led to unjustifiable outsourcing of epistemic responsibility. Governments have singled out the rating agencies as nearly official sources of information about credit risks, whose verdicts investors are legally bound to take seriously. As a result, investors have become less interested in forming their own judgements about these risks. Instead of encouraging epistemic virtues, regulation has dumbed investors down, and inexcusably so. That is what I argue here at any rate.

I start with a brief discussion of Jason Kawall's view of other-regarding epistemic virtues. I show that for all its ingenuity his view misses an essential difference between epistemic and non-epistemic other-regarding virtues: the need for the beneficiary to cooperate. I introduce the concept of *interlucency* to show what this requirement amounts to, and illustrate this by means of a case about stock market recommendations that is also interesting in its own right. I then turn to the credit rating agencies and regulation.

Other-regarding epistemic virtues

Kawall groups the other-regarding epistemic virtues in three categories.[11] Two categories are, I believe, best seen as 'meta-virtues'; echoing Zagzebski's suggestion, Kawall calls them the virtue of being a *good teacher* and the virtue of being a *good listener* or *critic*. The third category contains honesty, sincerity, integrity, creativity and other traits inspiring people to communicate in virtuous ways. Like non-epistemic other-regarding virtues, these virtues are constitutive of the good life. Kawall expresses himself slightly more conditionally here than in the

---

[10] Battaly, 'Teaching intellectual virtues'. Also see *Journal of Philosophy of Education*, 47, 2 (2013) (special issue).
[11] Kawall, 'Other-regarding epistemic virtues'.

non-epistemic case, writing that 'the development of other-regarding virtues *may* constitute part of the epistemic flourishing and wellbeing of an epistemic agent' and that '[a]n epistemic agent who focuses exclusively on self-regarding epistemic virtues (gaining knowledge and justified beliefs for herself alone) *could* be a deficient epistemic agent to the extent that she is a member of a community'.[12]

Kawall advances a number of arguments in defence of this claim. The first argument that other-regarding epistemic virtues are essential elements of *eudaimonia* looks at science. Scientists typically think of themselves as contributing to a 'common body' of knowledge rather than a mere 'personal stock' of knowledge'.[13] Kawall seems to imply that their doing so is essential. It is, he thinks, part of a scientist's good life to work for the sake of the scientific community. Secondly, communities value acquiring new knowledge more than acquiring old or irrelevant knowledge. Kawall illustrates this claim by comparing a person discovering a new species in the Amazon basin with a person memorizing an entire encyclopaedia. The latter's cognitive accomplishments may, if anything, be admired; but the former's epistemic contributions will be genuinely valued; and what we value in the former's contributions is, according to Kawall, other-regarding virtues. Kawall's third argument for other-regarding epistemic virtues uses a case due to Jonathan Kvanvig.[14] Kvanvig asks us to imagine two agents S and T who are completely identical with respect to the knowledge they possess. What S knows T knows, and what T knows S knows. The only difference between the two is that S has acquired the knowledge all by herself, whereas T has learnt everything from S. Kvanvig claims that S is a 'superior cognitive being' than T.[15] Kawall agrees, and he believes that S's cognitive superiority can be adequately explained by other-regarding epistemic virtues; for S 'has developed other-regarding epistemic virtues which [T] appears to entirely lack'.[16] Furthermore, Kawall seems to suggest, without other-regarding epistemic virtues it would be impossible to explain Kvanvig's judgement, and that is why we need them. Kawall's fourth and final argument takes a case of a very good teacher inspiring students to become genuinely interested in and curious about the topics

---

[12] Kawall, 'Other-regarding epistemic virtues', 260; emphasis added.
[13] Kawall, 'Other-regarding epistemic virtues', 268.
[14] Kvanvig, *Value of knowledge*, 148.   [15] Kvanvig, *Value of knowledge*, 148.
[16] Kawall, 'Other-regarding epistemic virtues', 271.

she teaches. What Kawall values about the teacher is that she 'contributes to a surplus of true beliefs over false beliefs ... among her students and community'.[17] Again, other-regarding epistemic virtues are needed to explain this.

One may find fault with the diagnosis Kawall gives of specific cases. I do not, for example, think that Kvanvig's case necessarily suggests that T lacks other-regarding epistemic virtue. T may just as well have failed to carry out investigative actions because of a lack of self-regarding epistemic virtues or a lack of opportunity for research. (In the latter case, S is not rightfully called *cognitively superior* to T.) Most people know most of what they know about maths the way T knows things. They learn maths from others; but this does not mean that they lack other-regarding epistemic virtue. Furthermore, Kawall's approach to epistemic virtue is, I think, rather highbrow, making it difficult to apply it to simpler forms of knowledge we attempt to acquire. Only a few of us are scientists; most of us, however, want to know how to prepare a meal or drive a car. We encountered these problems in Chapter 2, where I proposed an alternative to Jason Bachr's view of personal intellectual worth because of its being too intellectualist to capture knowledge acquisition outside the domain of science. It is not so much a desire for wisdom, but a desire for profit that leads businesses to engage in research activities, and I do not see any reason to judge these activities as less virtuous. The idea of instrumental epistemic value I submitted as an alternative to Bachr's view is not immediately applicable to other-regarding virtues, however, if people gain knowledge as instrumental to their own goals only. Up to now the instrumental value of epistemic virtues has been in their contribution to gaining knowledge. What knowledge others acquire was important only in so far as it influenced our own knowledge or our ability to gain knowledge. I have somewhat neglected this point at various stages of the book, perhaps rather care-lessly speaking about the epistemic generosity of a CEO, for instance, without making it clear that, as a virtue, the generosity of CEOs does not directly contribute to realizing their own private goals but rather those of the company. Generosity may truly be a nuisance to a CEO whose mainspring is to get rich. Yet generosity can be consistently viewed as an instrument to reaching particular goals. Despite my disagreement with

---

[17] Kawall, 'Other-regarding epistemic virtues', 271.

Kawall, his theory of other-regarding virtues does contain a suggestion as to how these goals could be developed further. We have to think of these goals as arising out of a *community*.[18] Kawall's example is the scientific or academic community furthering science. But nothing in the concept of community prohibits us from applying it to business. Indeed this is exactly what a flourishing Aristotelian tradition in ethics has begun to examine, viewing firms as communities contributing to the common good in ways that transcend individual *eudaimonia*.[19] What Kawall refers to as *community*, in business consequently becomes the corporation, the partnership, the firm. A firm acquires epistemic virtue among other things by ensuring that the individual epistemic virtues of employees match the demands placed upon these employees by the specific way in which their job contributes to realizing corporate goals set by its directors. Some of the required epistemic virtues will be self-regarding. A person working in the research and development department cannot do without love of knowledge. Some of the virtues, however, will be other-regarding, such as CEO generosity.

One might object that generosity does not necessarily contribute to every corporate goal, strictly speaking. Hiding things from investors may sometimes be better advice if strict maximization of shareholder value is one's goal. When the aim is to derive other-regarding epistemic virtues from community goals, we should not therefore consider the corporation as a community in isolation. Corporations operate within larger environments. As we have seen, even Milton Friedman, who is generally viewed as one of the most uncompromising advocates of shareholder value maximization, assigned lexicographic priority to two other goals, namely, law and ethics. It is the responsibility of corporate executives to earn as much as possible for the owners of the firm provided they conform to 'the basic rules of the society, both those embodied in law and those embodied in ethical custom'.[20] What I should say therefore is that the epistemic virtue of generosity for a CEO originates in the corporate goals together with these 'basic rules of society'. The corporation is still the community from which other-regarding epistemic virtues arise; the rules of the society in which the corporation functions place conditions on the goals this community can develop.

[18] Kawall, 'Other-regarding epistemic virtues', 272.
[19] Sison, 'Common good theory'.   [20] Friedman, 'Social responsibility', 33.

Generosity

Let me now turn to generosity. Kawall seems to claim that other-regarding virtues do not require us to ensure that our audiences understand what we say:

Honesty is a virtue, and we have duties to testify clearly, etc. in a fashion which should help others to gain true beliefs. But we need not guarantee that our testimony will be accepted. Compare – there is a moral other-regarding virtue of benevolence, even if we cannot guarantee that, e.g., money we donate will be used for food and not bombs.[21]

First difference from non-epistemic virtue

This is plausible if it refers to our inability to *force* our testimony or beliefs upon another person. It is implausible if the position stems from a reticence to explore the further consequences of other-regarding epistemic virtues. One way to see this is to turn to Robert Roberts and Jay Wood, who define generosity as a disposition to give freely, for the purpose of benefiting the receiver. Their definition includes generosity (giving) and good stewardship, the two dimensions of Aristotle's liberality.[22] Despite the definition's straightforwardness, what epistemic generosity motivates and enables one to do is far from obvious. When epistemically generous people give information to others, they do not lose what they give, unlike non-epistemically generous givers. This does not mean, however, that giving information comes at no cost. The costs of sharing knowledge about music or tennis with my neighbours will probably amount to nothing more than the time spent on it. Buyers who freely share with a dealer in second-hand cars the maximum price they want to pay, however, will certainly end up paying too much. Adopting the austere picture of epistemic virtue propounded by the personal intellectual worth view makes it rather difficult to develop a concept of generosity that is sensitive to this issue. This is one of the reasons why I explore a view of epistemic virtue based on instrumental epistemic value. What type of information sharing generosity amounts to in business typically depends on the particular non-epistemic ends that generosity is

---

[21] Kawall, 'Other-regarding epistemic virtues', 274.
[22] Roberts and Wood, *Intellectual virtues*, 286–304.

supposed to contribute to, and obviously no business enterprise has as an end the hastening of its own demise by helping its competitors.

This is one difference between epistemic and non-epistemic generosity: one does not necessarily lose what one gives if the gift is knowledge, but that is not to say that giving epistemic gifts can never harm the giver. Another difference is that one only succeeds in giving an epistemic gift if the recipient of the gift cooperates in certain ways. Money given to a charitable organization is a gift, even if it the organization misspends it; it is a gift once the charity's bank account has been credited. Sending an item of information to a person does not, however, entail that the sender has made an epistemic gift.

Second difference from non-epistemic virtue

To see this, I move to investment recommendations, which are provided by stock market analysts. Analysts give recommendations about company equity. The format is quite rigid, allowing them to choose exactly one of the following five possible recommendations: *strong sell*, *sell*, *hold*, *buy* and *strong buy*. When an analyst has a hold recommendation on Royal Dutch Shell it suggests, one would think, that one should not sell shares in Royal Dutch Shell if one owns them, but should not buy them either. What else can *holding* shares mean? All the same, one should take the hold recommendation as a recommendation to *sell*. Analyst recommendations show a shift of scale (called *stock recommendation bias*) not unlike that of a tennis coach consistently characterizing terrible shots as 'not bad'. Less than 5 per cent of all recommendations are recommendations to sell. Of all recommendations, 95 per cent are as a consequence either neutral or positive. This cannot be what the analysts mean. In reality hold recommendations are recommendations to get rid of the shares, and only 'very bad' shares get sell or strong sell recommendations.[23]

Institutional investors (insurance companies, pension funds, large endowments, etc.) are fully aware of the bias.[24] They sell after a hold recommendation, buy after strong buy recommendations and do nothing after buy recommendations. Small, non-professional investors trading

---

[23] Malmendier and Shanthikumar, 'Are small investors naive?'
[24] S. Iskoz, 'Essays in financial economics', MIT Sloan School of Management (2003), dspace.mit.edu/bitstream/handle/1721.1/16969/53484012.pdf.

on their personal accounts do not discount the bias, however. They take analyst recommendations literally, to their potential disadvantage. (The issue of stock recommendation bias is very different from the issue of whether analysts can outperform the market.) There seems to be no evidence to support the claim that small investors' lack of knowledge of the bias is the result of analysts intentionally deceiving them.[25] I offer the diagnoses that their lack of knowledge is caused by miscommunication and failures of epistemic generosity and what I shall call *interlucency*.

I first sketch a game-theoretical model of investment recommendations. Using modelling techniques from linguistics, the interaction between analysts and investors may be viewed as one between speakers (or senders) and hearers (or recipients).[26] Analysts have three 'strategies' to choose from, which they can use to communicate their advice. They may use an upwardly biased strategy U, a literal strategy L, and a downwardly biased strategy D. Investors, in turn, may interpret analysts at face value and use a strategy l, or they may interpret them as being upwardly or downwardly biased, with corresponding strategies u and d. The most natural outcome arises when both analysts and investors 'play' their literal strategies; but adopting biased strategies U and u, or D and d, in no way disrupts communication. Converging on U and u is exactly what analysts and large investors do.

I now turn to a defence of the second claim about the difference between epistemic and non-epistemic virtues. Generous people share knowledge with others. Sharing knowledge is more than merely sending a particular message in a linguistic game; it is sending a message that hearers are in the position to use to increase their knowledge. This is no different from non-epistemic virtue. I am not really generous if in response to a demand for transportation I offer my car for use by a person who is unable to drive. Genuine generosity in such a case would lead me to offer the person a lift. Similarly, epistemically generous people adjust the way they communicate to their audience and try to ensure they use the speaker strategy that the hearers are likely to match.

This leads to an interesting difference from non-epistemic generosity because it also requires active cooperation from the recipient. For

---

25 Malmendier and Shanthikumar, 'Are small investors naive?'
26 Traces of such models can be found in Lewis, *Convention* and Schiffer, *Meaning*. Also see Stalnaker, 'Common ground'.

beneficiaries of non-epistemic generosity to benefit from generous gifts, they only need to accept them. If you accept the lift someone offers you, or if you do not pay back the money you receive in your bank account, generosity has done its work in an unmediated or immediate way, whatever use you may make of the money. Epistemic generosity, by contrast, uses language as a medium only and the gift is not the mere utterance of words. If someone gives you advice, you have to interpret the linguistic utterances in which the advisor has cast the advice. This may go wrong because you may interpret the message incorrectly.

One may object that this is also true of non-epistemic generosity. Non-epistemically generous financial aid to, say, famine victims causes similar problems if it fails to reach the victims. This problem is more accurately described, however, as one in which the gift was not used in the way the giver intended. The problem with epistemic generosity is not that the gift is misused, but rather that no gift has been given as long as the recipient fails to interpret the linguistic utterance correctly. The investor first has to interpret a hold recommendation as a recommendation to *sell*. It is subsequently up to the investor to decide whether to use this 'gift' as it was intended, to misuse it, or not to use it at all.

A consequence of reasoning along these lines is that to be epistemically generous, people must express themselves in ways that the beneficiaries of their generosity understand. This in turn requires that the recipients provide the senders with relevant feedback, especially when, as in the case of stock recommendations, common words acquire uncommon meanings. (Uncommon words acquiring common or uncommon meanings is much less of a problem because recipients can easily spot uncommon words and ask for clarification.)

Let us return to the example of analyst recommendations, and let us suppose that a particular analyst believes that investors should rid their portfolios of Royal Dutch Shell equity. To communicate this advice the analyst has to choose a communication strategy such as U, L or D. Epistemically virtuous analysts choose a strategy they believe the recipients interpret as a recommendation to sell the shares. It is important to note that this does not exclude any of the three strategies. As we have seen, when analysts and institutional investors communicate and interpret via upwardly biased ways and coordinate on choosing U and u, analysts get the recommendation across. A true mark of epistemic generosity is that the sender has reasons to think that the recipient uses the correct strategy; and to examine whether such reasons are available requires that the sender actively track the recipient's understanding. The sender cannot do this, however, unless the recipient is sufficiently open about her interpretation. The recipient has to acknowledge receipt of the message and must try to make clear how she understands the message. Both sender and recipient have to contribute to sufficient openness concerning the communication and interpretation strategies they use in order that epistemic generosity gets off the ground. Contributing to such openness by tracking understanding, acknowledging receipt, providing feedback and so on is what I call *interlucent* senders and recipients do.

Personal one-to-one communication between finance practitioners and customers, and to a lesser extent telephone conversations and email correspondence, are ways of communication that allow interlucency. Advisers talking to clients have ample opportunity to track understanding. Carefully listening to clients is often sufficient to spot errors in understanding. It is evident that a client's stated intention to sit still after having received a hold recommendation betrays a clear misunderstanding, and a virtuous adviser seizes the opportunity to set this right. By contrast, unilateral communication using web sites, information leaflets and other forms of written documentation offers less space for interlucency. Senders never know whether the intended recipients read the web sites and brochures. They have little room for tracking the recipients' understanding. Recipients who fail to understand have no way to gain clarification, except by face-to-face communication.

Interlucency may be conceived of as an epistemic virtue. To avoid communicative misunderstanding, interlucent people try to place themselves in the position of others and adopt their perspective. They pay due attention to what others say, but they also actively signal their own interpretation in order to allow their communication partners to provide feedback on these interpretations or to adapt their communication strategies. Should we conclude that stock market analysts show insufficient concern for interlucency? That would be going fast. In describing my shots as 'not bad', my tennis coach by no means fails to help, as long as I understand what he means. Epistemic generosity is entirely compatible with understatement, hyperbole or other figures of speech, where they do not obscure communication. Given that institutional investors are perfectly capable of understanding analyst recommendations, the case against the analysts is fairly weak. Secondly, epistemically temperate *private* investors realize that they do not fully grasp much of what they read. They know that recommendations from such consumer organizations as Which? or the Consumers Union should be taken with a grain of salt. Temperate people do not make their purchasing choices entirely dependent on what others say. Only a mild degree of curiosity suffices for private investors to consult web sites and articles explaining the stock recommendation bias (and also, by the way, the sheer lack of evidence backing the added value of analyst recommendations). Private investors following analyst recommendations without any further thought are in any case somewhat naive.[27]

This conclusion may be disappointing: why do we need a theory of other-regarding epistemic virtues in business if stock market analysts can get off so easily? Let me clarify. In earlier chapters I have already shown that other-regarding epistemic virtues are crucial to business, but I did so without turning to recent work in virtue epistemology. As the discussion of knowledge sharing in Chapter 5 made clear, no business enterprise can do without epistemically generous employees. In some way, the present chapter is more concerned with the *limits* of epistemic virtue. It is tempting to use the theory of epistemic virtue to make grand claims about the informational duties of professionals in the financial services industry towards clients and prospective customers. It is tempting to blame accountancy firms, banks, credit rating agencies, insurance companies, mortgage lenders, pension funds and governments for having provided us with so little and such obscure information, and it is equally tempting to find fault with analysts who fail to ensure that their audience understands their recommendations. I shall defend the view that though the temptation is understandable, it is misplaced. This, I hope, is not only interesting in and of itself, but also provides insights that are relevant to regulation. I argue that outsourcing epistemic responsibility is something that regulators should be reluctant to do.

Credit ratings

While stock market analysts are an important source of information for financial markets, credit rating agencies and accountants play more pronounced roles. It is chartered accountants who write the official auditors' reports that corporate annual reports are legally bound to

---

[27] Malmendier and Shanthikumar, 'Are small investors naive?'

include to make the documents valuable to banks, shareholders and tax officials, among others; and it is credit rating agencies that are designated by many governments as the sole authoritative source of credit risk. If an argument for other-regarding epistemic virtue among stock market analysts fails, one may still hope to make a case for such virtues in credit rating and accountancy. This chapter considers the raters, and shows that the case for other-regarding virtues is weak because governments have rather clumsily outsourced epistemic responsibility. The next chapter turns to the accountant, showing that the case for outsourcing epistemic responsibility is stronger once one considers that management and accountant form a joint epistemic agent.

Credit risk: asserting creditworthiness

It is useful to distinguish three functions of credit rating agencies, namely, estimating credit risk, monitoring issuers and, thanks to regulation, exerting influence on the management of regulated institutional funds. First, their role is to furnish investors with estimations of the credit risk. *Credit risk* captures the risk that the issuer of a security (e.g., the corporation borrowing money) will fail to pay interest and/or repay the loan. It excludes such things as the risk that markets will turn unfavourable (market risk) or that no one will want to buy or sell the securities (liquidity risk). Credit rating agencies express their judgements of credit risk in letter combinations, ranging from the top-ranking AAA (for Standard and Poor's, and Fitch) and Aaa (for Moody's) to the D of default or bankruptcy. In the case of government debt, credit rating agencies also incorporate an estimation of the willingness to pay because, unlike companies, countries may decide not to pay back their loans when they think this will prevent social or political unrest.

Martha Poon describes the rating procedure in four steps.[28] The process starts with a primary analyst developing a preliminary rating on the basis of the financial statements provided by the issuer of the security. The credit rating agency then meets the issuer's representatives for discussion. During the third step of the process the credit rating agency develops a short report detailing and motivating the decision. The final step is that a committee is set up, including the primary analyst and the managing director, as well as other analysts, managers and staff

[28] Poon, 'Rating agencies', 283.

members with relevant knowledge. The committee votes on the final rating. The agency sends the final rating together with the report to the issuer. In principle issuers can appeal to the ratings decision, but they hardly ever do so. A press release finally publishes the rating.

Monitoring: directing management

A second role is that of *monitoring* the issuers. Credit rating agencies attempt to influence corporate or political decision making and they do this, not by participating in the issuer's decision making process, but by verbal means only: their ratings. The agencies review ratings every twelve to eighteen months. In the meantime, however, the primary analyst can put issuers on *watch lists* and provide *outlooks* about them, showing the concerns the agency has about the short- and medium-term development of their creditworthiness. Warning investors of potential ratings changes, these instruments may be perceived by the issuers as signals of problems that must be resolved to prevent a real down-grade.[29] Perhaps this sounds rather far-fetched as a method of active monitoring. Theoretical and empirical work in economics, however, shows that agencies use watch lists and outlooks as part of an implicit contract between agencies and issuers, the terms of which stipulate that issuers shall do their best to avoid future downgrades.[30] Particularly for issuers with low perceived creditworthiness, watch lists fulfil this coer-cive function rather well.[31]

Stamps of approval: directing investors

But how much value do ratings have to investors? Standard and Poor's emphasizes that its ratings have to be interpreted as providing informa-tion on the relative ranking of issuers, and so does Fitch. Moody's states that '[t]here is an expectation that ratings will, on average, relate to subsequent default frequency, although they typically are not defined as precise default rate estimates'; perhaps slightly inconsistently it describes its ratings also as 'relative'.[32] Empirical work on credit rating

[29] Bannier and Hirsch, 'The watchlist'.
[30] Boot et al., 'Coordination mechanisms'.
[31] Bannier and Hirsch, 'The watchlist'.
[32] www.moodys.com/ratings-process/Understanding-Moody-s-Corporate-Bond-Ratings-And-Rating-Process/002005001.

agencies demonstrates that the ratings the big three agencies give to corporate and government bonds correspond rather accurately with default probability, suggesting that they offer more than a mere relative ordering of credit risk. Triple A amounts to a 0.5 per cent probability of default, whereas the highly speculative B- (Standard and Poor's) and B3 (Moody's) amount to 49.2 and 48.3 per cent.[33] But in contrast to what many investors thought before the subprime mortgage meltdown started, ratings do not have the same meaning across different classes of securities. Baa corporate bond ratings from Moody's were associated with a default probability of 2 per cent over the period 1983–2005; collateralized-debt obligations with the same rating had a twelve times higher likelihood of 24 per cent that they would default.[34]

It is important to realize that the fact that ratings accurately reflect default probabilities offers no proof of their added value. Research on the determinants of bankruptcy shows that numerous measures may be used to approximate credit ratings rather accurately on the basis of publicly available information. This is a severe blow to the accomplishments of the agencies, given that they claim to have superior information obtained privately in off-the-record conversations with the issuers themselves. These publicly available determinants include standard financial ratios of a firm's profitability, liquidity, solvency and size, but also measures of corporate governance (ownership structure and the way the firm is managed) and board independence, and a number of macroeconomic factors such as the growth of gross domestic product.[35] Lawrence White observes more technically that the correlation between credit ratings and default rate referred to above can also be obtained by looking at publicly available information about bond spreads, which is roughly the difference between what one gets from the bond and what one gets from a 'risk-free' benchmark such as US treasury bonds or Libor. As White concludes, '[t]he question of what true value the major credit rating agencies bring to the financial markets remains open and difficult to resolve'.[36] For all we know, they may, as Paul Krugman suggests above, be useless.

---

[33] Zhou, 'Credit rating and corporate default'.
[34] Strier, 'Rating the raters', 539.
[35] A classic paper is Altman, 'Corporate bankruptcy'. See Bhojraj and Sengupta, 'Bond ratings and yields' and Löffler, 'Rating through the cycle'.
[36] White, 'Credit rating agencies', 219.

That some investors do respond to changes in a security's rating despite the fact that ratings can be approximated on the basis of publicly available information seems hard to square with the hypothesis of efficient markets. (One version of the efficient market hypothesis is roughly that prices reflect all publicly available information.) A possible explanation of why investors respond (and also why, as they do, they respond more intensely to downgrades than to upgrades) leads us to a third function that credit rating agencies fulfil, besides informing investors about credit risk and monitoring the issuers of securities.[37] The letter judgements (AAA, AA+, etc.) play this third role as a consequence of a peculiar bit of financial regulation. In the 1930s US state governments started referring to credit ratings in their prudential regulation of pension funds. They also developed regulations prohibiting banks from investing in speculative investment securities, the sort of things popularly called *junk bonds*. This development has never stopped. Today the investment decisions of pension funds, health insurance companies, banks and many other financial services firms are severely curtailed, throughout the world, by rules that refer directly to the ratings published by a relatively small group of officially registered and accredited rating agencies.[38] When a security's rating changes, managers of such institutional funds may consequently have to change their positions, even in cases where they have formed a different estimate of credit risk from the rating agency's.

The three roles that credit rating agencies play can be neatly summarized in philosophical terminology deriving from speech act theory developed by John Austin and John Searle.[39] We use words and sentences to carry out many disparate sorts of things such as asserting, ordering, promising, expressing emotions, pronouncing a couple 'man and wife', or directing people.[40] Most straightforwardly, ratings are *assertions of creditworthiness*. When Standard and Poor's gives a B+ rating to Austin Martin this is nothing other than the statement that the default probability of this company is around 32 per cent. Secondly, rating agencies provide *directives of management*. An example is Standard and Poor's informing Sainsbury about the measures that management should take to avert a potential downgrade:

[37] White, 'Credit rating agencies'.   [38] White, 'Credit rating agencies'.
[39] Austin, *How to do things*. Searle, 'Illocutionary acts'.
[40] Searle, 'Illocutionary acts'.

A weakening of [Sainsbury's] financial profile due to poor trading or capital investments and capital returns not fully mitigated by improvements in earnings could lead us to lower the ratings. Conversely, we could consider a positive rating action if Sainsbury achieved and maintained [funds from operations to debt ratios] of more than 25%.[41]

Thirdly, the agencies issue *directives of investment*. If Standard and Poor's gives Hilton a rating of BB-, as it once did, investors bound by regulation must be particularly careful if a one-notch downgrade to B+ leads them to sell the bonds, because then the hotel chain will verge close to *junk*.

Compromising epistemic virtue

Why did regulators endow the rating agencies with the authority to issue directives of investment? A little history may help us here. The predecessors of credit rating agencies were *credit reporting firms* such as the famous Mercantile Agency, founded in the United States in 1841. They expanded their activity particularly after the US Civil War, when demand increased for reliable information about the 'credit behaviour' of companies and individual businesspeople. Trade and mercantile exchange started flourishing during that period, and much of the trade took place on the basis of trade credit. A buyer receives *trade credit* when a seller sells something but does not require the buyer to pay upon delivery but gives her, say, ninety days to pay. Trade credit is essential when, due to seasonal fluctuations in the buyer's cash flow, no payment can be made right away but only after the buyer has sold products to her own customers. Sellers only extend trade credit to buyers they have reason to trust. Credit reporting agencies therefore started gathering information that merchants could use to determine the trustworthiness of companies, using sheriffs, businesspeople, bank cashiers and other 'correspondents' as sources of information.[42]

In the first two decades of the twentieth century, credit reporting firms changed in important respects. Until then they had specialized in providing information, leaving the ultimate judgements about creditworthiness to their clients. Around 1910, however, they began to publish

[41] www.standardandpoors.com/ratings/articles/en/us/?assetID=1245193708812#ID2603.
[42] Olegario, *Culture of credit*.

their own verdicts of creditworthiness and to adopt the letter system still in use today. The mid-1920s ratings from Moody's, covering almost all of America's corporate bonds, are an example. Governments found these verdicts reliable enough to include them in prudential regulation aimed at mitigating the effects of the crash of 1929 and the subsequent depression. In 1931, for example, the US Office of the Comptroller of the Currency, an important American regulator, introduced the distinction between *investment* and *non-investment grade* securities and determined that non-investment grade securities must be treated differently (as bearing higher risk) on a bank's balance sheet. Only five years later, an outright prohibition of banks investing in speculative securities followed, where the meaning of *speculative* had to be determined by officially recognized credit rating agencies.[43]

It may be suspected that this development was inspired by the 1933 Glass-Steagall Act, or else by the general regulation-friendly sentiment that gave rise to the Act. But we see increased reliance on rating agencies in times of deregulation too. Since 1989, for example, American pension funds have been allowed to invest in asset-backed and mortgage-backed securities with high ratings, and in 2001 the Federal Deposit Insurance Corporation significantly weakened the capital requirements that banks in the United States have to satisfy concerning mortgage-backed securities receiving ratings of AA and above, from 8 per cent to only 1.6 per cent.[44] Even though outside the United States the role of credit rating agencies is of a more recent date, rather similar pictures come out of Europe and elsewhere. All in all 'the creditworthiness judgements of [credit rating agencies have] attained the force of law', as Lawrence White once said.[45]

One may suspect that when agencies are granted such power it places enormous epistemic responsibility on them. This may change, however, once we recall that the added information value of credit ratings is dubious because they can be replicated on the basis of publicly available information. If ratings are just like horoscopes in that they do not add new information to what we already know, requiring epistemic virtue of raters is wide of the mark. One may blame astrologers for a lack of almost any epistemic virtue, but this is appropriate only if they seriously

---

[43] White, 'Credit rating agencies'.
[44] Pagano and Volpin, 'Credit ratings failures'.
[45] White, 'Credit rating agencies', 213.

conceive of what they deliver as genuine predictions. Most writers of astrology columns, however, seem to understand quite well that the game they play is a different one.

The comparison is perhaps a bit tendentious, but it does suggest that rather than blaming raters for a lack of epistemic virtue, the pressing issue is whether we should endow them with such epistemic powers. Lloyd Blankfein, then CEO of Goldman Sachs, once stated that

> too many financial institutions and investors simply outsourced their risk management. Rather than undertake their own analysis, they relied on the rating agencies to do the essential work of risk analysis for them ... This overdependence on credit ratings coincided with the dilution of the coveted triple A rating. In January 2008, there were 12 triple A-rated companies in the world. At the same time, there were 64,000 structured finance instruments, such as collateralized debt obligations, rated triple A.[46]

This indictment sounds largely true. Most astrologers only acknowledge their limited aims quite implicitly, but most people do not take horoscopes seriously. Credit rating agencies are, as we saw above, rather clear about their stated ambitions, but most of their clients use the ratings in ways that go beyond these ambitions. It is worth stressing that, like the readers of astrology columns and the users of stock recommendations, investors could have known more about the limitations of the ratings. Treating triple A rated structured debt securities as though they had a yield curve commonly associated with triple A rated corporate bonds was, as Philippe Jorion states, an 'act of blind faith in the credit rating', which is an expression of a lack of epistemic temperance.[47]

Jorion made this comment in the context of a discussion of the Swiss financial services firm UBS. UBS employees rashly believed that the agencies were capable of deriving ratings of the quality they were used to obtaining for corporate and government bonds. The employees knew, however, that the agencies were much less experienced at rating structured finance than rating corporate debt. The precise extent of credit risk seems to have left them cold at any rate. Despite being large enough to assign a team of economists to the task of comparing structured finance and corporate debt ratings, UBS apparently did not have the corporate curiosity to do so, nor to investigate the

---

[46] Quoted by Pagano and Volpin, 'Credit ratings failures', 404.
[47] Jorion, 'Lessons from the credit crisis', 929.

creditworthiness of issuers itself. This research would have been costly because obtaining information about all the underlying mortgages of a mortgage-backed security requires data that were only available from commercial data providers. But UBS could have done it. Moreover, as Jorion also observes, UBS employees failed to ask even the simplest questions. How, for example, can a mortgage-backed security be assigned the triple A status of a riskless security and at the same time deliver a yield *much* higher than the Libor, a shining example of risk-lessness? The correlation between risk and return is the most funda-mental principle of finance. A lack of epistemic courage may have led financial economists at UBS (and many other financial services firms) not to ask the obvious question: how can structured debt securities increase expected return and simultaneously stay almost risk free?

The discussion of the UBS case has drawn us into the topic of out-sourcing epistemic responsibility. I defend the view that when regulation forces business to outsource epistemic responsibility to other organiza-tions, epistemic virtues are in danger. Credit rating is used here as an example. If governments prohibit investors from investing in bonds characterized in terms of the credit risk as estimated by officially desig-nated credit rating agencies, evaluating credit risk is no longer something that investors have reason to do themselves. This affects epistemic vir-tues. One might object that this is not very relevant as long as it does not influence investment behaviour among investors. Economists provide evidence, however, that the inflated ratings of structured debt securities contributed to a greater appetite for these products among investors.[48] Structured finance products are hard to disentangle, and without the ratings many investors would have found them too intricate to trade. Without the ratings, there would probably have been much less demand for them.

Love

Let me now turn to the virtues, love of knowledge to begin with. Outsourcing epistemic activities to credit rating agencies leads to a situation where regulated investors have little incentive themselves to probe the credit risk of securities they trade. The aggregate result of this is a decrease in epistemic activity, because absent such regulation more

[48] Pagano and Volpin, 'Credit ratings failures'.

parties would research credit risk themselves. Moreover, the methods a rating agency employs are largely unknown outside the agency. This decreases the quality of the research. Unlike the academic ideal of peer review and openness fostering informed and rational discussion, rating agencies keep their methods to themselves. This makes it more difficult to put their hypotheses to the test and is also likely to lead to an unnecessary doubling of work.

The sheer complexity of structured finance products exacerbates this. A typical mortgage-backed security comprises hundreds or thousands of mortgages with different sorts of real estate as collateral. To assess the risks of such securities, raters have to assess, among other things, the magnitude of the correlation between the risks of the underlying assets (the collateral). It matters whether, say, all real estate is from Florida or from places scattered throughout the United States. The documentation that comes with mortgage-backed securities (the *prospectuses*) generally only contains statistical information about the average underlying mortgage, not about all individual mortgages. This is not enough to determine the correlation of risk, far from it, and data have to be purchased from data providers. Credit rating agencies were not very keen on doing research here, and investors themselves had no incentive either. Not until 2007, for example, did Moody's start requesting the simplest detailed data about the borrowers of mortgages such as the loan to value ratio, the borrower's credit score, and the borrower's debt to income level. These, however, are the most important indicators of a mortgage's credit risk.[49] An additional complexity is that the credit risk of mortgage-backed securities is determined not just by the risk that borrowers will default on their mortgage (the risk that they cannot repay), but also by the risk that they will pay back too early (and that the lender earns less interest than expected). Estimating prepayment risk is, however, mathematically complex.[50]

Moreover, overwhelming evidence shows that a large majority of triple A rated structured debt had underlying loans (the things out of which the structured bonds were constructed) that barely made it to investment grade, which Efraim Benmelech and Jennifer Dlugosz aptly

---

[49] J. Mason and J. Rosner, 'Where did the risk go? How misapplied bond ratings cause mortgage backed securities and collateralized debt obligation market disruptions' (2007), papers.ssrn.com/sol3/papers.cfm?abstract_id=1027475.
[50] Agarwal et al., 'Optimal mortgage refinancing'.

describe as sheer *alchemy*, deriving as it does gilt-edged ratings out of junk bonds.[51] More empirical research has to be carried out to examine this suggestion; as it stands, however, we have some initial indications that love of knowledge was not omnipresent.

Justice

Secondly, open-mindedness and epistemic justice are hardly fostered by a regime in which regulators bestow epistemic authority on particular companies. Regulated investors are forced by law to consider the rating agencies as the official source of information concerning credit risk. This largely obviates the need to consider what other sources say. A rating above the junk bond status is the only mark of approval an investor needs. This is aggravated by the issuer-pays compensation model. Issuers pay to get their securities rated; they are effectively the sponsors of the research that credit rating agencies carry out. To see why this is unlikely to contribute to epistemic virtue, consider pharmaceutical research. Drug studies funded by pharmaceutical companies show a systematic bias towards outcomes that favour the sponsor. Sponsored research is more likely to report positively on tested drugs.[52] This phenomenon has not been thoroughly investigated in other industries, but a recent study by Andreas Milidonis suggests that bond ratings suffer from similar biases.[53] Milidonis investigated bond ratings for the American insurance industry, where both issuer-pays and investor-pays ratings are available. He did not directly examine whether issuer-paid agencies should be described as merely interested in currying the favours of the issuers, but he did find something that is epistemologically relevant all the same. Changes in ratings from issuer-paid agencies follow upon changes in ratings from investor-paid agencies; in other terms, issuer-paid agencies are not in the epistemic vanguard.

Independent evidence bolstering this claim may be obtained from observing the ways in which credit rating agencies developed the mathematical modelling techniques that play a fundamental role in rating structured securities. (I should point out that we do not know very much

---

[51] Benmelech and Dlugosz, 'The alchemy of CDO ratings'.
[52] Lexchin et al., 'Pharmaceutical industry sponsorship' is a frequently cited meta-analysis.
[53] Milidonis, 'Compensation incentives'.

about these models because they are trade secrets, but we know enough to develop a reasonable hypothesis.) In 2004, Moody's decided to introduce a new model for particular structured debt securities. Interviews between a Bloomberg journalist and former employees reveal that rather than stemming from a desire to increase accuracy, the reason for the shift was a desire to ease ratings standards. More structured securities would receive gilt-edged ratings to please their issuers. After Moody's had split from Dun and Bradstreet it became listed on the New York Stock Exchange in 2000. From then on, concerns about profitability and shareholder interests took centre stage, and for the first time in the history of the firm senior management received compensations partly in terms of stock options.[54]

I do not wish to suggest that it is beyond dispute that gaining market share was the prime motivation underlying the revision of the rating models; the urge for reform may well have come from a realistic assessment that the traditional techniques of binomial expansion used for many structured products had become less suited to novel products having less diversified and more correlated collateral. That the new models lent themselves very nicely to doling out higher ratings attracting a new clientele, enlarging a hitherto rather small market share, does not make this suggestion very plausible, though. An unpublished study by Simi Kedia, Shivaram Rajgopal and Xing Zhou indeed suggests a strong link.[55] They discovered that after Moody's flotation on the stock market its ratings became decidedly more favourable than Standard and Poor's ratings.

Temperance

A third virtue to suffer is epistemic temperance. Philippe Jorion has pointed out that many risk management approaches have difficulties incorporating *unknown unknowns*. Examples are regulatory interventions in the form of trading restrictions or other market developments inspired by regulation, but also socio-political events or environmental

[54] K. Selig, 'Greed, negligence, or system failure? Credit agencies and the financial crisis', Case Studies in Ethics, The Kenan Institute for Ethics at Duke University, kenan.ethics.duke.edu/wp-content/uploads/2012/07/Case-Study-Greed-and-Negligence.pdf.
[55] S. Kedia, S. Rajgopal and X. Zhou, 'Did going public impair Moody's credit ratings?' (2013), papers.ssrn.com/sol3/papers.cfm?abstract_id=2343783.

catastrophes. Epistemically temperate risk assessment always leaves open the possibility that no decent quantifiable estimation of risk can be delivered for lack of information. Credit rating agencies did not, however, decide to withhold a judgement of credit risk on the grounds that the security was too complex; they did not characterize securities as *not rateable*.[56] They always rated. But where saying 'We don't know' is not a possible outcome of inquiry, organizational support for epistemic temperance is severely decreased.

Courage

Excluding the possibility of ending up with no rating at all decreases the scope for practising epistemic temperance. In a similar way, excluding certain ratings changes compromises epistemic courage. Moody's, for example, stated that it will never engage in 'unnannounced multinotch ratings changes'.[57] The firm will never radically change its mind about an issuer's creditworthiness, allegedly to avoid disturbing financial markets or risking their relationship with issuers or investors. This is an intriguing, if flawed, argument. Epistemologists discuss whether one might adopt certain beliefs or hold on to certain beliefs for practical rather than epistemic reasons. Is it acceptable that I adopt a belief that, say, someone was killed accidentally rather than murdered if this avoids the riots that may result from bringing the murderer to justice? And if so, is it morally justifiable to do so on such grounds? This case may be difficult, and when ratings changes may lead to riots or even to wars, the agencies are certainly in an unenviable position. The answer to the questions, however, is easy to give if their motivation stems from concerns about the risk of losing their clients. One needs epistemic courage to downgrade an issuer when one's business depends on the issuer's willingness to pay the business.

Generosity

Finally, I turn to other-regarding virtues. Regulation has led to a situation where the need for genuine communication between the senders

---

[56] Diomande et al., 'Public credit rating agency'. Jorion, 'Lessons from the credit crisis'.
[57] Quoted by Dooley, 'Overhaul ratings process'.

and recipients of information has almost entirely disappeared. Agencies endowed with official epistemic authority that are paid by the issuers of the securities rather than the investors have little in the way of motivation to obtain feedback from the end users of their ratings, very much unlike the predecessors of the credit rating agencies, the credit reporting agencies. Moreover, the credit rating agencies may find it difficult to imagine what it means for investors not to understand the rating. The rating being only the letter combination it is (and regulation being quite clear about what that requires), what topics are there for them to discuss? A lack of generosity and interlucency, however, may be discerned in the fact that investors do not respond to ratings in the way they would rationally be expected to do if ratings had a completely unequivocal meaning. A fair amount of evidence indicates that investors respond asymmetrically to ratings changes. Most studies find that upgrades have no effects, but downgrades do.[58] Several theories are in the frame for an explanation of this phenomenon. Downgrades are more informative than upgrades if raters search more intensely for 'bad news' or if issuers provide 'good news' more readily themselves.[59] Others have suggested that investors respond to downgrades more than is rationally warranted.[60] The correct explanation need not detain us here. The fact is that raters do not interpret ratings literally as expressions of default probability.

To reiterate a point made earlier, it is true that around 2005 ample documentation was available showing that ratings were not comparable across asset classes, but time and again the rating agencies insisted that their models provided uniform rating measures. Standard and Poor's stated in 2007 that

[o]ur ratings represent a uniform measure of credit quality globally and across all types of debt instruments. In other words, an 'AAA' rated corporate bond should exhibit the same degree of credit quality as an 'AAA' rated securitized issue.[61]

Moody's and Fitch made similar claims. But as we saw, historical data reveal a very different story, making a rating of Baa from Moody's for

---

[58] Gonzales et al., 'Market dynamics'.
[59] Jorion and Zhang, 'Information effects'.
[60] Dichev and Piotroski, 'Bond ratings changes'.
[61] Quoted by Pagano and Volpin, 'Credit ratings failures', 207.

structured bonds more than ten times as likely to default as a corporate bond.[62]

Testimony

This conclusion is strengthened once we turn to *testimonial* knowledge. Within the theory of knowledge, two sources of knowledge and justification are distinguished. The most obvious source is perception. I know that I am sitting in front of my computer because I see that I am. Much of our knowledge, however, does not come to us through our senses. That sharks are dangerous and that Beethoven and Hegel were born in the same year I learned from other people. This kind of knowledge is called *testimonial knowledge* or *knowledge by testimony*. It is the sort of knowledge gained by reading books, asking experts, hiring consultants, listening to parents and teachers.

For testimony to be an acceptable ground for belief it has to be trustworthy, and it has to be perceived as trustworthy. But there are various kinds of obstacles to perceived trustworthiness. The most obvious obstacle arises when sources of testimony employ substandard belief formation policies. A source that does not possess genuine knowledge about a matter (owing to its not having carried out investigations in epistemically virtuous ways, for example) cannot help anyone to gain knowledge about it. Credit rating agencies using substandard research methodologies are therefore not trustworthy.

Another obstacle arises when the recipient fails to *perceive* the trustworthiness of the source. Sometimes this is caused by the recipient's being overly sceptical. Suppose that an unsubstantiated prejudice leads me to refuse to believe whatever analysts or raters tell me. Then I never trust their evidence and judgements, reliable though they may be. But in the case of the rating agencies, a more likely cause of a failure to establish a perception of trustworthiness is that the agencies are not particularly generous with information about the methodologies that underlie their ratings. To perceive an individual or organization as a trustworthy source of knowledge about a particular topic, one needs evidence of expertise. One needs indications that the source is knowledgeable in the relevant domain. That is quite difficult in the case of credit rating agencies. It is hard to find out exactly how agencies arrive at their ratings.

---

[62] Strier, 'Rating the raters'.

Little information is available about the people responsible for a rating, their expertise and their rating success record. A great deal of the mathematical and computational methodology is hidden from our eyes. Rating agencies compete, among other things, on their methods, and consequently they consider their methods to be trade secrets. But if we cannot determine an organization's trustworthiness, we should not trust it. Regulators can see that they cannot see how raters arrive at their judgements. Unlike methods in medicine, what credit ratings do to determine credit risk is something at which we can only guess. In such a case trust should be suspended. We simply lack the information we need to place our trust rationally. Outsourcing epistemic responsibility to parties that keep their methods secret flies in the face of common sense.

This is not the only reason why outsourcing epistemic responsibility is misplaced. Determining trustworthiness is also made difficult by a second phenomenon: *ratings shopping*. The idea is simple. An issuer of a security applies for a rating to each of the three main agencies, compares the ratings and decides to publish the most favourable rating only. Ratings shopping, it seems, occurred quite widely. In an interview with *Wall Street Journal* reporters in 2008, Brian Clarkson, Moody's Investors Service President at the time, said: 'There is a lot of rating shopping that goes on ... What the market doesn't know is who's seen certain transactions but wasn't hired to rate those deals.'[63] Even if rating agencies were entirely epistemically virtuous, ratings shopping would likely lead to inflated and untrustworthy ratings. Given sufficiently complex securities, even experts exercising epistemic virtue will disagree about credit risk. We find this in health care too, when medical specialists disagree in 'hard cases'. The public can accommodate differences whenever all views are made public and are easily accessible. In the case of ratings, however, issuers only publish the most favourable rating.[64] This makes it impossible to compare ratings and as a result this leads to a systematic upward bias among published ratings.[65]

That regulators allow issuers of securities to shop for the best rating is, besides the methodologies being trade secrets, a serious obstacle to perceiving the trustworthiness of the agencies. A third argument against

---

[63] Quoted by Lucchetti, 'Bond-rating shifts'.
[64] Skreta and Veldkamp, 'Ratings shopping'.
[65] Griffin et al., 'Rating shopping or catering?'

outsourcing epistemic responsibility to rating agencies is their issuer-pays compensation model. Several authors view this as a source of conflicts of interest. This may be too harsh. A conflict of interest arises, in John Boatright's useful definition, whenever 'a personal or institutional interest interferes with the ability of an individual or institution to act in the interest of another party, when the individual or institution has an ethical or legal obligation to act in that other party's interest'.[66] For there to be a conflict of interest in the present situation, credit rating agencies must have an ethical or legal obligation to act in the interest of potential buyers and sellers of rated securities. It is not clear, however, that such obligations exist. Legal obligations they probably do not have. Courts grant them First Amendment protection of free speech. Ethical obligations may follow from the fact that particular investors are by regulation forced to rely on the ratings, but the analogy with astrology, together with the fact that these investors have the resources to research credit risks themselves, does not make this immediately evident. It is hardly plausible to maintain that when a government decides to enforce laws obligating pilots to rely on their horoscopes instead of meteorologists when it comes to weather forecasts, this places ethical obligations on the astrologers writing the columns.

Even though the case for conflicts of interest is weak, the issuer-pays model still endangers trustworthiness because it leads to a situation where the interests of the testimonial sources of information and the recipients of information are not aligned. A recent article by John Griffin, Jordan Nickerson and Dragon Yongjun Tang addresses this issue under the heading of *ratings catering*.[67] Ratings catering is related to ratings shopping in the sense that it happens when issuers request ratings from more than one rater, but it differs in that the assumption of rater honesty is lifted. In the model of Griffin and his colleagues, rating agencies adjust initial ratings upwardly (and dishonestly) when the issuer shows that competing agencies have rated the security more favourably. The sample includes 716 collateralized triple A debt obligation tranches that were rated by Standard and Poor's and Moody's in the period 1997–2007, so the usual caveats apply. The conclusion is that a lenient Standard and Poor's is likely to be followed by Moody's,

---

[66] Boatright, 'Conflicts of interest', 219.
[67] Griffin et al., 'Rating shopping or catering?'

and vice versa. This is a consequence of the issuer-pays compensation scheme, which decreases the ratings' trustworthiness.

Outsourcing epistemic responsibility

We outsource epistemic responsibility more often than not. We rely on the judgements of accountants, legal advisers, doctors, consumer organizations and so on because we do not have the time, the skills and the money to do all the research ourselves. This is not wrong; testimony is an acceptable source of knowledge. But we should choose our sources of testimony with care, and when governments designate particular sources as the sole or ultimate source of information this is only justified if their trustworthiness is beyond rational doubt. It may be that some of the effects of outsourcing epistemic responsibility surveyed in this chapter are not as easy to detect as I suggest. Without knowledge of empirical research, for instance, it is not immediately evident that there is a mismatch between what ratings are claimed to express and how investors interpret them. No theoretical sophistication is needed, however, to see that one should not place trust in organizations whose methods one cannot check and compare with others.

The argument I develop here may still appear convoluted. It may be objected that I have only shown that outsourcing epistemic responsibility does not foster virtue without making the claim that this is wrong. It may be said that although legislators have made investors increasingly dependent on the published 'opinions' of credit rating agencies, one may object to blaming the agencies for a lack of generosity and interlucency. I think one can always defend the *prima facie* case in favour of epistemic virtue. Unless one is playing a game, and nothing else, one's claims should be backed by evidence obtained in epistemically virtuous ways. This applies to astrologers too. But I have a different aim. In Chapter 5 we saw that companies can help their employees practise epistemic virtue along three lines: virtue-to-function matching, organizational support for virtue and organizational remedies against vice. This chapter shows in a sense that, like companies, governments too influence epistemic virtues among citizens and companies. I did not develop a theory of how regulators can encourage epistemic virtue because the strategies they can use are very similar to the strategies that companies have at their disposal. Rather I looked at credit rating agencies. They have received ample criticism from commentators, and I do not wish to downplay the relevance of the critiques. But if we are to blame a party in the first place, our blame should be directed at those governments that forced investors to outsource credit risk assessment to companies of which the trustworthiness is hard to determine.

Summary

Chapters 3 and 5 looked into a number of conceptual and empirical issues to do with individual and corporate epistemic virtues. I defended a view of epistemic virtue as instrumentally contributing to *eudaimonia*, and I analysed corporate epistemic virtue in terms of virtue-to-function matching, organizational support for virtue and organizational remedies against vice. The present chapter continued this investigation by looking at other-regarding epistemic virtues. But it also did something else. Not until the present chapter had I asked the question of whether we can normatively expect individuals or corporations to care for virtue. It may be quite nice to possess epistemic virtues as a character trait, but what could be the justification of requiring others to practise them, or to criticize others if they do not? It is true that from a job description epistemic virtues often readily follow; the minimal normative assumptions about the purpose of a firm, however, barred the derivation of corporate virtue from corporate purpose. If a corporation is merely a nexus of voluntary contracts of equal and freely consenting people, what reason could we have to blame them for running their business foolishly? They will soon be pushed out of the market by more virtuous competitors.

It is important to see that the applicability of the theory of epistemic virtues – and corporate epistemic virtues in particular – is independent of the minimal assumptions I prefer to make. Many commentators hold on to the view that banks are there to safeguard the private property of citizens and to foster their freedom in line with recent ethical ideals of corporate citizenship. If that is your view, then the case for epistemic virtue in finance is made more quickly.

But not too quickly. In this chapter I defended the claim that even though the credit rating agencies were far removed from being exemplars of epistemic virtue, government regulators deserve even harsher epistemic criticism. The analogy between horoscopes and credit ratings was perhaps a bit over the top. Yet it did serve the purpose of showing the recklessness of outsourcing epistemic responsibility to corporations whose testimonial trustworthiness regulators had not cared to examine sufficiently thoroughly. The more general lesson was that for it to be safe to outsource epistemic responsibility to a corporation with regard to a particular subject matter (assessment of credit risk in the case of the rating agencies), we have to ascertain two things. First, of course, that the corporation is a trustworthy source of information concerning the subject matter. Part of the task here is also to establish that the corporation adds any informational value in the first place. This is all very plain, but already at this stage the regulators failed to pass the test. But secondly, we must be confident that outsourcing responsibility to the corporation will not have undesirable side effects. In the case of the rating agencies, outsourcing responsibility did have such effects, one of which was a lower than desirable degree of epistemic competition: when three American agencies are in the position to give official stamp of approval assessments of credit risk, what incentive would you have to assess these risks for yourself?

Next to the credit rating agencies and the stock market analysts discussed earlier in this chapter, accountants are viewed as an important source of information to financial markets. Recent and not so recent accounting scandals may suggest that outsourcing epistemic responsibility to accountants should meet similar scepticism. The next chapter examines this question. By doing so, it also places other-regarding epistemic virtues – the main theme of this chapter – in a more constructive light.

8 | *Case study III: scores and accounts*

Accountancy is a puzzling profession with a puzzling remuneration model. Like physicians, lawyers and engineers, accountants enjoy the right to self-regulation and monopoly because of the specific function they fulfil in society. Unlike physicians, lawyers and engineers, however, accountants are not paid by the beneficiaries of their services. Physicians are paid by the people whose health they improve. But accountants are paid by the firms they audit rather than by those in whose interest it is to have objective information about the audited firms: banks, shareholders, governments and many others. The author of a survey article wryly likens this to what would happen if butchers hired their own meat inspectors, 'with the power to set their prices and fire [their inspectors] if they do not like the inspection reports issued'.[1]

It would at first appear that accountancy and credit rating are in the same boat. But unlike raters, accountants see themselves as members of a profession; and within accountancy, professional codes of conduct are meant to offer a solution to the puzzle, albeit one of which the success is as yet undecided. Many other solutions have been put forward, including government auditing, auditing tax and having large investors pay the fees of the accounting houses.[2] Although some of the alternative regimes have a lot to recommend them, most are so radical as to make it impossible to predict the consequences of their implementation. Instead of proposing yet another remuneration model, the idea that underlies this chapter is to proffer a solution that, inspired by the theory of epistemic virtues, takes it as given that accountants are paid by the firms they audit despite the firms not being the primary beneficiaries of the accountants' services. I develop a view of auditing according to which corporate management and accountants jointly form an epistemic agent whose task it is to provide information about the firm's

---

[1] Armstrong, 'Ethical issues in accounting', 155.
[2] Armstrong, 'Ethical issues in accounting' briefly summarizes the debate.

annual performance. Accountants, in this model, play the role, not of providing information, but of providing justification, where the term is used in the epistemological sense we encountered in Chapter 2. I show that professional codes of conduct can be seen as exhortations to epistemic virtue. A brief case study drawn from work by Matthew Gill among chartered accountants in the City of London concludes the chapter, showing the pertinence of other-regarding epistemic virtues.

The case study of Madoff and Markopolos illustrated one aspect of the theory of corporate epistemic virtues, namely, how accurate virtue-to-function matching helps employees to do the work that their role in business requires. The present case study likewise examines one instance of other-regarding virtue, the theme broached in the previous chapter. The argument developed there was mainly negative, its conclusion being that overreliance on the financial industry's cultivating other-regarding virtues easily leads to unjustifiable outsourcing of epistemic responsibility. This negative conclusion may arouse the feeling that other-regarding epistemic virtues are less important than self-regarding epistemic virtues, despite the fact that I emphasized the relevance of other-regarding epistemic virtues in earlier chapters. Examining other-regarding epistemic virtues within the accountancy profession should allay this feeling. It defends the thesis that other-regarding epistemic virtues are a defining element of the accountancy profession.

Professional accountants

Accountancy is a profession. But what is a profession? And what is the role of professional codes of conduct? I briefly survey the current view of professionalism here. The starting point of most analyses is that members of a profession fulfil a particular and clearly described function in society, as lawyers contribute to a well-functioning legal system and medical practitioners provide adequate health care.[3] A precondition for carrying out this function leads to another characteristic of professions. Members of a profession must possess a high degree of practical expertise. They possess high levels of specific and often practical skills and knowledge that require intense, lifelong training to

---

[3] The present treatment owes much to Cowton, 'The ethics challenge' and Duska et al., *Accounting ethics*.

maintain. Thirdly, professionals are not supposed to act out of merely selfish concerns.[4] Expectations of a decent salary may be among the reasons why someone decided to study medicine and continues to practise; the non-selfishness condition requires, however, the daily motivation of professionals to be serving their clients and society at large. Fourthly, in contrast to the sale of cars, in which everyone is allowed to engage, auditing firms or working in the operating theatre is restricted to those holding a professional licence. Professions are monopolies. Governments grant the right to monopoly to the professional body, and typically defend this as the best or most likely way to ensure that the profession best fulfils its social function. With the right to monopoly comes the right to self-regulation, defended in similar ways. What counts as the educational background of a professional (or what counts, in the medical profession, as the treatment of a particular disease) is best left to the profession itself to decide, or so the argument goes. Finally, even though professional membership is a precondition for working as a professional, membership as such is a wholly voluntary affair. No one is forced to become a physician or a lawyer. When graduates of professional schools become members of a profession, they assume a number of additional duties (professional obligations) that are typically enshrined in professional codes of conduct. They contain principles and rules that go beyond the ethical obligations every human being has, and these principles and rules are binding on all professionals. But professionals assume these additional duties voluntarily, and any professional dissatisfied with the obligations can leave the profession.

What about accountancy? Accountants carry out an increasingly diverse range of tasks. The activities of chartered accountants or certified public accountants are consultancy, tax advice, auditing, and reviewing financial statements. Management accountants work as executives or in middle management functions of business corporations. Their work requires the setting of performance targets (budgeting) as well as internal reporting and auditing. Management accountants also work on external reporting, providing information to shareholders and other interested parties. Government accountants, in turn, work for various tax offices. It is tempting to conclude from this multifarious list that accountancy is not a genuine profession. That probably goes too far. First of all,

---

[4] This point is especially emphasized by Duska et al., *Accounting ethics*, 66–79.

accountancy does require a body of specific, highly technical knowledge and expertise, which needs continuous refinement and updating. Accountancy does, moreover, enjoy the right to monopoly and self-regulation, membership is voluntary, and detailed special obligations are described in professional codes of conduct. Finally, many accounting graduates find employment outside of public accounting. Yet the attest function of audit and review forms a solid basis to build a case for considering accountancy a profession. Adequate mechanisms of audit and review are an essential precondition for business in capitalist societies. Firms produce balance sheets and information about their profits and losses and their cash flows, but readers of these documents should not take them seriously until accountants have audited them.

It is important to dwell a little more on the non-selfishness condition. Ronald Duska, Brenda Duska and Julie Ragatz claim that accountancy satisfies this condition.[5] They believe that accountants have a social responsibility, among other things, to give precedence to the client's interests above their own. Thus they seem to suggest identifying the accountants' clients as the prime beneficiaries of social responsibility. By doing that, however, they risk missing the connection between the non-selfishness condition and the social function of the accountancy profession, which is not so much to serve their clients but, by auditing their clients, to serve their clients' stakeholders. Non-selfishness, as the authors view it, rules out such practices as gaining extra income by doing more work than necessary. Promoting your own interests at your clients' expense certainly sits ill with the non-selfishness condition. What makes these acts wrong is not, however, related to the specific social function of accountancy, and must rather be explained in terms of breach of contract, which any business ought to avoid. The non-selfishness condition, by contrast, rules out such practices as conspiring with the client against the general public. (Duska and his co-authors do recognize the need for accountants to serve the social aim, but the difference from my account is that I interpret non-selfishness as a condition on how they treat their beneficiaries rather than their clients.) Practices euphemistically described as *creative accountancy* and *earnings management* may be in the selfish interests of client and accountant alike, but they harm the interests of the true beneficiaries of the auditing services because they do not provide them with an accurate picture of

---

[5] Duska et al., *Accounting ethics*.

the firm's financial situation. Accountants should not, in the words of the late Lord Justice Harman, be 'witch-doctors ... willing to turn their hands to any kind of magic'.[6]

Joint epistemic agents

Recall the epistemological concept of justification. I explained in Chapter 2 that knowledge requires justification. For me to know that there is a bittern at the bottom of the garden requires not only that I believe it, but also possess justification for believing that there is one. Moreover, the belief has to be true. What justification amounts to is a matter of intense debate, which should not occupy us here. Suffice it to say that justification requires that one possesses evidence for one's belief.

The starting point of the analysis is that accountants and corporate management together form an epistemic agent that is a source of testimonial knowledge about the performance of the firm. Within this joint epistemic agent, management and accountants do not play the same role. The accountancy firm produces a report, which is typically a standard statement of one or two pages appended to the company's annual report. As such, the firm's accountants do not themselves provide a large amount of information or data. It is the task of corporate management to provide most of the data about assets, liabilities and capital, profits and losses, cash flows and so on. Rather than producing information, the accountants produce justification. To be sure, this is a to-and-fro process in which accountants suggest changes to the report if no adequate information can be produced to back the statements made by corporate management; management tries to provide the desired information so as to avert making changes. But if management does not provide the desired information and does not accept the suggested changes, accountants must ultimately resign from the task in order not to give an unjustified stamp of approval. What accountants in the end have to do is to ensure that the annual report provides readers with justified claims about the firm's state of affairs.

The closeness of provider and justifier of information is doubtless a locus of potential moral friction, and several scholars have argued that

---

[6] Quoted in Sampson, *The new anatomy of Britain*, 503.

it is the main aim of professional codes of conduct to mitigate this. More generally, they see accountancy as fraught with *moral hazard*. Moral hazard arises when an *agent* is acting on behalf of a *principal*. An example of a principal–agent relationship arises in retirement planning when a portfolio manager invests money on behalf of the clients (future pensioners, that is). The clients have little opportunity to examine the quality of the investment decisions that the manager takes. Only when they reach retirement age will they know how well the manager did. Managers, however, may be too lazy or egoistic to do what is best for their clients, or they may just be incompetent. The principal–agent relationship, then, allows for the possibility that professionals provide lower quality services to their clients and beneficiaries than they get paid for, without the clients being able to monitor the professionals' work.

At least in part, professional codes are meant to diminish moral hazard.[7] I should say, however, that the effectiveness of codes is disputed: codes are no guarantee against scandals; codes frequently lack adequate enforcement mechanisms; codes do not always play a role in actual professional decision making; codes, in particular in accountancy, tend to focus disproportionately on quality assurance rather than public interest; codes are sometimes seen as not going far enough in protecting the public interest; codes in some cases even plainly prescribe unethical rather than ethical behaviour; and codes mostly focus on rules rather than moral character.[8] Research into codes of conduct does not unequivocally discredit codes on all counts, though. Some scholars emphasize, for example, that though codes offer no panacea for moral hazard problems, they do build a professional identity by making explicit what public function the profession is supposed to fulfil, what kinds of activities and obligations this function entails, and what demands from society and clients are justified and unjustified.[9] This is certainly the view that underlies codes in accountancy. Consequently, if the view of accountants as justifiers is plausible, we should expect epistemic themes to be running through accountancy codes.

---

[7] See, e.g., Jamal and Bowie, 'Theoretical considerations'.
[8] Ragatz and Duska, 'Financial codes of ethics'. Lere and Gaumnitz, 'The impact of codes'. Jamal and Bowie, 'Theoretical considerations'. Velayutham, 'The accounting profession's code'. Adams et al., 'Confidentiality decisions'. Melé, 'Ethical education in accounting'.
[9] Frankel, 'Professional codes'.

Codes of conduct

To test this hypothesis I use an analysis of codes of conduct by Julie Ragatz and Ronald Duska, who examined a number of codes in the financial services industry, accountancy codes among them, and showed that much of the content of these codes can be reduced to the following seven values: integrity, objectivity, competence, fairness, confidentiality, professionalism and diligence.[10] I use their analysis to show that most of these values place stringent demands on epistemic virtue.

The conditions of professionalism and diligence are perhaps the most difficult to interpret in epistemic terms. Professionalism compels an accountant to uphold the reputation of the profession and to abstain from acting in ways that may discredit it. This includes such things as treating clients with respect and consideration, and continuously striving to improve the quality of the services the profession renders. Professionalism is not as such an epistemic condition, albeit epistemically virtuous accountants deliver better professional services. The same is true of diligence. Epistemic virtues help an accountant to work in a diligent, careful and efficient manner, but diligence as such is not an epistemic concept.

But the remaining five conditions do have clear epistemic interpretations. Let me start with integrity. Ragatz and Duska take the example of the code of the American Institute of Certified Public Accountants (AICPA), which requires its members to perform their professional responsibilities with the highest sense of integrity, with integrity probably being a 'super virtue' incorporating not only the ideas of autonomy and wholeness, but also trustworthiness.[11] Trustworthiness is an essential precondition for accountants to be justifiers. Without the audit report, a firm's stakeholders have much less reason to believe what the annual report claims, in particular when they suspect corporate management may not have resisted the temptation to provide a more positive view of the firm than is warranted.

Accountants, moreover, are required to remain objective and independent, and to avoid conflicts of interest. These are important ideals for professionals guided by a non-selfishness condition. Accountants encounter two sorts of risk. One arises from conflicts of interest.

[10] Ragatz and Duska, 'Financial codes of ethics'.
[11] Ragatz and Duska, 'Financial codes of ethics'.

Accountants serving two masters endanger the objectivity of their verdicts. Another risk is epistemic. When accountants are unrealistically optimistic or overly confident about their judgements and fail to show sufficient epistemic sobriety, objectivity and independence are endangered. An example may be drawn from research on sampling methods that accountants use to retrieve documents and data from their clients. Accountants as justifiers may feel that they can draw conclusions after they have done some *haphazard* sampling, so called because they determine the sample themselves rather than by means of randomization tools. This often results in unconscious selection biases decreasing the objectivity or the independence of their views, suggesting that epistemically temperate accountants will select their samples more randomly.[12]

The condition of competence, in turn, is secured by requiring both mastery of a common stock of professional knowledge and by lifelong learning programmes. AICPA accountants have to earn credits lest their professional membership be discontinued. To be sure, competence as such is not an epistemic virtue. In order to be aware of the need for continuous education, however, accountants must have a clear sense of their own fallibility; and this requires epistemic humility. They have to be aware of the limitations of their knowledge and skills. I should point out, however, that humility does not always come easily. Accountants tend to overestimate their own knowledge and skills as well as the knowledge and skills of their subordinates.[13]

The fairness requirement deals with situations in which accountants come under conflicting pressures from clients, credit grantors, employers, governments, investors and others depending on the accountant's justificatory role. The solution recommended by the AICPA code is that members acknowledge that the interests of the various people and organizations are best served when they fulfil their responsibility to the public. It is important to note that whereas the view from epistemic virtue concurs with the previous three elements of the professional codes (integrity, objectivity, competence), the element of fairness must be re-evaluated. Satisfying the interests of the stakeholders may conflict with the exercise of epistemic virtues when the interests of the accountant's client (the audited firm) are given too much weight. I provide an illustration of this phenomenon shortly when I sketch a case in which a

---

[12] Hall et al., 'Haphazard sampling'. Power, 'From common sense to expertise'.
[13] Kennedy and Peecher, 'Judging auditors' technical knowledge'.

concrete accounting decision (capitalizing an item on the balance sheet of a firm) is in the interest of the client, but goes against the interests of the prime beneficiaries of the annual report, the firm's bank in particular. This does not show that fairness is always at odds with a concern for epistemic integrity, nor does it show that epistemic justice or fairness should be jeopardized in certain cases. It does show, however, that fairness should not lead accountants to give *equal* weight to the interests of their clients and the beneficiaries of their services. Accountants work *with* clients, but *for* beneficiaries such as banks or shareholders. In accountancy, client interests do not come first.

The final requirement prescribes that no public accountant must disclose confidential information without the client's consent. This requirement has come under pressure in the wake of the global financial crisis.[14] The joint epistemic agent model of accountancy does not support a radical departure from it, though. Confidentiality is essential if corporate management and accountants are to form a joint epistemic agent. Management fearing that their accountants may publicize information at will hesitates to share sensitive information with the accountants; and it is exactly the function of the accountants to ensure that sensitive information is reflected in the accounts. Management may disagree with the accountants about the way the information should be reflected in the accounts, and if the disagreement persists, accountants should have the courage to consider ending the relation, as a last resort, to show they are no longer willing to play their justificatory role. Disclosure of confidential information is not, however, compatible with their justificatory role.

To summarize, the view proposed here regards corporate management and accountants as jointly forming an epistemic agent where corporate management provides data and the accountants justification. Neither the company nor the accountants can on their own provide trustworthy testimonial evidence about the company. People will not generally perceive the company as making a true and reliable statement because it has a potential interest in presenting a partial picture of its performance. Reasonably sceptical investors and other interested parties have reason to be suspicious of the firm's statements and to hold open the possibility that the figures have been embellished in ways serving the firm's ends but not necessarily those of the readers. Without

---

[14] Association of Chartered Certified Accountants, 'Audit under fire'.

corporate management, however, the accountants do not have access to the relevant data. On their own, accountants are incapable of delivering much information.

Expectation gap

The model of the joint epistemic agent explains how corporate management and accountants together form a source of testimonial knowledge for banks, shareholders, governments and others. It is clear, however, that this epistemic agent is not always going to be a *trustworthy* source. The critical accounting literature has demonstrated that when a society increasingly resorts to auditing (teaching audits, clinical audits, environmental audits, etc.) the risk is that auditing will bring us nothing more than what Michael Power has rightly and famously called 'shallow rituals of verification'.[15] It has also been argued that the statutory monopoly enjoyed by accountants does not mesh well with the very limited duty of care required of them.[16] More generally, the standard view of accountancy as merely providing an opinion of the firm's financial performance has come under scrutiny in this literature on such grounds as that

[c]ontrary to the profession's preferences, the meaning of audit has been associated with fraud detection, warning of impending bankruptcy, guaranteeing the accuracy of information and financial soundness, etc.[17]

The general public, in other words, expects more from an audit than a mere opinion on the financial statements of a firm. The standard view and the view of the general public diverge into what is called the *expectation gap*.[18]

While I do not dispute the usefulness of toughening fraud detection and the like, fraud detectors are hardly going to be very effective as long as they are paid by the firms they have to monitor. It is also difficult to see whether bridging the expectation gap is compatible with the confidentiality requirement. Informing the general public about an impending bankruptcy may well clash with this condition. Perhaps there are

---

[15] Power, *The audit society*, 123.   [16] Cousins et al., *Auditors*.
[17] Sikka et al., 'Expectations gap', 303.
[18] Liggio, 'The expectation gap'. An empirical study is Porter, 'The audit expectation-performance gap'.

good reasons to change the status quo compensation scheme altogether, but as long as we stick to it we have to find different ways to train accountants about the general public's expectations. Accountants who are sensitive to their true beneficiaries keenly realize that the firms they audit are *not* their primary intended audience. As far as accountants can meet public demands, they must meet them; but where they realize that they are unable to meet them, they must make clear that the public demands placed on them are excessive. Accountants with a concern for their audience practise other-regarding epistemic virtues and emphasize, for example, that the confidentiality requirement prohibits them from communicating sensitive information and that their role is the more limited one of providing justification.

Accounting options

Accountants not only benefit from exercising other-regarding virtues when they communicate with intended audiences – which they do only every so often. Other-regarding virtues are also important in the daily dealings accountants have with colleagues and clients. A case study by Matthew Gill offers highly instructive insights here.[19] Gill interviewed chartered accountants working in large practices in the City of London about a hypothetical case involving the accounts of Champion Chicken, a supplier of ready-cooked rotisserie chickens to supermarkets in Britain.

This is the case. Champion Chicken is negotiating new terms of credit as it has faced some financial difficulties recently. Its bank, London Money, has requested it to cut costs and has helped finance a more efficient roasting facility. There were some start-up problems with this facility, however, which resulted in a loss of £0.4 million worth of overcooked and unusable chickens. The management of the firm capitalized the item together with the other costs related to the facility, but did not mention the overcooked chickens in the account's draft version (the preliminary version that a firm's finance department prepares for the accountant). (It is unimportant here what *capitalization* precisely amounts to; some details will be provided shortly.) The accountants were asked what they would do if they were Champion Chicken's accountant. Some of their responses vividly illustrate the potential consequences of a lack of concern for other-regarding epistemic virtues.

---

[19] Gill, *Accountants' truth*.

To begin with let us survey the accounting options they have. The overcooked chickens can be capitalized (as management suggests) on the balance sheet; and they can treated as an expense on the profit and loss account. Typical things to capitalize are so-called *current and fixed assets* such as cash, inventory, buildings and equipment. Deducting the current liabilities from the assets provides insight into the value of the firm. By contrast, typical things to treat as an expense on a profit and loss account are costs incurred to produce, market, distribute or sell things. Deducting these costs from the turnover the firm has generated gives insight into the profits the firm has made. The question is, in other words, whether the overcooked chicken should be seen as diminishing the firm's assets or diminishing its profit.

Capitalized, the overcooked chickens are incorporated in the costs of a fixed asset (the roasting facility) and will be depreciated over a certain time period, just as computer equipment depreciates over time. The overcooked chickens do not, then, count as an expense on the profit and loss account, and therefore do not influence Champion Chicken's profit. The other option is that the overcooked chickens appear as an expense. Here several variations are possible. The item may be subsumed under cost of sales in the profit and loss account, or it may appear on a separate line devoted to exceptional costs; and, if taken as an exceptional item, it may appear before or after operating profit. It is unimportant for current purposes what the rationale behind these options is. What is important is to realize, however, that Gill designed the scenario in such a way that capitalization leads to a profit of £0.2 million, and expensing to a loss of £0.2 million, and that depending on the way the item was expensed, it leads to differences in operating profit (profit before deduction of interest and tax) and/or cost of sales.

It is patently obvious that capitalizing is attractive for Champion Chicken because its bargaining power over London Money, their bank, is stronger if it can show profit. But capitalizing is also rather dubious. It is as though one buys a lorry and adds it to one's firm's assets (which is understandable) together with the costs incurred to get it fixed after it was damaged in an accident (which is not so understandable). When answering Gill's question of what he would do if he happened to be the company's accountant, one respondent noted that management's decision to capitalize the item is acceptable if accompanied by exhaustive verbal explanations in the report. He suggested, however, that Champion Chicken 'sell it up a bit' to the readers of the annual report and add the 'reasonably open disclosure' that the facility item simply includes 'half a million pounds of stock used to guarantee that the best quality stuff comes out'.[20]

Epistemically generous accountants do not suggest 'selling it up a bit'. They rather try to steer the middle course between explaining all the details of the facility and 'selling it up a bit'. They are acutely aware of the fact that the prime beneficiary of their work is not Champion Chicken or its management, but London Money, among others. Epistemic generosity does not require complete disclosure. Apart from the fact that full disclosure is impracticable because it makes the annual report much longer, generous accountants acknowledge that Champion Chicken has no obligation to incriminate itself. But the 'reasonably open disclosure' suggested by Gill's respondent lands the accountant at the other extreme. Rather than suggesting ways to 'sell it up', epistemically generous accountants keep the beneficiaries in mind and require more information to be included about the causes of the losses in order to justify capitalizing the item, if they approve of capitalization in the first place.

Only one of Gill's respondents was so astute as to conjecture that the overcooked chickens betoken a 'fundamentally wrong' process of financial control, and he explicitly considered the possibility that Champion Chicken might be trying to hide theft, fraud or mismanagement.[21] As the discussion of the expectation gap revealed, the beneficiaries of the information expect accountants to investigate the plausibility of exactly this kind of explanation, and to keep in mind that, irrespective of whether an item is capitalized or expensed, it is important to explain the costs a firm has incurred, especially when an atypical item is capitalized or when an exceptional item appears in the accounts. Such a form of curiosity was rather scarce, Gill observed.

Although Gill found that most respondents rejected management's decision to capitalize the overcooked chickens, their decisions to expense them were again largely guided by the interests of Champion Chicken rather than the prime beneficiaries of the accounts, the bank. One particularly problematic lack of other-regarding virtue is the following:

You've got to manage the expectations of [London Money] and demonstrate to them, by way of … sufficient disclosure in the accounts, that this is a

---

[20] Gill, *Accountants' truth*, 43.   [21] Gill, *Accountants' truth*, 46.

one-off cost. And you know, you could say, 'and during the year, four hundred thousand of stock was written off due to initial,' I don't know quite how you'd say it without making it sound horrendous, but 'initial production runs and blah blah blah' [*sic*].[22]

Gill captures the spirit of this and similar responses in the following way. He notes that most accountants wish to 'get the numbers right', which for most means expensing the item. All the same he observes that his respondents are willing to act as a 'business advisor to recommend that the events to which [the] numbers relate be interpreted in words on the same page'.[23] It is in this process of interpretation that accountants give greater weight to the client's interests than to the real beneficiaries of the information. This lack of sensitivity towards the prime audience shows a lack of other-regarding epistemic virtues. Accountancy codes contain numerous principles and rules encouraging accountants to act virtuously. As we have seen, these requirements are largely concerned with self-regarding virtues. While accountants cannot play their role of justifiers adequately if they do not practise epistemic courage, temperance, justice and other virtues, the upshot of this case study has been that for accountants to fully address the needs of their beneficiaries, accountants should also nurture other-regarding virtues.

[22] Gill, *Accountants' truth*, 48 [23] Gill, *Accountants' truth*, 49.

Conclusion

In Martin Scorsese's *The Wolf of Wall Street*, Mark Hanna initiates novice Jordan Belfort over lunch into the rites of brokering, the profession Belfort has recently joined. Belfort's illusions are quickly dispelled. Brokers know as little about the stock market as their clients. 'You know what *fugazi* is?', Hanna asks. Belfort knows the slang. '*Fugazi*. It's fake.' That is how Hanna explains the trade. Brokers do not work for their clients. Their aim is to pocket the commissions.

The scene is as hilarious as it is worrying. What are these people doing if they are only interested in getting rich? Their excessive desire to become rich is certainly disgraceful. What worries me more, however, is their acknowledgement of incompetence – or better, the fact that there seems to be no need for competence on Wall Street in the first place. That we pay people whose sole motive is to become rich is something we may resent. That we pay people for faking services is utterly disturbing. I am afraid the dialogue would hardly fit any other sector better than finance. Doctors, lawyers, carpenters, architects, fishermen, engineers – imagine them describing their work as *fugazi*, their expertise as fake, their skills as useless. You will not be able to do that. But our imagination effortlessly populates the financial services industry solely with egoistic buzzards.

In the course of this book we have seen that this is not entirely groundless. There are serious questions to be asked about the informational value provided by credit rating agencies or stock market analysts. Regulators have shown little interest in uncovering financial crime. Clients did not bother to look into the terms of their mortgages. Loan officers are often more interested in their own career prospects than in monitoring their clients. At the same time it cannot be denied, however, that banks, insurance companies and pension funds deliver services that we need, but that are hard or impossible for individuals to obtain without professional assistance. It is likely that my amateur portfolio of shares will occasionally beat the results of professionals, for mere statistical reasons. On the stock market I may be as good as any 'professional' – *fugazi*, nothing more. But unless I am rich enough to shoulder the risks, I desperately need health insurance. The same holds for a bank account and retirement plan. We just cannot do without finance, and we cannot do it ourselves.

The simple view, according to which finance practitioners work with complex concepts and use impenetrable jargon only to obfuscate the absence of any serious intellectual inquiry, is dangerous for two reasons. First, as I have just said, a lot of intellectual work is needed if a bank or insurance company is to do well what it has to do. Secondly, because the simple view is so easily set aside as a caricature, one might forget that the extent to which it is true is perhaps greater than one might think. I am sure that the simple view is at the back of the minds of quite a few people working for supervisory authorities around the world. You will not, however, find them actually treating finance correspondingly. In the end, regulators do not really believe the simple view when they regulate, and we do not believe the simple view when we take out insurance or save money in a bank account.

This book has made a start at investigating the applications of epistemic ethics to finance. Most virtue epistemologists have advocated views of epistemic virtue that emphasize the intrinsic value of gaining knowledge, wisdom and understanding. This has led to enormous progress in epistemology and ethics, and the present book could not have been written had these theories not been developed over the past two or three decades. Most people in finance are not very interested in such intrinsically valuable epistemic goods most of the time, though. One contribution of this book is to have shown that this is not the end of epistemic virtue. It is rather the beginning.

The book's conclusions can be summed up in the following two claims, paralleling the remarks from the previous paragraphs. First, if a particular practice in finance has true informational value, epistemic virtues are called for. We have seen that epistemic virtues are indispensable for clients if they are to be more effective decision makers who assume responsibility for meeting their needs and satisfying their desires, in line with the argument for liberty that has figured in the background of the book. I have shown that financial due diligence is unlikely to work in the hands of people who lack epistemic courage, sobriety, open-mindedness and an inexhaustible degree of inquisitiveness or love of knowledge. At the corporate level, corporate epistemic virtues are needed. Managers must hire employees who have the epistemic virtues required by the job; they have to match virtues to functions. Managers, moreover, must provide organizational support for the practice of virtue. If your job requires you to weigh ingredients carefully and accurately, you need a pair of scales and sufficient time to use them, and you need colleagues who do not poke fun at your precision but recognize your scalesmanship as instrumental to the firm's goals. And if individual virtue cannot be developed further or is just plain absent, managers must introduce clever strategies to remedy vice. We have seen some examples of this, including an intricate probabilistic rotation scheme among loan officers that countered their tendency to monitor the creditworthiness of their clients in epistemically unsoberminded ways.

Secondly, however, we must also acknowledge that recommending epistemic virtue is sometimes totally senseless. We should not recommend epistemic virtue where knowledge has little chance of being produced. Astrology was the pet example. In finance, we must ask ourselves whether the world is going to be better if stock market analysts or credit raters embrace temperance and other epistemic virtues. I believe the answer is negative. This has important practical repercussions. I have argued that regulators should avoid outsourcing epistemic responsibility to sources of knowledge that do not deserve our trust. Policymakers turning credit rating agencies into official spokespeople of credit risk do not do what they should do.

This book can only be the beginning of an attempt at interdisciplinary research on epistemic virtue. An awful lot still has to be done to develop its ideas further. Philosophers and behavioural researchers have to team up. Following the Groningen style, which resists armchair navel-gazing as much as unreflectively frivolous experimentation performed in isolation from conceptual research, one way to progress is to return to the common roots of philosophy and the social sciences. This is not to deny the importance of decent experimental and conceptual work, but I think the most revealing ways to make sense of the world around us combine philosophical and empirical research.

A research agenda? Although I am quite confident that most of the links I have forged between epistemic virtue and social scientific research are plausible, we need to know much more. So far I have only been able to make use of research findings the relevance of which to epistemic virtue theory was accidental. The research had not been carried out with virtue epistemological questions in mind. Rather than sketching an agenda let me give a brief example of how I think we should proceed. It shows how philosophical questions stimulate new empirical research.

In Chapter 3 I discussed the concept of financial literacy. People are financially literate to the extent that they know the difference between bonds and shares, real and nominal value, simple and compound interest, and more. Research into financial literacy is claimed to have great social relevance. The more people know, the better their decisions are. Or so it seems. I agree that this claim is plausible. But there is hardly any empirical evidence for it. Why?

I think the obvious reason is that empirical researchers hesitate to address an issue that is normative through and through. What is it that determines whether someone's decisions are 'better'? Social scientists become uneasy and move on to more neutral or descriptive terrains, which is a shame. Philosophers can help. They can show how to analyse normative concepts that social scientists can subsequently operationalize. This is what we need to understand what 'better' financial planning means. This is also what we need to deepen our understanding of a host of things discussed in this book. Some examples are, at the individual level: racism and sexism among loan officers; at the corporate level: the relation between individual dishonesty and corporate epistemic injustice; at the regulatory level: the dangers of outsourcing epistemic responsibility. Epistemic virtues do not offer a foolproof all-in warranty against false or incomplete beliefs and other forms of epistemic mishap. Cases illustrating this fact abound. We looked into the Financial Services Authority's failures to communicate with British citizens in understandable ways, and we saw that even fully virtuous citizens were likely to misunderstand the authority's explanation of the difference between defined-contribution and defined-benefit retirement plans. Yet epistemic virtue certainly helps.

Glossary

Argument for liberty an argument backing various policies of deregulation, liberalization and privatization on the grounds that this would lead to increased personal responsibility and preference satisfaction

Belief perseverance a bias making people stick to their beliefs even when they are confronted with important counterevidence

Bond a loan to a company (*corporate bond*) or country (*government bond*)

Chief executive officer (CEO) the managing director of a firm, its most prominent director

Chief financial officer (CFO) the financial director of a firm

Confirmation bias the tendency to interpret as evidence for the views one holds what is actually counterevidence

Consequentialism an approach defining normative concepts (e.g., virtues) in terms of properties of the consequences of actions

Corporate virtue a virtue possessed by a corporate entity by means of *virtue-to-function matching*, *organizational support for virtue* and *organizational remedies against vice*

Courage the virtue enabling one to perform investigative actions bearing a certain amount of risk when they are necessary for gaining knowledge that one needs

Credit rating agency an agency such as Standard and Poor's, Moody's or Fitch that assesses *credit risk*, which is the risk that issuers of corporate bonds, government bonds and structured finance securities (e.g., mortgage-backed securities) will not repay their loans

Decision situation a situation of choice faced by an agent, determined by a set of available actions with consequences of varying likelihood, over which the agent has preferences and beliefs

Deontology an approach to normative ethics in which the concept of duty is central

Disbelief one disbelieves a proposition if one believes that its negation is true

Doxastic stance an attitude towards a proposition of belief, disbelief or suspension of belief

Epistemic action an action consisting of inquiry concerning some proposition leading to evidence justifying the adoption of a correct belief concerning the proposition

Epistemic virtue an acquired character trait motivating and enabling its possessor to gain instrumentally valuable knowledge

Eudaimonia the 'good life'

Financial due diligence a process to determine the potential risks of investments using qualitative methods (e.g., screening) and quantitative methods (models from financial mathematics)

Generosity the virtue to share knowledge freely, but not in ways that unjustifiably harm one's own interests; the primary example of an other-regarding virtue

Hubris a particular instance of lack of humility

Humility the virtue to defer inquiry to others when their level of relevant knowledge is higher, but not to hesitate to claim epistemic authority when justified

Instrumental epistemic value the view that knowledge is valuable in so far as it helps people to reach goals

Interlucency the virtue of contributing to maximally successful communication by signalling one's understanding to the speakers (if one is a hearer) and by tracking the understanding of the hearers (if one is a speaker)

Intrinsic value the value that something has for its own sake

Investigative action an action performed to gain information or evidence concerning a particular subject matter; one of the three elements of an epistemic action

Joint epistemic agent management and accountants form a joint epistemic agent in which the former provides information and the latter justification

Justice the virtue not to ignore relevant bits of evidence in one's inquiry, to be open-minded

Justification knowledge differs from mere true belief in that when one knows something one bases one's belief on evidence that justifies one's belief

Love of knowledge the virtue that makes one investigate and adopt beliefs only when one possesses evidence justifying it; inquisitiveness, curiosity

Monitoring the process of continuously assessing and sometimes influencing the credit risk of a bank's clients (active or passive monitoring by loan officers) or issuers of securities (by credit rating agencies)

Mortgage-backed security a structured finance product consisting of hundreds or thousands of mortgages structured along particular tranches with allegedly different risk characteristics

Option a contract to buy or sell a particular asset (e.g., shares) at or before a given point in time (the *expiration date* of the option) at a given price (the *exercise* or *strike price*)

Other-regarding virtues virtues of which the beneficiaries are other people

Overconfidence a tendency to have a greater degree of confidence in one's own capacities than justified

Securities bonds, shares, options and so on

Self-regarding virtues virtues of which the possessor is the main beneficiary

Share a piece of equity or ownership of a firm, also called *stock*

Suspension of belief one suspends belief regarding a particular statement if one neither believes nor disbelieves it

Temperance the virtue to devote the right degree of investigation to a particular issue, not to hasten to a conclusion, but not to be too reticent to reach a conclusion at all either

Testimony in contrast to, for instance, knowledge obtained by perception, one gains testimonial knowledge when trustworthy others inform one about a particular subject matter

References

Adams, B., F. Malone and W. James, 'Confidentiality decisions: the reasoning process of CPAs in resolving ethical dilemmas', *Journal of Business Ethics*, 14 (1995), 1015–20.

Adams, R. *A theory of virtue: excellence in being for the good* (Oxford University Press, 2006).

Advisory Committee on the Future of Banks in the Netherlands, 'Restoring trust' (2009).

Agarwal, S., J. Driscoll and D. Laibson, 'Optimal mortgage refinancing: a closed-form solution', *Journal of Money, Credit and Banking*, 45 (2013), 591–622.

Aikin, S. and J. Clanton, 'Developing group-deliberative virtues', *Journal of Applied Philosophy*, 27 (2010), 409–24.

Alchian, A. and H. Demsetz, 'Production, information costs, and economic organization', *American Economic Review*, 62 (1972), 777–95.

Aldridge, A., '*Habitus* and cultural capital in the field of personal finance', *Sociological Review*, 46 (1998), 1–23.

Altman, E., 'Financial ratios, discriminant analysis and the prediction of corporate bankruptcy', *Journal of Finance*, 23 (1968), 589–609.

Alzola, M., 'Character and environment: the status of virtues in organizations', *Journal of Business Ethics*, 78 (2008), 343–57.

Anderson, M. and P. Escher, *The MBA oath: setting a higher standard for business leaders* (New York: Portfolio, 2010).

Andrews, E., *Busted: life inside the great mortgage meltdown* (New York: Norton, 2009).

Anonymous, 'Confessions of a risk manager', *The Economist*, 7 August 2008.

Anscombe, G., 'Modern moral philosophy', *Philosophy*, 33 (1958), 1–16.

Aquinas, *Summa theologiae* (Cambridge University Press, 2006).

Argandoña, A., 'Beyond contracts: love in firms', *Journal of Business Ethics*, 99 (2011), 77–85.

Argote, L. and P. Ingram, 'Knowledge transfer: a basis for competitive advantage in firms', *Organizational Behavior and Human Decision Processes*, 82 (2000), 150–69.

Aristotle, *Ethica Nicomachea* (Oxford University Press, 1963).

206

Arjoon, S., 'Virtue theory as a dynamic theory of business', *Journal of Business Ethics*, 28 (2000), 159–78.

Armour, J., H. Hansmann and R. Kraakman, 'What is corporate law?' in R. Kraakman, J. Armour, P. Davies, et al. (eds.), *The anatomy of corporate law: a comparative and functional approach* (Oxford University Press, 2009), pp. 1–34.

Armstrong, J., 'Evidence-based advertising: an application to persuasion', *International Journal of Advertising*, 30 (2011), 743–67.

Armstrong, M., 'Ethical issues in accounting', in N. Bowie (ed.), *The Blackwell guide to business ethics* (Oxford: Blackwell, 2002), pp. 145–64.

Artzrouni, M., 'The mathematics of Ponzi schemes', *Mathematical Social Sciences*, 58 (2009), 190–201.

Arvedlund, E., *Madoff: the man who stole $65 billion* (London: Penguin, 2009).

Association of Chartered Certified Accountants, 'Audit under fire' (London, 2011).

Atkins, R., 'A look back at financial innovations', *Financial Times*, 14 May 2013.

Austin, J., *How to do things with words* (Oxford University Press, 1962).

Babutsidze, Z., 'How do consumers make choices? A survey of evidence', *Journal of Economic Surveys*, 26 (2012), 752–62.

Baehr, J., *The inquiring mind: on intellectual virtues and virtue epistemology* (Oxford University Press, 2011).

Baertschi, B., 'Defeating the argument from hubris', *Bioethics*, 27 (2013), 435–41.

Baker, J., 'Virtue and behavior', *Review of Social Economy*, 67 (2009), 3–24.

Bannier, C. and C. Hirsch, 'The economic function of credit rating agencies: what does the watchlist tell us?', *Journal of Banking and Finance*, 34 (2010), 3037–49.

Barber, B. and T. Odean, 'Online investors: do the slow die first?', *Review of Financial Studies*, 15 (2002), 455–87.

Barberis, N. and R. Thaler, 'A survey of behavioral finance', in G. Constantinides, M. Harris and R. Stulz (eds.), *Handbook of the economics of finance, vol. 1* (Amsterdam: Elsevier, 2003), pp. 1053–128.

Bar-Gill, O., 'The law, economics and psychology of subprime mortgage contracts', *Cornell Law Review*, 94 (2009), 1073–152.

Battaly, H., 'Teaching intellectual virtues', *Teaching Philosophy*, 29 (2006), 191–222.

'Epistemic self-indulgence', *Metaphilosophy*, 41 (2010), 214–34.

Bazerman, M. and A. Tenbrunsel, *Blind spots: why we fail to do what's right and what to do about it* (Princeton University Press, 2011).

Beadle, R. and K. Knight, 'Virtue and meaningful work', *Business Ethics Quarterly*, 22 (2012), 433–50.

Behrman, J., O. Mitchell, C. Soo and D. Bravo, 'How financial literacy affects household wealth accumulation', *American Economic Review*, 102 (2012), 300–4.

Benmelech, E. and J. Dlugosz, 'The alchemy of CDO credit ratings', *Journal of Monetary Economics*, 56 (2009), 617–34.

Berkowitz, M., 'The Madoff paradox: American Jewish sage, savior and thief', *Journal of American Studies*, 46 (2012), 189–202.

Bernard, C. and P. Boyle, 'Mr. Madoff's amazing returns: an analysis of the split-strike conversion strategy', *Journal of Derivatives*, 17 (2009), 62–76.

Bertland, A., 'Virtue ethics in business and the capabilities approach', *Journal of Business Ethics*, 84 (2009), 25–32.

Bhattacharya, U., A. Hackethal, S. Kaesler, B. Loos and S. Meyer, 'Is unbiased financial advice to retail investors sufficient? Answers from a large field study', *Review of Financial Studies*, 25 (2012), 975–1032.

Bhojraj, S. and P. Sengupta, 'Effect of corporate governance on bond ratings and yields: the role of institutional investors and outside directors', *Journal of Business*, 76 (2003), 455–75.

Blodget, H., 'Fairfield Greenwich Group's amazing due diligence practices', *Business Insider*, 1 April 2009.

Blumenberg, H., 'Neugierde und Wissenstrieb: Supplemente zur *curiositas*', *Archiv für Begriffsgeschichte*, 14 (1970), 7–40.

Boatright, J., 'Conflicts of interest in financial services', *Business and Society Review*, 105 (2000), 201–19.

Bolton, P., M. Brunnermeier and L. Veldkamp, 'Leadership, coordination and corporate culture', *Review of Economic Studies*, 80 (2013), 512–37.

Boot, A., T. Milbourn and A. Schmeits, 'Credit ratings as coordination mechanisms', *Review of Financial Studies*, 19 (2006), 81–118.

Brigley, S., 'Business ethics in context: researching with case studies', *Journal of Business Ethics*, 14 (1995), 219–26.

Brown, A., *Personal responsibility: why it matters* (London: Continuum, 2009).

de Bruin, B., 'We and the plural subject', *Philosophy of the Social Sciences*, 39 (2009), 235–59.

Buchanan, A., 'Philosophy and public policy: a role for social moral epistemology', *Journal of Applied Philosophy*, 26 (2009), 276–90.

Buie, E. and D. Yeske, 'Evidence-based financial planning: to learn … like a CFP', *Journal of Financial Planning*, 11 (2011), 38–43.

Bull, C. and A. Adam, 'Virtue ethics and customer relationship management: towards a more holistic approach for the development of "best practice"', *Business Ethics: A European Review*, 20 (2011), 121–30.

Burton, D., *Financial services and the consumer* (London: Routledge, 1994).

Calvet, L., J. Campbell and P. Sodini, 'Measuring the financial sophistication of households', *American Economic Review*, 99 (2009), 393–8.

Carlin, B. and D. Robinson, 'Financial education and timely decision support: lessons from Junior Achievement', *American Economic Review*, 102 (2012), 305–8.

Carlson, L., J. Rossiter and D. Stewart, 'Comments on J. Scott Armstrong's "Evidence-based advertising: an application to persuasion"', *International Journal of Advertising*, 30 (2011), 769–94.

Carroll, A., *Business and society: ethics and stakeholder management* (Cincinnati: South-Western, 1989).

'The pyramid of corporate social responsibility: towards the moral management of organizational stakeholders', *Business Horizon*, July–August (1991), 39–48.

Carter, S., *Reflections of an affirmative action baby* (New York: Basic Books, 1991).

Charlier, S., K. Brown and S. Rynes, 'Teaching evidence-based management in MBA programs: what evidence is there?', *Academy of Management Learning and Education*, 10 (2011), 222–36.

Cheng, P., Z. Lin and Y. Liu, 'Do women pay more for mortgages?', *Journal of Real Estate Finance and Economics*, 43 (2011), 423–40.

Cloyd, C. and B. Spilker, 'The influence of client preferences on tax professionals' search for judicial precedents, subsequent judgments and recommendations', *Accounting Review*, 74 (1999), 299–322.

Coady, D., *What to believe now: applying epistemology to contemporary issues* (Chichester: Wiley, 2012).

Coase, R., 'The nature of the firm', *Economica*, 4 (1937), 386–405.

Code, L., 'Toward a "responsibilist" epistemology', *Philosophy and Phenomenological Research*, 45 (1984), 29–50.

Cohan, W., *Money and power: how Goldman Sachs came to rule the world* (London: Allen Lane, 2011).

Cohen, D. and L. Prusak, *In good company: how social capital makes organizations work* (Harvard Business School Press, 2001).

Cohen, N., 'FSA rejects call for pension compensation', *Financial Times*, 3 August 2004.

Collins, J., 'Financial advice: a substitute for financial literacy?', *Financial Services Review*, 21 (2012), 307–22.

Conner, M. and J. Clawson, *Creating a learning culture: strategy, technology, and practice* (Cambridge University Press, 2004).

Courchane, M., B. Surette and P. Zorn, 'Subprime borrowers: mortgage transitions and outcomes', *Journal of Real Estate Finance and Economics*, 29 (2004), 365–92.

Cousins, J., A. Mitchell, P. Sikka and H. Willmott, *Auditors: holding the public to ransom* (Basildon, Essex: Association for Accountancy and Business Affairs, 1998).

Cowton, C. 'Accounting and the ethics challenge: re-membering the professional body', *Accounting and Business Research*, 39 (2009), 177–89.

Crane, A. and D. Matten, *Business ethics* (Oxford University Press, 2003).

Culp, C. and J. Heaton, 'Returns, risk and financial due diligence', in J. Boatright (ed.), *Finance ethics: critical issues in theory and practice* (Hoboken: Wiley, 2010), pp. 85–101.

Curzer, H., 'Aristotle's account of the virtue of temperance in Nicomachean Ethics III. 10–11', *Journal of the History of Philosophy*, 35 (1997), 5–25.
'Aristotle's much maligned *megalopsychos*', *Australasian Journal of Philosophy*, 62 (2006), 131–51.

Dalkir, K., *Knowledge management in theory and practice* (Amsterdam: Elsevier, 2005).

Dedman, B., 'The color of money', *Atlanta Journal Constitution*, 1–5 May 1988.

DeMartino, G., *The economist's oath: on the need for and content of professional economic ethics* (Oxford University Press, 2011).

Deshmukh, S., A. Goel and K. Howe, 'CEO overconfidence and dividend policy', *Journal of Financial Intermediation*, 22 (2013), 440–63.

Dichev, I. and J. Piotroski, 'The long-run stock returns following bond ratings changes', *Journal of Finance*, 54 (2001), 173–203.

Dietz, R. and D. Haurin, 'The social and private micro-level consequences of homeownership', *Journal of Urban Economics*, 54 (2003), 401–50.

Diomande, M., J. Heintz and R. Pollin, 'Why US financial markets need a public credit rating agency', *Economist's Voice*, 6 (2009), 1–4.

Disney, R. and J. Gathergood, 'Financial literacy and consumer credit portfolios', *Journal of Banking and Finance*, 37 (2013), 2246–54.

Dobos, N., 'Neoliberalism: is this the end?', in N. Dobos, C. Barry and T. Pogge (eds.), *Global financial crisis: the ethical issues* (Basingstoke: Palgrave, 2011), pp. 63–81.

Dobson, J., 'Alasdair MacIntyre's Aristotelian business ethics: a critique', *Journal of Business Ethics*, 86 (2009), 43–50.

Dombret, A. and H. Kern, *European retail banks: an endangered species? Survival strategies for the future* (Weinheim: Wiley, 2003).

Dooley, J., 'Moody's investors service cuts back on plan to overhaul ratings process', *Wall Street Journal*, 13 February 2002.

Doris, J., 'Persons, situations and virtue ethics', *Noûs*, 32 (1998), 504–30.

Drake, M. and J. Schlachter, 'A virtue-ethics analysis of supply chain collaboration', *Journal of Business Ethics*, 82 (2008), 851–64.

Driskill, R. 'Deconstructing the argument for free trade: a case study of the role of economists in policy debates,' *Economics and Philosophy*, 28 (2012), 1–30.

Driver, J., *Uneasy virtue* (Cambridge University Press, 2001).
  'The conflation of moral and epistemic virtue', *Metaphilosophy*, 34 (2003), 367–83.
Duménil, G. and D. Lévy, *The crisis of neoliberalism* (Harvard University Press, 2010).
Duska, R., B. Duska and J. Ragatz, *Accounting Ethics* (Hoboken: Wiley, 2011).
Easterbrook, F. and D. Fischel, *The economic structure of corporate law* (Harvard University Press, 1991).
Eenkhoorn, P. and J. Graafland, 'Lying in business: insights from Hannah Arendt's "Lying in politics"', *Business Ethics: A European Review*, 20 (2011), 359–74.
Elkington, J., *Cannibals with forks: the triple bottom line of 21st century business* (Chichester: Capstone, 1997).
Engel, K. and P. McCoy, 'A tale of three markets: the law and economics of predatory mortgage lending', *Texas Law Review*, 80 (2002), 1255–382.
Feldman, S., 'The high cost of not finding information', *KMWorld*, 13 (2004).
Ferguson, N., *The ascent of money* (London: Allen Lane, 2008).
Fitzpatrick, W., *Teleology and the norms of nature* (New York: Garland, 2000).
Fontrodona, J. and A. Sison, 'The nature of the firm, agency theory and shareholder theory: a critique from philosophical anthropology', *Journal of Business Ethics*, 66 (2006), 33–42.
Foster, D. and H. Young, 'Gaming performance fees by portfolio managers', *Quarterly Journal of Economics*, 125 (2010), 1435–58.
Francis, J., 'What do we know about audit quality?', *The British Accounting Review*, 36 (2004), 345–68.
Frankel, M., 'Professional codes: why, how, and with what impact?', *Journal of Business Ethics*, 8 (1989), 109–15.
Freeman, R., *Strategic management: a stakeholder approach* (Boston: Pitman, 1984).
Freeman, R., L. Stewart and B. Moriarty, 'Teaching business ethics in the age of Madoff', *Change*, November–December (2009), 37–42.
French, P., 'The corporation as a moral person', *American Philosophical Quarterly*, 16 (1979), 207–15.
  Corporate ethics (Fort Worth: Harcourt, 1995).
Fricker, M., *Epistemic injustice: ethics and the power of knowing* (Oxford University Press, 2009).
  'Group testimony? The making of a collective good informant', *Philosophy and Phenomenological Research*, 84 (2012), 249–76.
Friedman, B., *Human values and the design of computer technology* (Cambridge University Press, 1997).

Friedman, D., K. Pommerenke, R. Lukose, G. Milam and B. Huberman, 'Searching for the sunk cost fallacy', *Experiencing Economics*, 10 (2007), 79–104.

Friedman, M., 'The social responsibility of business is to increase its profits', *New York Times Magazine*, 13 September 1970.

Galbraith, J., *The new industrial state* (London: Hamish Hamilton, 1967).

Garland, H., 'Throwing good money after bad: the effect of sunk costs on the decision to escalate commitment to an ongoing project', *Journal of Applied Psychology*, 75 (1990), 728–31.

Gaurav, S., S. Cole and J. Tobacman, 'Marketing complex financial products in emerging markets: evidence from rainfall insurance in India', *Journal of Marketing Research*, 48 (2011), 150–62.

Gaus, G., 'The idea and ideal of capitalism', in G. Brenkert (ed.), *Oxford handbook of business ethics* (Oxford University Press, 2009), pp. 73–99.

Gerardi, K., L. Goette and S. Meier, 'Numerical ability predicts mortgage default', *PNAS*, 110 (2013), 11267–71.

Gerring, J., *Case study research: principles and practices* (Cambridge University Press, 2007).

Gershoff, A. and G. Johar, 'Do you know me? Consumer calibration of friends' knowledge', *Journal of Consumer Research*, 32 (2006), 496–503.

Gert, B., 'Moral arrogance and moral theories', *Philosophical Issues*, 15 (2005), 368–85.

Gervais, S., J. Heaton and T. Odean, 'Overconfidence, compensation contrasts and capital budgeting', *Journal of Finance*, 66 (2011), 1735–77.

Gettier, E., 'Is justified true belief knowledge?' *Analysis*, 23 (1963), 121–3

Gibson, K., *Ethics and business: an introduction* (Cambridge University Press, 2007).

Gilbert, M., *On social facts* (London: Routledge, 1988).
    Sociality and responsibility: new essays in plural subject theory (Lanham: Rowman and Littlefield, 1999).
    A theory of political obligation: membership, commitment, and the bonds of society (Oxford University Press, 2008).

Gill, M., *Accountants' truth: knowledge and ethics in the financial world* (Oxford University Press, 2009).

Goel, A. and Thakor, A., 'Overconfidence, CEO selection and corporate governance', *Journal of Finance*, 63 (2008), 2737–84.

Goff, S., 'FSA critical of lenders' advice to borrowers', *Financial Times*, 9 January 2007.

Gomez-Lobo, A., 'The ergon inference', *Phronesis*, 34 (1989), 170–84.

Gonzales, F., R. Haas, R. Johannes, M. Persson, L. Toledo, R. Violi, C. Zins and M. Wieland, 'Market dynamics associated with credit ratings: a literature review', *Banque de France Financial Stability Review*, 4 (2004), 53–76.

Gowri, A., 'On corporate virtue', *Journal of Business Ethics*, 70 (2007), 391–400.

Graafland, J., 'Do markets crowd out virtues? An Aristotelian framework', *Journal of Business Ethics*, 91 (2009), 1–19.

Grandori, A., *Epistemic economics and organization: forms of rationality and governance for a wiser economy* (London: Routledge, 2013).

Grant, R., 'Toward a knowledge-based theory of the firm', *Strategic Management Journal*, 17 (1996), 109–22.

Gray, J., 'Bi-polar: college education and loans to small businesses headed by black females', *Review of Black Political Economics*, 39 (2012), 361–71.

Griffin, J., J. Nickerson and D. Tang, 'Rating shopping or catering? An examination of the response to competitive pressure for CDO credit ratings', *Review of Financial Studies*, 27 (2013), 2270–310.

Griffin, M., 'Motivating reflective citizens: deliberative democracy and the internal deliberative virtues', *Journal of Value Inquiry*, 45 (2011), 175–86.

Griffith-Jones, S., J. Ocampo and J. Stiglitz (eds.), *Time for a visible hand: lessons from the 2008 world financial crisis* (Oxford University Press, 2010).

Hackethal, A., M. Haliassos and T. Japelli, 'Financial advisors: a case of babysitters?', *Journal of Banking and Finance*, 36 (2012), 509–24.

Hall, T., A. Higson, B. Pierce, K. Price and C. Skousen, 'Haphazard sampling: selection biases induced by control listing properties and the estimation consequences of these biases', *Behavioral Research in Accounting*, 24 (2012), 101–32.

Harman, G., 'No character or personality', *Business Ethics Quarterly*, 13 (2003), 87–94.

Harris, H., 'Is love a management virtue?', *Business and Professional Ethics Journal*, 21 (2002), 173–84.

Hartman, E., 'Virtue, profit and the separation thesis: an Aristotelian view', *Journal of Business Ethics*, 99 (2011), 5–17.

Harvey, D., *A brief history of neoliberalism* (Oxford University Press, 2005).

Hayward, M., D. Shepherd and D. Griffin, 'A hubris theory of entrepreneurship', *Management Science*, 52 (2006), 160–72.

Heaton, J., 'Managerial optimism and corporate finance', *Financial Management*, 31 (2002), 33–45.

Hekman, D., K. Aquino, B. Owens, T. Mitchell, P. Schilpzand and K. Leavitt, 'An examination of whether and how racial and gender biases influence customer satisfaction', *Academy of Management Journal*, 53 (2010), 238–64.

Henriques, D., *The wizard of lies: Bernie Madoff and the death of trust* (Oxford: Oneworld, 2011).

Hertzberg, A., J. Liberti and D. Paravisini, 'Information and incentives inside the firm: evidence from loan officer rotation', *Journal of Finance*, 65 (2010), 795–828.

Hirshleifer, D., A. Low and S. Teoh, 'Are overconfident CEOs better innovators?', *Journal of Finance*, 67 (2012), 1457–98.

HM Treasury, 'Reforming financial markets' (London: The Stationery Office, 2009).

van der Hoven, J. and N. Manders-Huits, 'Value-sensitive design', in J. Olsen, S. Pedersen and V. Hendricks (eds.), *A companion to the philosophy of technology* (Oxford: Blackwell, 2010), pp. 477–80.

Howard, D., J. Gazmararian and R. Parker, 'The impact of low health literacy on the medical costs of Medicare managed care enrollees', *American Journal of Medicine*, 118 (2005), 371–7.

Hume, D., *A treatise of human nature: being an attempt to introduce the experimental method of reasoning into moral subjects* (London: Noon, 1739).

Hurka, T., 'Why value autonomy?', *Social Theory and Practice*, 13 (1987), 361–82.

Huse, M., *Boards, governance and value creation: the human side of corporate governance* (Cambridge University Press, 2007).

Hynes, R. and E. Posner, 'The law and economics of consumer finance', *American Law and Economic Review*, 4 (2002), 168–207.

Jamal, K. and N. Bowie, 'Theoretical considerations for a meaningful code of professional ethics', *Journal of Business Ethics*, 14 (1995), 703–14.

Jankélévitch, V., *Traité des vertus* (Paris: Bordas, 1949).

Jensen, M., *A theory of the firm: governance, residual claims, and organizational forms* (Harvard University Press, 2003).

Jensen, M. and W. Meckling, 'Theory of the firm: managerial behaviour, agency costs and ownership structure', *Journal of Financial Economics*, 3 (1976), 305–60.

Jones, T., 'Ethical decision making by individuals in organizations: an issue-contingent model', *Academy of Management Review*, 16 (1991), 366–95.

Jones, T., 'Numerous ways to be an open-minded organization: a reply to Lahroodi', *Social Epistemology*, 21 (2007), 439–48.

Jones, T. and W. Felps, 'Shareholder wealth maximization and social welfare: a utilitarian critique', *Business Ethics Quarterly*, 23 (2013), 207–38.

Jorion, P., 'Risk management lessons from the credit crisis', *European Financial Management*, 15 (2009), 923–33.

Jorion, P. and G. Zhang, 'Information effects of bond rating changes: the role of the rating prior to the announcement', *Journal of Fixed Income*, 16 (2007), 45–59.

Kahneman, D., *Thinking, fast and slow* (London: Allen Lane, 2011).

Kaplan, R., 'What to ask the person in the mirror', *Harvard Business Review*, 85 (2007), 86–95.

Katrougalos, G., 'Constitutional limitations of privatization in the USA and Europe: a theoretical and comparative perspective', *Constellations*, 7 (2010), 407–25.

Kawall, J., 'Other-regarding epistemic virtues', *Ratio*, 15 (2002), 257–75.

Kennedy, J. and M. Peecher, 'Judging auditors' technical knowledge', *Journal of Accounting Research*, 35 (1997), 279–93.

Klein, N., *The shock doctrine: the rise of disaster capitalism* (New York: Metropolitan Books, 2007).

Kvanvig, J., *The value of knowledge and the pursuit of understanding* (Cambridge University Press, 2003).

Lahroodi, R., 'Collective epistemic virtues', *Social Epistemology*, 21 (2012), 281–97.

Lawrence, D., F. Pazzaglia and K. Sonpar, 'The introduction of a non-traditional and aggressive approach to banking: the risks of hubris', *Journal of Business Ethics*, 102 (2011), 401–20.

Lehrer, E., 'Subprime borrowers: not innocents / Pro: willing customers', *Bloomberg Businessweek*, 12 December 2007.

Leininger, W., 'The fatal vote: Berlin versus Bonn', *Finanzarchiv*, 50 (1993), 1–20.

Lere, J. and B. Gaumnitz, 'The impact of codes of ethics on decision making: some insights from information economics', *Journal of Business Ethics*, 48 (2003), 365–79.

Lewis, D., *Convention: a philosophical study* (Harvard University Press, 1969).

Lexchin, J., L. Bero, B. Djulbegovic and O. Clark, 'Pharmaceutical industry sponsorship and research outcome and quality: systematic review', *Business Management Journal*, 326 (2003), 1–10.

Liebowitz, J. and C. Yan, 'Knowledge sharing proficiencies: the key to knowledge management', in C. Holsapple (ed.), *Handbook on knowledge management, vol. 1* (Berlin: Springer, 2004), pp. 409–24.

Liggio, C., 'The expectation gap: the accountant's Waterloo', *Journal of Contemporary Business*, 3 (1974), 27–44.

Lintner, J., 'The valuation of risk assets and the selection of risky investments in stock portfolios and capital budgets', *Review of Economics and Statistics*, 47 (1965), 13–37.

List, C., 'The theory of judgment aggregation: an introductory review', *Synthese*, 187 (2012), 179–207.

Löffler, G., 'An anatomy of rating through the cycle', *Journal of Banking and Finance*, 28 (2004), 695–720.

Lorsch, J., 'Board challenges 2009', in W. Sun, J. Steward and D. Pollard (eds.), *Corporate governance and the global financial crisis: international perspectives* (Cambridge University Press, 2011), pp. 165–87.

Lucchetti, A., 'Bond-rating shifts loom in settlement', *Wall Street Journal*, 4 June 2008.

MacIntyre, A., *After virtue: a study in moral theory* (London: Duckworth, 1981).

Mäki, U., 'Economics imperialism: concepts and constraints', *Philosophy of the Social Sciences*, 39 (2009), 351–80.

Malmendier, U. and D. Shanthikumar, 'Are small investors naive about incentives?', *Journal of Financial Economics*, 85 (2007), 457–89.

Malmendier, U. and G. Tate, 'CEO overconfidence and corporate invest ment', *Journal of Finance*, 60 (2005), 2661–700.
  'Does overconfidence affect corporate investment? CEO overconfidence measures revisited', *European Financial Management*, 11 (2005), 649–59.
  'Who makes acquisitions? CEO overconfidence and the market's reaction', *Journal of Financial Economics*, 89 (2008), 20–43.

Mandell, L. and L. Schmid Klein, 'Motivation and financial literacy', *Financial Services Review*, 16 (2007), 105–16.

Manson, N. and O. O'Neill, *Rethinking informed consent in bioethics* (Cambridge University Press, 2007).

Marcum, J., 'The epistemically virtuous clinician', *Theoretical Medical Bioethics*, 30 (2009), 249–65.

Markopolos, H., *No one would listen: a true financial thriller* (Hoboken: Wiley, 2010).

Matten, D. and A. Crane, 'Corporate citizenship: toward an extended theoretical conceptualization', *Acadamy of Management Review*, 30 (2005), 166–79.

Mayer, C., K. Pence and S. Sherlund, 'The rise in mortgage defaults', *Journal of Economic Perspectives*, 23 (2009), 27–50.

Mazzucato, M., 'Towards a fairer capitalism: let's burst the 1% bubble', *Guardian*, 15 January 2013.

McCormack, L., C. Bann, J. Uhrig, N. Berkman and R. Rudd, 'Health insurance literacy of older adults', *Journal of Consumer Affairs*, 43 (2009), 223–48.

McGee, S., 'Choosing a financial advisor: who can you trust with your money?', *Guardian*, 17 October 2013.

Melé, D., 'Ethical education in accounting: integrating rules, values and virtues', *Journal of Business Ethics*, 57 (2005), 97–109.
  'Integrating ethics into management', *Journal of Business Ethics*, 78 (2008), 291–7.

Messick, D. and M. Bazerman, 'Ethical leadership and the psychology of decision making', *Sloan Management Review*, 37 (1996), 9–22.

Milidonis, A., 'Compensation incentives of credit rating agencies and predictability of changes in bond ratings and financial strength ratings', *Journal of Banking and Finance*, 37 (2013), 3716–32.

Mill, J. S., *Principles of political economy: with some of their applications to social philosophy* (London: Parker, 1848).

Miller, S., 'Social institutions', in *Stanford Encyclopedia of Philosophy* (2007). 'Korruption, kollektive Verantwortung und internationale Finanzinstitutionen', in V. Zanetti and D. Gerber (eds.), *Kollektive Verantwortung und internationale Beziehungen* (Frankfurt: Suhrkamp, 2010), pp. 185–217. *The moral foundations of social institutions: a philosophical study* (Cambridge University Press, 2010).

Mills, M., 'The discussions of ANDREIA in the Eudemian and Nicomachean Ethics', *Phronesis*, 25 (1980), 198–218.

Misra, S., 'Is conventional debriefing adequate? An ethical issue in consumer research', *Journal of the Academy of Marketing Science*, 20 (1992), 269–73.

Moloney, N., 'Financial services and markets', in R. Baldwin, M. Cave, and M. Lodge (eds.), *Oxford handbook of regulation* (Oxford University Press, 2010), pp. 437–61.

Montmarquet, J., *Epistemic virtue and doxastic responsibility* (Lanham: Rowman and Littlefield, 1993).

Moore, G., 'Corporate character: modern virtue ethics and the virtuous corporation', *Business Ethics Quarterly*, 15 (2005), 659–85. 'Re-imagining the morality of management: a modern virtue ethics approach', *Business Ethics Quarterly*, 18 (2008), 483–511.

Morgenson, G., 'Inside the Countrywide lending spree', *New York Times*, 26 August 2007.

Nash, L., *Good intentions aside: a manager's guide to resolving ethical problems* (Harvard Business School Press, 1990).

Nevicka, B., F. ten Velden, A. de Hoogh and A. van Vianen, 'Reality at odds with perceptions: narcissistic leaders and group performance', *Psychological Science*, 22 (2011), 1259–64.

Nielsen, R., 'Whistle-blowing methods for navigating within and helping reform regulatory institutions', *Journal of Business Ethics*, 112 (2013), 385–95.

Noe, T. and H. Young, 'The limits to compensation in the financial sector', in N. Morris and D. Vines (eds.), *Capital failure: rebuilding trust in financial services* (Oxford University Press, 2014), pp. 65–78.

Nonaka, I. and H. Takeuchi, *The knowledge-creating company: how the Japanese companies create the dynamics of innovation* (Oxford University Press, 1995).

Nuyen, A., 'Vanity', *Southern Journal of Philosophy*, 37 (1999), 613–27.

O'Connor, M., 'The Enron board: the perils of groupthink', *University of Cincinnati Law Review*, 71 (2003), 1233–320.

Olegario, R., *A culture of credit: embedding trust and transparency in American business* (Harvard University Press, 2006).

O'Neill, O., 'Trust, trustworthiness, and accountability', in N. Morris and D. Vines (eds.), *Capital failure: rebuilding trust in financial services* (Oxford University Press, 2014), pp. 172–89.

Osborne, A., 'Pension victims accuse government of hypocrisy', *Daily Telegraph*, 19 September 2007.

Pagano, M. and P. Volpin, 'Credit ratings failures and policy options', *Economic Policy* 25 (2010), 401–31.

Palanski, M., S. Kahai and F. Yammarino, 'Team virtues and performance: an examination of transparency, behavioral integrity and trust', *Journal of Business Ethics*, 99 (2010), 201–16.

Pauly, M., 'Changing the rules of play', *Topoi*, 24 (2005), 209–20.

Petit, V. and H. Bollaert, 'Flying too close to the sun? Hubris among CEOs and how to prevent it', *Journal of Business Ethics*, 108 (2012), 265–83.

Pflaging, J., 'Enterprise collaboration: the big payoff', *KMWorld*, 1 September 2001.

Pieper, J., *Vom Sinn der Tapferkeit* (Leipzig: Hegner, 1934).

Poon, M., 'Rating agencies', in K. Knorr Cetina and A. Preda (eds.), *Oxford handbook of the sociology of finance* (Oxford University Press, 2012), pp. 272–92.

Porter, B., 'An empirical study of the audit expectation-performance gap', *Accounting and Business Research*, 24 (1993), 49–68.

Posner, R., *Frontiers of legal theory* (Harvard University Press, 2004).

Pouivet, R., 'Moral and epistemic virtues: a Thomistic and analytical perspective', *Forum Philosophicum*, 15 (2010), 1–15.

Power, M., 'From common sense to expertise: the pre-history of audit sampling', *Accounting, Organizations and Society*, 17 (1992), 37–62.

The audit society: rituals of verification (Oxford University Press, 1999).

Powley, T. and B. Masters, 'FCA acts to head off UK interest-only mortgage crisis', *Financial Times*, 2 May 2013.

Pritchard, D., *Epistemic luck* (Oxford University Press, 2004).

'Virtue epistemology and the acquisition of knowledge', *Philosophical Explorations*, 8 (2005), 229–43.

Quiggin, J., *Zombie economics: how dead ideas still walk among us* (Princeton University Press, 2010).

Ragatz, J. and R. Duska, 'Financial codes of ethics', in J. Boatright (ed.), *Finance ethics: critical issues in theory and practice* (Hoboken: Wiley, 2010), pp. 297–323.

Rawwas, M., S. Arjoon and Y. Sidani, 'An introduction of epistemology to business ethics: a study of marketing middle-managers', *Journal of Business Ethics*, 117 (2013), 525–39.

Rest, J., *Moral development: advances in research and theory* (New York: Praeger, 1986).

Roberts, R. and J. Wood, *Intellectual virtues: an essay in regulative epistemology* (Oxford University Press, 2007).

Roberts-Witt, S., 'A "Eureka!" moment at Xerox', *PC Magazine*, 26 March 2002.

Roll, R., 'The hubris hypothesis of corporate takeovers', *Journal of Business*, 59 (1986) 197–216.

van Rooij, M., A. Lusardi and R. Alessie, 'Financial literacy and retirement planning in the Netherlands', *Journal of Economic Psychology*, 32 (2011), 593–608.

'Financial literacy and stock market participation', *Journal of Financial Economics*, 101 (2011), 449–72.

Rosen, F., 'The political context of Aristotle's categories of justice', *Phronesis*, 20 (1975), 228–40.

Russell, B., *History of western philosophy, and its connection with political and social circumstances from the earliest times to the present day* (London: Allen and Unwin, 1946).

Rutherford. M. and A. Buchholtz, 'Investigating the relationship between board characteristics and board information', *Corporate Governance*, 15 (2007), 576–84.

Ruzzene, A., 'Drawing lessons from case studies by enhancing comparability', *Philosophy of Social Sciences*, 42 (2012), 99–120.

Sampson, A., *The new anatomy of Britain* (London: Hodder and Stoughton, 1966).

Sarna, D., *History of greed: financial fraud from tulip mania to Bernie Madoff* (Hoboken: Wiley, 2010).

Scalet, S. and T. Kelly, 'The ethics of credit rating agencies: what happened and the way forward', *Journal of Business Ethics*, 111 (2012), 477–90.

Scheibehenne, B., R. Greifeneder and P. Todd, 'Can there ever be too many options? A meta-analytic review of choice overload', *Journal of Consumer Research*, 37 (2010), 409–25.

Schiffer, S., *Meaning* (Oxford University Press, 1972).

Schmid, H., D. Sirtes and M. Weber (eds.), *Collective epistemology* (Frankfurt: Ontos, 2011).

Schmittmann, S., 'Die Rolle des Chief Risk Officer unter Corporate-Governance-Gesichtspunkten', in K. Hopt (ed.), *Handbuch Corporate Governance von Banken* (Munich: Vahlen, 2011), pp. 481–92.

Schudt, K., 'Taming the corporate monster: an Aristotelian approach to corporate virtue', *Business Ethics Quarterly*, 10 (2000), 711–23.

Schwab, A., 'Epistemic humility and medical practice: translating epistemic categories into ethical obligations', *Journal of Medicine and Philosophy*, 37 (2012), 28–48.

Schwartz, B., *The paradox of choice: why more is less* (London: HarperCollins, 2004).

Searle, J., 'A classification of illocutionary acts', *Language in Society*, 5 (1976), 1–23.

Senge, P., *The fifth discipline: the art and practice of the learning organization* (New York: Doubleday Currency, 1990).

Sharpe, W., 'Capital asset prices: a theory of market equilibrium under conditions of risk', *Journal of Finance*, 19 (1964), 425–42.

Sheehy, P., 'On plural subject theory', *Journal of Social Philosophy*, 33 (2002), 377–94.

Shefrin, H., *Beyond greed and fear: understanding behavioral finance and the psychology of investing* (Harvard Business School Press, 1999).

Shiller, R., *Irrational exuberance* (Princeton University Press, 2000).

'Crisis and innovation', *Journal of Portfolio Management*, 36 (2010), 14–19.

Finance and the good society (Princeton University Press, 2012).

Sikka, P., A. Puxty, H. Willmott and C. Cooper, 'The impossibility of eliminating the expectations gap: some theory and evidence', *Critical Perspectives on Accounting*, 9 (1998), 299–330.

Silverman, D., 'Step into the office-less company', *Wall Street Journal*, 4 September 2012.

Sims, R. and J. Brinkmann, 'Enron ethics (or: culture matters more than codes)', *Journal of Business Ethics*, 45 (2003), 243–56.

Sison, A., 'Toward a common good theory of the firm: the Tasubinsa case', *Journal of Business Ethics*, 74 (2007), 471–80.

'Aristotelian corporate governance', in A. Brink (ed.), *Corporate governance and business ethics* (Dordrecht: Springer, 2011), pp. 179–202.

Skreta, V. and L. Veldkamp, 'Ratings shopping and asset complexity: a theory of rating inflation', *Journal of Monetary Economics*, 56 (2009), 678–95.

Solomon, M., '*Groupthink* versus *The wisdom of crowds*: the social epistemology of deliberation and dissent', *Southern Journal of Philosophy*, 44 (2006), 28–42.

Solomon, R., 'Corporate roles, personal virtues: an Aristotelean approach to business ethics', *Business Ethics Quarterly*, 2 (1992), 317–39.

Ethics and excellence: cooperation and integrity in business (Oxford University Press, 1992).

'Victims of circumstances? A defense of virtue ethics in business', *Business Ethics Quarterly*, 13 (2003), 43–62.

Sosa, E., 'The raft and the pyramid: coherence versus foundations in the theory of knowledge', *Midwest Studies in Philosophy*, 5 (1980), 3–26.

Sparks, C. and J. Tulloch, *Tabloid tales: global debates over media standards* (Lanham: Rowman and Littlefield, 2000).

Stalnaker, R., 'Common ground', *Linguistics and Philosophy*, 25 (2002), 701–21.

Staw, B., 'Knee deep in the big muddy: a study of escalating commitment to a chosen course of action', *Organizational Behavior and Human Performance*, 16 (1976), 27–44.

Steger, M. and R. Roy, *Neoliberalism: a very short introduction* (Oxford University Press, 2010).

Stein, M., 'Unbounded irrationality: risk and organizational narcissism at Long Term Capital Management', *Human Relations*, 56 (2003), 523–40.

Stevenson, D., 'New UK listed ETFs', *Financial Times*, 25 June 2009.

Stiles, P. and B. Taylor, *Boards at work: how directors view their roles and responsibilities* (Oxford University Press, 2001).

Stout, L., *The shareholder value myth: how putting shareholders first harms investors, corporations, and the public* (San Francisco: Berrett-Koehler, 2012).

Strier, F., 'Rating the raters: conflicts of interest in the credit rating firms', *Business and Society Review*, 11 (2008), 533–53.

Taylor, G. and S. Wolfram, 'Self-regarding and other-regarding virtues', *Philosophical Quarterly*, 18 (1968), 238–48.

Tennyson, S., 'Consumer's insurance literacy: evidence from survey data', *Financial Services Review*, 20 (2011), 165–79.

Tiberius, V. and J. Walker, 'Arrogance', *American Philosophical Quarterly*, 35 (1998), 379–90.

Tirole, J., 'Corporate governance', *Econometrica*, 69 (2001), 1–35.

Trottmann, C., 'Studiositas et superstitio dans la Somme de Théologie de Thomas d'Aquin: enjeux de la défiance à l'égard des "sciences curieuses"', in G. Federici-Vescovini, G. Marchetti, O. Rignani and V. Sorge (eds.), *Ratio et superstitio: essays in honor of Graziella Federici Vescovini* (Louvain-La-Neuve: Brepols, 2003), pp. 137–54.

Velayutham, S., 'The accounting profession's code of ethics: is it a code of ethics or a code of quality assurance?', *Critical Perspectives on Accounting*, 14 (2003), 483–503.

van de Ven, B., 'An ethical framework for the marketing of corporate social responsibility,' *Journal of Business Ethics*, 82 (2008), 339–52.

Wagner, R., 'To think . . . like a CFP', *Journal of Financial Planning*, 3 (1990), 36–41.

Walker Naylor, R., C. Droms and K. Haws, 'Eating with a purpose: consumer response to functional food health claims in conflicting versus complementary information environments', *Journal of Public Policy and Marketing*, 28 (2009), 221–33.

Weiss, H. and P. Knight, 'The utility of humility: self-esteem, information search and problem-solving efficiency', *Organizational Behaviour and Human Performance*, 25 (1980), 216–23.

Whetstone, J., 'How virtue fits within business ethics', *Journal of Business Ethics*, 33 (2001), 101–14.

White, L., 'Markets: the credit rating agencies', *Journal of Economics Perspectives*, 24 (2010), 211–26.

Wicks, A., 'On MacIntyre, modernity and the virtues: a response to Dobson', *Business Ethics Quarterly*, 7 (1997), 133–5.

Williams, B., *Ethics and the limits of philosophy* (London: Fontana, 1985).

Williams, W., 'The argument for free markets: morality vs. efficiency', *Cato Journal*, 15 (2004), 179–89.

Zagzebski, L., *Virtues of the mind: an inquiry into the nature of virtue and the ethical foundations of knowledge* (Cambridge University Press, 1996).

Zhang, P., 'Board information and strategic tasks performance', *Corporate Governance*, 18 (2010), 473–87.

Zhou, C., 'Credit rating and corporate default', *Journal of Fixed Income*, 3 (2001), 30–40.

Index

Access International Advisors, 143
accountancy, 59, 69, 79–80, 132, 184,
  185–8, 189, 190–2, 197
action, 3, 38, 40, 41, 52, 69
  see also epistemic action
Adams, Robert, 67–8
advice, 73, 74, 81, 101, 102–3, 160–1,
  162–4
Agarwal, Sumit, 102, 103–4
alchemy, 174
alpha of an asset, 146
Altmann, Ros, 90–2
Amromin, Gene, 103–4
analyst recommendations, 160–1,
  162–4
Andrews, Edmund, 94
Anscombe, Elizabeth, 45
Apple, 119
Aquinas, St Thomas, 13, 52, 65, 75
Aristotle, 1, 45, 46, 62, 65, 80, 83, 86,
  115, 159
Armour, John, 29
arrogance. *See* humility
articles of association, 111
assertions of creditworthiness, 168
asset partitioning, 29
astrology, 153, 171
Austin, John, 168

Baehr, Jason, 12, 46, 47, 48–50, 61–2,
  67–8, 154
bank, 2, 3, 6, 7, 8, 32, 33–5, 42, 88, 94,
  98, 99, 106, 117, 128, 130, 131,
  133, 135, 168, 170, 182
banker. *See* bank
Banker's Oath, 4
bankruptcy, 167
Barber, Brad, 85–6
Bar-Gill, Oren, 95–8

Barnier, Michel, 132
Battaly, Heather, 154
behavioural economics, 8, 15, 42, 49,
  52, 85, 119
belief, 39, 40, 45, 47, 48, 53, 54, 55–6,
  57–60, 64, 76, 80, 114, 126, 178
Ben-David, Itzhak, 103–4
benevolence, 154
Benmelech, Efraim, 173
beta of an asset, 146
bias, 8, 15, 52, 81, 82, 89, 97–8, 102,
  104, 130, 131, 160, 174, 191
Black, Fisher, 88–9
Black-Scholes model, 88–9
Blair, Tony, 37
Blankfein, Lloyd, 171
board of directors, 26, 30, 31, 46, 108,
  113, 117–18, 130, 132, 188
Boatright, John, 180
Bollaert, Helen, 87
bonus, 8, 9, 128–9
Brown, Alexander, 37, 38
Buchanan, Alan, 12
Buffett, Warren, 88
bylaws, 111

Cadbury Committee, 113
capital asset pricing model
  (CAPM), 146
capitalization, 195
carefulness. *See* interlucency; love of
  knowledge
Carroll, Archie, 24
Carter, Steven, 83, 100
CEO hubris, 87–8
certificate of incorporation, 111
character-based virtue epistemology,
  45
Cheng, Ping, 98

CPSIA information can be obtained at www.ICGtesting.com
Printed in the USA
LVOW04*2359020215

425435LV00003B/95/P